Civil society

The term 'civil society' has in recent years enjoyed something of a vogue. Social scientists in many countries have enthusiastically endorsed it as an ideal model of social organisation, but from an anthropological point of view this seems odd. How can an elusive idea that is clearly European in origin – and which, on closer scrutiny, throws little light even on the current social realities in Europe – gain the status of a universal prescriptive model?

Civil society is nowadays conventionally defined in terms of mediating institutions between the family and the state. It is often represented as a distinct private sphere and equated with the voluntary or non-governmental sector. The contributors to *Civil Society* challenge such narrow definitions in the light of ethnographic research. They argue for a broader understanding of civil society, encompassing everyday social practices and power relations, and paying close attention to the many material constraints that influence shared moralities and ideologies.

Drawing on case materials from the United States, Britain, four of the former communist countries of Eastern Europe, Turkey and the Middle East, Indonesia, China and Japan, the studies presented here demonstrate the contribution that anthropology can make to the current debate in the social sciences. They also add up to an exciting renewal of the agenda for political anthropology.

Chris Hann is Professor of Social Anthropology and Dean of Social Sciences at the University of Kent at Canterbury. **Elizabeth Dunn** is a doctoral candidate at Johns Hopkins University, Baltimore.

European Association of Social Anthropologists

The European Association of Social Anthropologists (EASA) was inaugurated in January 1989, in response to a widely felt need for a professional association which would represent social anthropologists in Europe, and foster co-operation and interchange in teaching and research. As Europe transforms itself in the 1990s, the EASA is dedicated to the renewal of the distinctive European tradition in social anthropology.

In the same series:

Revitalizing European Rituals
Jeremy Boissevain

Other Histories
Kirsten Hastrup

Alcohol, Gender and Culture
Dimitra Gefou-Madianou

Understanding Rituals
Daniel de Coppet

Conceptualizing Society
Adam Kuper

General Anthropology
Edited by Teresa del Valle

Nature and Society
Philippe Descola and Gísli Pálsson

Grasping the Changing World
Edited by Vaclav Hubringer

Civil society

Challenging western models

**Edited by Chris Hann
and Elizabeth Dunn**

London and New York

First published 1996
by Routledge
11 New Fetter Lane, London EC4P 4EE

Simultaneously published in the USA and Canada
by Routledge
29 West 35th Street, New York, NY 10001

Routledge is an International Thomson Publishing company.

© 1996 Chris Hann and Elizabeth Dunn for selection and
editorial matter; © the contributors for individual chapters

Typeset in Times by
Ponting–Green Publishing Services, Chesham, Bucks
Printed and bound in Great Britain by
Clays Ltd, St Ives PLC

British Library Cataloguing in Publication Data
A catalogue record for this book is available from the
British Library.

Library of Congress Cataloging in Publication Data
A catalogue record for this book has been requested.

ISBN   0–415–13218–5 (hbk)
ISBN   0–415–13219–3 (pbk)

Contents

Contributors

David G. Anderson is Lecturer in Arctic Anthropology at the University of Alberta.

Michał Buchowski is Lecturer at the Institute of Ethnology and Cultural Anthropology, Adam Mickiewicz University, Poznań.

Elizabeth Dunn is a doctoral candidate at the Department of Anthropology, Johns Hopkins University, Baltimore.

John Flower is a doctoral candidate at the Department of History, University of Virginia.

Chris Hann is Professor of Social Anthropology, University of Kent at Canterbury.

John Knight is Honorary Research Fellow, University of Kent at Canterbury.

Pamela Leonard recently obtained her Ph.D. from the Department of Social Anthropology, University of Cambridge.

Peter Loizos is Reader in Social Anthropology at the London School of Economics.

Annika Rabo is Lecturer at the Department of Social Science, Linköping University.

Steven Sampson is Research Fellow, University of Copenhagen.

Leo Schmit is Lecturer at the International Institute for Asian Studies, University of Leiden.

Susanne Spülbeck is a doctoral candidate at the Technical University of Berlin.

Jenny B. White is Lecturer at the Department of Sociology and Anthropology, University of Nebraska.

Acknowledgements

Most of the papers in this volume are revised versions of presentations made at the workshop we convened at the third meeting of the European Association of Social Anthropologists (EASA), held in Oslo in June 1994. The general subject of this meeting was 'Perspectives on Moralities, Knowledge and Power'. David Anderson, Pamela Leonard and John Flower, and Peter Loizos were not present in Oslo but have prepared chapters for this collection that significantly enhance its range and value. Mihály Sárkány was present and made valuable contributions to the workshop; unfortunately he was unable to write for this volume. Our thanks to the organisers of the EASA meeting, especially Signe Howell, to all the contributors for their cooperation, and to Yana Johnson for her help in preparing the final typescript.

CMH
ED

Introduction
Political society and civil anthropology
Chris Hann

> Under communism the nations of Eastern Europe never had a 'civil society.' A 'civil society' exists when individuals and groups are free to form organizations that function independently of the state, and that can mediate between citizens and the state. Because the lack of civil society was part of the very essence of the all-pervasive communist state, creating such a society and supporting organizations independent of the state – or NGOs – have been seen by donors as the connective tissue of democratic political culture – an intrinsically positive objective.
>
> (Wedel 1994: 323)

The subject of civil society has stimulated much research and lively debates within and across several academic disciplines in recent years. Contributions from anthropologists have been few and far between, and it is not hard to see why. There is something inherently unsatisfactory about the international propagation by western scholars of an ideal of social organisation that seems to bear little relation to the current realities of their own countries; an ideal which, furthermore, developed in historical conditions that cannot be replicated in any other part of the world today. I shall suggest that the term is riddled with contradictions and the current vogue predicated on a fundamental ethnocentricity. It is therefore no surprise that most anthropologists have hitherto ignored it.

One apparent exception turns out to confirm the rule. Ernest Gellner (1994) provides an enthusiastic endorsement of civil society as a model of social organisation. Gellner's model differs from pervasive neo-liberal approaches by acknowledging the need for an effective guarantor state (to prevent excesses of 'insider-dealing'). In fact he endorses a kind of pluralist system, based on a mixed economy as it used to exist in countries like Britain. However, he does so not as an anthropologist but as a social philosopher writing squarely within the traditions of the European enlightenment. When Gellner considers non-European societies, notably those of the Islamic world, he does so in even more abstract terms, without investigating ethnographic particulars.

So, perhaps the most obvious agenda for anthropological contributions to the civil society debates would be precisely to particularise and to make concrete: to show how an idea with its origins in European intellectual discourse has very different referents, varying significantly even within European societies. This agenda would also be concerned with analogues to the discourse of civil society in non-European cultural traditions, and with the interaction of these specific cultural ideas with the putative universalism of civil society as this idea is exported across the globe. Ethnographic research would focus on how these ideas are manifested in practice, in everyday social behaviour.

In clarifying this anthropological agenda, I find it helpful to use the following preliminary distinctions, as drawn recently by Adam Seligman (1992: 201–6 *passim*). He passes quickly over civil society as 'slogan', judging this to be an ephemeral, journalistic usage. The most common such usage, as we shall see, is that which posits civil society as locked into a zero-sum opposition to 'the state'. Some anthropologists have none the less realised the force of the slogan usage: Steven Sampson suggests in this volume that civil society is part of the 'magic' of the current transition in Eastern Europe, and Gellner himself recognises the power of the term as a 'shining emblem' (1994: 1). The second usage identified by Seligman is 'civil society' as a positive, analytic term for the social sciences, with concrete referents that can be investigated through empirical research. He has himself contributed to such research through his work on eighteenth-century America. Others, however, deny the possibility of strict definition and find the term confusing or redundant analytically: for example, Krishan Kumar has concluded that the idea of civil society is 'seductive but perhaps ultimately specious' (1994: 130). Seligman's third sense (which, like other writers on this topic, he frequently blurs with the second) concerns civil society as a normative concept, a distinctive vision of a desirable social order. The recent work of Keith Tester lays heavy emphasis on this normative dimension. Presenting the concept as 'the self-image of modernity', Tester argues that it is deeply implicated in the foundation of the social sciences (1992: 51). Historians of social anthropology may wish to consider how such arguments might be applied to their discipline. However, most anthropologists will be primarily interested in investigating civil society as a term that has some purchase on social reality, and not solely in terms of what

Tester calls 'the hermeneutic stakes' (1992: 1). Anthropologists will be interested in the normative dimension, but they will not necessarily expect the values espoused in the texts of intellectual élites to correspond closely to the practices of these groups; and the values and practices of other groups are likely to be different again.

The contributors to this volume address civil society in all of these dimensions. They do so in particular ethnographic contexts, and no simple consensus emerges. The term poses problems for political anthropology, but it may also open up new opportunities. In the following sections I look first at the trajectory of the term as it has evolved from origins in early modern European political thought through to the recent astonishing renewal or reinvention of these traditions. After this foray into the history of ideas and a brief consideration of the East European scene, I then turn to some of the ethnographic materials presented by the other contributors to this volume. Perhaps the most important general points to emerge are: (1) that civil society debates hitherto have been too narrowly circumscribed by modern western models of liberal-individualism, and (2) that the exploration of civil society requires that careful attention be paid to a range of informal interpersonal practices overlooked by other disciplines. Taken together, these studies show that anthropologists have much to contribute in the investigation of moral aspects of power, cohesion and social order in contemporary societies. At the end of the day, debates about civil society lead us to a renewed awareness of the fusion of the moral, the social and the political in the constitution of all human communities.

FROM EIGHTEENTH-CENTURY IDEAL TO TWENTY-FIRST-CENTURY REALITY

There are now plenty of works about the career of the idea of civil society and I shall not attempt to provide a detailed account (see Cohen and Arato 1992; Hall 1995; Keane 1988; Kumar 1993; Seligman 1992; Tester 1992). Most scholars trace the origins of civil society back to early modern European political thought, and more specifically to the concept of a private legal realm as it emerged in the work of Hobbes and Locke in England.[1] Perhaps a more rewarding starting point for anthropologists is the way civil society was viewed by the great figures of the Scottish Enlightenment in the second half of the eighteenth century. In the work of Ferguson, for example, we find the tensions and the paradoxes that have remained critical to the usefulness of the term down to the present day. The fundamental tension is that between particular and universal interests, between the selfish goals of individual actors and the need for some basic collective solidarity in a moral community. Ferguson resolves the tension through taking a view of human nature that amounts, in the words of Adam Seligman, to a 'naive anthropology of moral sentiments and natural sympathy' (1992: 205). This resolution becomes even more implausible and unrealistic in the much larger and more differentiated societies of the industrial age. The extension of citizenship in the modern world is based on the notion that individuals have sacrosanct rights. But this universalism is deeply prejudicial to the maintenance of trust and sociability in the realms where individuals interact. Later thinkers have placed less emphasis on 'moral affections' and 'natural sympathies', and stressed instead the virtues of a pluralism that is founded on equal and autonomous individual citizens. Seligman argues persuasively that this shift from an emphasis on the moral constitution of society to an emphasis on the universalist discourse of citizenship 'undermines that concrete mutuality and shared components of the moral community upon which trust is based' (1992: 12). Hence today's call for a return to civil society.

Seligman's paradoxes stem from his insistence that 'the universal (i.e. ethical) solidarity of a community of citizens rests on the moral inviolability of each individual' (1992: 146), rather than in some shared realm of sociability, as emphasised by Ferguson. It is arguable as to whose anthropology is more naive here. What seems clear is that the 'individualist' model, with its impoverished understanding of social relationships, became increasingly strong in intellectual discourses in the nineteenth century. It is exemplified in neo-classical economics, but similar 'rational choice' foundations have underpinned wide areas of social science, and anthropology itself has not been immune.

Of course, by no means all the thinkers who developed the notion of civil society in the nineteenth century were liberals or methodological individualists. The ground for the dominant modern tendency to draw a very sharp dichotomy (not drawn by Ferguson) between civil society and the state was laid out in the philosophy of Hegel. This opposition was taken over by Marx, who also follows Adam Smith in identifying civil society primarily with economic interaction through the market. But in Marx's view, in contrast to Smith, civil society is an illusion that needs to be unmasked. The apparent freedom of action it grants to the individual serves in reality to disguise underlying realities of class exploitation. The capitalist state, instead of resolving the tensions of civil society, merely cements the power of the ruling class. Citizens are hopelessly fragmented, alienated from each other and from their 'species-being', as well as from the means of production and the product of their labour.

No less significant than the contributions of Hegel and Marx are those of Tocqueville. A democrat who extolled the virtues of the 'habit of association', Tocqueville is the key figure in the modern 'liberal-individualist' approach. He also offers a narrower specification of 'political society', by which he means the activities of the population as it engages actively with matters of government and power. In this approach, both political society and the state are distinct from civil society, that is, the private relationships between citizens and their myriad non-political associations. I shall return to these distinctions below.

The recent literature contains many shades of opinion, but most contributions draw on the two central strands that took shape in the nineteenth century. The Marxist strand was creatively reworked by Gramsci, who argued that the struggle to transcend the inequalities of class society can only proceed following careful analyses of culture and ideology among the masses of civil society. But it is the liberal strand that has become almost hegemonic in the most recent debates. These two strands in western thinking about civil society might seem to be sharply opposed, in that one emphasises the reality of class exploitation while the other privileges freely associating individuals. But they also have a good deal in common. Both identify civil society with realms outside the power of the state, and emphasise economic life as such a realm. Even more importantly, both strands assume the universality of modern western notions of the person, what Seligman calls the 'autonomous agentic individual' (1992: 5); the Marxist tradition merely allows these atoms to be aggregated to form social classes. The tripartite schema recently elaborated by Cohen and Arato (1992), distinguishing civil society equally from the market and from the state, offers a fresh synthesis of these strands (for further discussion see David Anderson's chapter in this volume). But none of these accounts leaves room for the exploration of alternative forms of social relationship to those assumed by liberal-individualism, of culturally specific patterns of generating trust in human communities that are growing ever more crowded and complex.

From this brief outline we can see that civil society has meanings today that are quite different from those it had in the eighteenth century. The dominant meaning – which several contributors understandably refer to as the 'classical' meaning, even though the key elements are post-enlightenment – has come to be that which ties civil society to liberal individualism and sees it in opposition to the state. The standard definitions of civil society explain it as a space between families and kin groups on the one hand, and the modern state on the other. (Thus an anthropologist studying a small-scale society in which kinship was the principal mode of social organisation would have no need of this concept.) As Seligman shows, it emerged at a particular moment in the history of western societies, strongly marked by Protestant theology, when the scale of social organisation was much larger than could be managed by kin groups alone, but still small enough to permit trust and solidarity between individuals. Although the individual is the privileged moral agent, the social context is none the less crucial. Since the eighteenth century, the precarious social balance which produced the idea of civil society has, according to Seligman, been destroyed in one of two ways. In the western countries themselves, the universalism of modern citizenship has made trust too 'abstract', and therefore unworkable. Elsewhere, exclusivist nationalism and sectarianism are the factors that make social trust impossible. The result is an impasse, from which sloganising and nostalgia for the eighteenth-century scale of social organisation offer no prospect of escape.

Obviously the debates about civil society are closely linked to other debates: about modernity itself, and (only slightly less grandiose) about individualism, pluralism, the boundaries between public and private, and so on. The ground of these debates has shifted, sometimes dramatically. For example, whereas the *civil* was classically opposed to the *religious*, several chapters in this volume point to close connections between civil society and religious culture. Again civil society has historically been cast as a private realm in opposition to the public realm of the state, but for many modern feminists the private is equated with the domestic and the familial – leaving civil society firmly in the public sphere. (The need for a gendered approach to civil society is argued by several contributors to this volume, particularly Annika Rabo.) We tend to think today of civil society in terms of a national society, its boundaries fixed by those of a state. Yet this, too, is a far cry from older usages, and many social scientists have begun to find it unhelpful to postulate society as some kind of 'block' in the Durkheimian sense (see Kuper 1992). The latest phase in the long history of debate, associated with the end of the cold war and the unravelling of superpower conflicts, casts civil society in the role of David against the Goliath of the modern state, epitomised by the bureaucratic apparatus of state socialism. We should recognise that this phase has as much to do with trends in the west as with changed realities elsewhere. The welfare state seems less and less able to fulfil its responsibilities, but the very fact that formally it has expanded and accepted such a wide range of social tasks has tended to increase the isolation of individual citizens, leaving them bereft of other sources of collective identity and security. The appeal of the old idea of civil society is thus understandable. However, despite much heady talk of 'world civil society' in the context of globalisation, there is as yet no sign of any plausible alternative to the state as the primary institutional framework within which security and solidarity can be established in late-twentieth-century social conditions.

An awareness of the shifts in European intellectual debate, and of the common rootedness of the dominant modern strands in a specifically western theory of autonomous individuals, should alert us to the errors and dangers of exporting models of civil society to non-western societies. It is even possible that other traditions of thought might have something to offer us in the modern west: in other words, that anthropological investigations may offer an escape from Seligman's impasse, through providing critiques of his western bias and opening up the alternatives available in other cultural traditions.

CIVIL SOCIETY IN EASTERN EUROPE

My own views about civil society have been coloured particularly by its use in the context of the transformation of Eastern Europe. Indeed this was the principal terrain on which the popularity of the term became firmly established in the 1980s. I was, and remain, very sceptical of the way 'society' was invoked by some 'dissident' intellectuals and by various commentators outside the region to imply that Eastern European populations were united in their opposition to socialist governments. In this discourse, civil society is a slogan, reified as a collective, homogenised agent, combating a demonic state. For example, Vaclav Havel argues that his socialist predecessors in power imposed a uniform model of central control upon society. According to Havel (1993), 'It is as easy to do that as it is to smash a piece of antique, inlaid furniture with a single blow from a hammer. But it is infinitely more difficult to restore it all, or to create it directly.'[2]

Later in the same article Havel argues that 'communism brought history, and with it all natural development, to a halt. . . . National and cultural differences were kept on ice.' Here again are metaphors that have been widely used since 1989, but can one really accept that East European societies were placed in some kind of deep freeze for forty years? It seems to me that there was in fact continuous movement and great diversity among and within each of the East European countries. In some countries, such as Poland (as shown in this volume by Buchowski; see also Wedel 1992 on the importance of 'social circles'), the range of social activities was very extensive. There were some important common traits in the 'eastern bloc', but a stark contrast with the allegedly natural and free development of 'civil society' in the west does not take us very far in understanding the changes wrought by socialism. Where Havel reviles 'the intrinsic tendency of communism to make everything the same', many East Europeans still, in spite of everything, feel that its fundamental motivations were the highly moral ones of increasing entitlements and making people more equal. It has always seemed to me that many citizens, especially in the countryside, were empowered in the socialist period, that is, they became better able to express their social identities, in conditions of relative material prosperity. (No doubt this is less true of Czechoslovakia than of some of its neighbours, while in extreme cases, such as Romania in the 1980s, this generalisation does not apply at all.) This is little understood in western countries because coverage of the region focuses on the high culture produced by intellectual élites, among whom Havel himself is an outstanding figure. However, millions of East Europeans, and not just a few former communist *apparatchiks*, have now shown in elections that they wish to preserve some of the radical changes which took place in their societies under socialism. They do not accept that the new élites have a monopoly of the moral high ground, since there is little evidence in either eastern or western countries that the *laissez-faire* prescriptions of those who equate the rhetoric of 'natural development' with that of 'market economy' can enable the majority of citizens to realise Havel's romantic and Utopian ideals.

Others have argued that the main distinguishing feature of the opposition to communism in Eastern Europe was its *anti-political* character (Konrád 1984). According to this view, the recent revolutions in Eastern Europe were the first in human history *not* to be concerned with establishing some form of rational Utopia. Hence the new post-communist political associations are not really like political parties at all, since the revolutions have made any kind of rational political order impossible. Instead, these societies are seen as characterised by un-fettered egoism and consumerism. Only individuals exist, and they are allegedly devoid of significant human relationships. A superficial in-spection of the East European scene lends some support to this analysis. In spite of multiparty elections and the vigorous promotion of market-oriented economic policies, it has not been easy to establish the rich network of associations outside of the state that comprises the essence of the romanticised western model of civil society. Sometimes this can be linked to the withdrawal of state subsidies: for example, movements such as the Young Pioneers have suffered from cuts and repression, though evidence from several countries indicates their continuing popularity among young people.

However, a model of social life as based on depoliticised, atomised individuals, attractive though it has been to some philosophers, is unlikely to be convincing to many anthropologists. The young people who no longer wear the uniforms of Pioneers are forming other relationships and networks, and sometimes they may seek support from appropriate levels of the state. The assumption of an overriding antagonism between state and society is futile. If these terms can serve at all, the task must be to investigate their complex and continuous interactions. This certainly should not be restricted to the mapping of political opposition to authoritarian regimes. Radical opposition to socialism was restricted to small, politically conscious fragments of populations, and it should also be remembered that many of those who struggled to change communist systems did so from space they managed to find *within* the state (including its large education and research establishments).

The errors in western diagnoses of the social conditions of late socialist societies have recently become very obvious. Levels of disaffection from the new élites are typically as high or higher than before. Havel himself writes of 'the post-communist nightmare'. Some people may feel that with the demise of communism they are better able to assert their individual rights, notably the right to own property. But for many citizens it is far from clear that their rights have been enhanced in any *substantive* way: the re-emergence of Rotary clubs is little consolation when you no longer have secure employment. In this volume the chapter by David Anderson highlights the discrepancy between formal-legal notions of universal *rights* and the substantive *entitlements* to which citizens had become accustomed under socialism, and which in retrospect they are coming to value more highly. Civil society is no longer, in the mid-1990s, the emotive slogan that it became for many East European intellectuals in the 1980s.

However, as the quote from Janine Wedel at the opening of this chapter suggests, the concept of civil society is now central to western aid programmes in Eastern Europe, linked intimately to privatisation aid. Steven Sampson's chapter in this volume explores the mechanics of the creation of civil society by external intervention, focusing on his own work in Albania. Cases such as this, where civil society is equated crassly with the expansion of the 'non-governmental organisation' sector, migh* lead one to dismiss the term as an irrelevance, or of interest only as a slogan, politically potent perhaps, but quite useless for the analysis of changing social organisations. Yet the more elusive the realisation of civil society becomes, the more its virtues seem to be extolled in some quarters and, in the case of Eastern Europe, the more blame is piled on to communists and their predecessors for making it so difficult to replicate the conditions of western civil society in the east. Although the popularity of the term is now fading in Eastern Europe, in many other parts of the world the expansion of democracy is articulated explicitly in terms of civil society. The term has been used in basically similar ways in recent work on Latin America and sub-Saharan Africa. Case materials in this volume range from Indonesia to the Arctic, and from Japan to Baltimore. Faced with this proliferation, it can no longer suffice simply to dismiss civil society rhetoric as an extension of the cold war and the rhetoric of totalitarianism (Hann 1990). Its obvious attractions to large numbers of people throughout the world establish a strong claim on anthropological attention. The appeal is all the more remarkable in that the dominant western model of civil society seems less conducive to social cohesion and successful economic performance than starkly opposed models of social order, such as those of East Asia. Perhaps the biggest puzzle is why so many people in the modern west have faith in this model and preach it to others, when it offers only a partial and misleading guide to the organisation of their own societies.

CONTENTS OF THIS VOLUME

We open in the west with the case of the United States. The American experience features prominently in Adam Seligman's essay, for he takes America to epitomise the principles of universalist individualism. This is related to the circumstances in which the American colonies developed, including the religious dimension of the society in its formative stages. American individualism has persisted to the present day, which explains why affluent élites in California beach towns can interact with members of an ethnically distinct underclass in terms of civil equality. The ethnographic vignette provided by Seligman to support this point contrasts starkly with the portraits he provides of daily life in Budapest and Jerusalem, where ethnic boundaries have fundamental consequences for interaction and social trust. Seligman is not seduced by American civility (if counter-evidence were needed, it was provided in abundance by the racial rioting that occurred in Los Angeles in the very year his book was published). He understands that very high rates of poverty and crime in the modern United States are connected with the obliteration of the public realm of sociability. The society that exemplifies pluralism and liberal democracy in the contemporary world is hardly a society of harmony: the moral and political constitution of the society reveal a profound lack of solidarity and trust, notably because of racial divides. Yet, for Seligman, the United States remains a *genuinely* universalist society, in contrast to what he terms the 'false universalism' of state socialist societies (1992: 177).

It is this American society that forms the backcloth to Elizabeth Dunn's chapter in this volume. The Mormons are a group that finds the American environment deeply unbearable, and successfully constructs an alternative based on family and faith. They are a community into which one may be born, but Dunn concentrates on the active maintenance of communal ties through the practice of gifting. Church members much of the time follow the standard rules of profit-maximising, liberal-individualist society, and some of them have become highly successful businessmen. But they also support each other, through *labour* that is kept immune from the principles of capitalist accounting. Through this device the qualities of cohesion and trust deemed to be lacking in the wider society are successfully established. Though American society as a whole is incapable of achieving this, it does provide the conditions in which the members of a religious minority are able to achieve a measure of transcendence, through a theology and a repertoire of practices which deny self-interest and celebrate the moral community.

As an evaluative term, civil society is closely linked to issues concerning the 'quality of life', and Peter Loizos considers some of the difficulties in assessing this quality in contemporary Britain. It is commonly alleged that government policies in the era associated with Margaret Thatcher, ostensibly committed to the 'free market' and to scaling down the activities of the 'nanny state', in fact led to a strengthening of central government. This was accompanied by the undermining of other associations and institutions, such as professional bodies and trade unions, universities, and so on. Some institutions gained autonomy in managerial terms, whilst simultaneously being subject to more stringent central control, typically by 'quangos', that is, centralised controlling organs staffed by government appointees rather than elected representatives. Mrs Thatcher, Loizos reminds us, did not have any strong concept of society. On the contrary, in a famous statement she declared that it did not exist – for her there were only individuals and families. The rhetoric was new, but Loizos is not so sure that any radical change in the quality of British civic life occurred in the 1980s. Instead

he highlights long-term continuities. He is concerned that liberal democratic societies like Britain do not do enough to educate their citizens, or
to create a minimal informed consensus about historical identity. Pressure
groups and new social movements can play a major role in rebuilding
civil society, but Loizos places particular emphasis on the critical role of
the media in providing a link between the personal and the state, thereby
fulfilling a vital sociological function in maintaining cohesion and a
democratic spirit in contemporary Britain. It is clear that British civil
society differs in important ways from the American – there is no single
contemporary western model.

It is a matter of regret that this volume contains no further case studies
from Western Europe (nor indeed from other parts of the world where
the idea of civil society has been extensively deployed, including Africa
and Latin America). We are fortunate, however, in having rich materials
from the central and eastern parts of Europe that have figured so
prominently in recent debates. Susanne Spülbeck's fieldwork in a
Thüringian village leads her, like Loizos, to emphasise long-term cultural
continuities, in this case in the patterns of interaction with strangers.
Contemporary attitudes towards Jewish refugees echo older stories about
witches. Spülbeck notes how the Stasi, the former East German secret
police, penetrated even inside the domestic realm to pit spouse against
spouse. She sees this as completing the communist obliteration of the
public sphere, in Habermas's sense. (One could also interpret this
material as exposing the general inadequacy of the public–private
dichotomy: after all, western states also intervene, sometimes dramatically, in personal and domestic life, though few would deny that the force
of this intervention was greater in the former communist countries.) In
the post-communist years it has been hard to find people willing to
participate in the building of trust and a new local politics. The villagers'
pervasive suspicion extends to the anthropologist, creating practical and
even ethical problems for the researcher. The background in the new
united Germany is one of high unemployment, one form of insecurity
that villagers did not have to concern themselves with in the socialist
period.

In the following chapter Michaø Buchowski shows that it is by no
means easy to formulate general theories about the former communist
countries. While Susanne Spülbeck sees no effective tier of associational
or civil life between the family and the East German state, Buchowski
sees a very great deal in communist Poland. While she sees the family
itself disintegrating under totalitarian pressure, he sees it as one of the
bulwarks of civil society. But it is by no means the only one, for along

with the unique strength of the church, many other associations, official and unofficial, flourished in communist Poland. These are liable to be overlooked by political scientists, but an anthropological approach reveals a well developed civil society long before 1989. Buchowski adapts Foucault's notions of governmentality to argue, *contra* Tocqueville, that everyday participation in a wide range of social activities, many of them linked more or less directly to the state, is an important element in the constitution of any society. Some of these might be dismissed as 'trivial' and irrelevant to civil society in the sense in which it is explored by Peter Loizos, but in the communist context, virtually all social behaviour had political implications. Buchowski elaborates the notion of *civic* society to refer to all activity that put pressure on the state, and shows how a complex dialectic led eventually to the demise of communist governmentality and the election of a non-communist government. He disagrees with some of my own negative reflections on the quality of life in post-communist society, though he acknowledges much apathy and passivity in the new situation. 'Amoral familism' (also discussed by Loizos) could now become an obstacle to progress toward higher forms of civil society, and different constituencies have contradictory expectations of the post-communist state.

Continuing the analysis of post-communist societies, David Anderson draws on his research in Northern Siberia to illustrate how the shift to a more individualist, universalist notion of citizenship in Russia has eroded civility and trust. Here, it would seem, people did not think of themselves as a collective 'we' in opposition to a socialist state, and so the kind of discourse established by Polish intellectuals around the concept of civil society could not arise. Anderson identifies an equivalent local discourse around the concepts of *kul'tura* and *demokratiia*, the former corresponding to the dimension of civic rights and the latter to bourgeois market economy. In the communist period many of the country's smaller ethnic groups benefited from policies that, while significantly restricting individual freedoms, also constituted positive discrimination that provided security, social services and well-being to these remote communities. The shift to a model that emphasises juridically equal individuals, linked to the imposition of market economy, has led to impoverishment and insecurity – in short, to the breakdown of trust that is now evident in the proliferation of criminal gangs and violence throughout the country.

Steven Sampson reports that in Albania a focus on concrete entitlements is characteristic of older people, rather than the dynamic young activists currently creating new non-governmental organisations with aid and assistance from abroad. This account of contemporary civil society in Albania is based on the anthropologist's personal involvement in the promotion of this ideal, on behalf of the government of Denmark. In practice, this has meant a focus on projects in the non-governmental sector, though the boundary is a difficult one to draw since many state-controlled bodies try to pass themselves off as autonomous in order to qualify for grant aid. The Albanian situation is perhaps the most extreme variant of a pattern that is general throughout Eastern Europe. Sampson argues persuasively that in studying the transition it is necessary to consider a wide range of actors, in the west as well as in the east. Inevitably, some Albanians seek to manipulate the purveyors of foreign aid for their own advantage and 'sustenance'. Sampson finds that the routine local assumptions of self-interest and 'clanship' are applied – often with good reason – to the western experts and advisers who fly in and out of Tirana. But he also finds that tremendous social energies have been unleashed in recent years. There is a marked gap between the kind of associations into which the westerners would like to see all that energy channelled, and what is actually happening in contemporary Albanian society (most of which remains invisible to the foreigners). There is no doubt that far-reaching changes have occurred in social life as a consequence of the new pattern of unequal power relations between east and west; yet traditional practices are simply not reducible to the organisational charts and business-school rhetoric that are being imposed by western agencies.

There is therefore a need to shift the debates about civil society away from formal structures and organisations and towards an investigation of beliefs, values and everyday practices. Such an approach is vigorously advocated by Jenny White, who describes some of the social problems faced by working-class women in the sprawling slums of Istanbul. These women do not develop formal organisations and their activities would be overlooked by conventional approaches to civil society, which privilege the kind of groupings established by the articulate middle classes. However a close ethnographic inspection of the informal coping strategies of these working women reveals not isolated individuals or households, but rich networks of friendship and mutual aid. These women have sought to ameliorate their social conditions through what White terms 'reciprocal associations'. As in Dunn's Mormon example, one gives without calculation and without expectation of a specific return. The resulting forms of 'free association' operate on a pragmatic basis and within a very traditional set of ideologies. They are quite unlike liberal-individualist models of civil society, based on contract and the market, but they should not be dismissed as 'primordial', determined by kinship, ethnicity or religion. Such 'informal associations' are to be found in all societies. They are highly variable culturally, and they are heavily influenced by local forms of the state. In this latter respect there is considerable variety within the Middle East, and it is therefore ethnocentric to make sweeping generalisations to the effect that civic (the term preferred by White) society is incompatible with Islam.

Annika Rabo provides further evidence of this diversity. Her own study of the gendered aspects of civil society in adjacent patriarchal regions of the Middle East lends supports to White's call for closer analysis of the state. A gendered perspective, valuable everywhere, has particular significance in the Middle East, where the position of women has long been central to representations of progress and of cultural tradition. The modernisation programmes of new states such as Syria and Jordan have had far-reaching effects on women, for example, in the spheres of education and labour-market participation. Both states have sought to create national citizens, and to a considerable extent they have succeeded. The Syrian one-party regime has pursued a model of progress very close to that of Eurasian socialism. Jordanian political rhetoric has been different: here patriarchy has retained a more traditional form, within a polity still dominated by the royal family. Rabo focuses on recent controversies concerning cultural authenticity and veiling, and finds that neither state has succeeded completely in controlling key symbols. Public activity that is channelled by religion and symbolised by the use of the veil certainly seems a far cry from modern western understandings of civil society; but Rabo's point is that use of the veil is actually a modern response, one which shows that women are taking a position against their state. She raises the possibility that more civil society of the western sort could have deleterious consequences for many women. Given the constraints, veiling may offer greater potential for liberation than 'state feminism' within an encompassing patriarchal ideology.

Leo Schmit also writes about a state, Indonesia, in which entrenched power-holders have recently had to respond to increased pressure for more open and pluralist forms of government. For him, civil society has a dual character – civic aspects that relate to politics and government at all levels, and economic aspects, related to the market and entrepreneurship. Ideas about participation and cooperation are influential in both aspects. The Indonesian state claims to have worked out an original alternative model to the liberal-individualist models associated with the modern west. Schmit finds that (contrary to Sampson's experience in Albania) major international agencies have been sympathetic to this aspiration and have provided both funding and a broad endorsement of its principles. However, Schmit's own assessment suggests that the technocratic consensus behind the 'politics of expertise' in Indonesia has already begun to break down, and that the new programmes, for all their emphasis on economic democracy and the deployment of civil energy in entrepreneurship, add up to a very risky strategy that is unlikely to succeed in emulating the most successful economies of East Asia. Putting it crudely, it would seem that the Indonesian state, aided and abetted by the development agencies, is trying to hold on to its own power through diverting pressures for political participation into economic activities. The balance is precarious, the military lurk in the background, and one likely outcome is intensified exclusionary pressure on the hitherto most powerful business group, the Sino-Indonesian community.

Chinese leaders, too, have for some time been anxious to promote economic growth without at the same time 'liberalising' the polity. The chapter by John Flower and Pamela Leonard presents materials from their work with a development project in rural Sichuan. The authors are critical of the tendency to apply to China a western notion of totalitarianism, and argue instead that state and society should be seen as part of a 'seamless field of moral interaction'. Villagers seek to maintain a balance between autonomy and involvement with the bureaucracy. They are reluctant to accept the 'gifting' strategy recommended by an American-funded private voluntary organisation as part of its project to increase the productivity of their goat-breeding programmes, because it does not make cultural sense to 'give' to the state. Instead they prefer to apply more rational, 'scientific' principles. Villagers are also the victims of a new wave of corruption that has overwhelmed local state agencies since the impact of market reforms. This impact has weakened the ties of mutual trust and undermined informal social relationships. However, villagers have sustained some kind of moral equilibrium through their historical memory, and this has been expressed in the revival of the religious institutions that were destroyed in the Maoist period.

Finally, John Knight presents materials from a mountain region in another East Asian state that invites comparisons both with China and with the west. Japan has made an astonishing success of capitalist economic development, while maintaining a strong state and principles of lifetime security of employment and respect for seniority that seem to contradict western economic logic. Knight goes behind the myths to explore some of the very practical dilemmas faced by the inhabitants of a 'rural municipality' that is very much a product of the government's social engineering. Members of older and younger generations have radically differing perspectives on the traditional forms of village life. An old man upholds the virtues of family ties and a specific cultural idiom that asserts the value of self-help. He is strongly opposed to dependency on the state or the local form of the state, the town-office. This is not surprising, because state programmes have threatened the material and political dominance of élite families like his own. A young girl, in contrast, feels stifled by the prospect of life in a backward and closed village community: she welcomes the civic initiatives taken by the town-office to promote new forms of collective solidarity. Although some of these new forms emphasise their 'voluntary' character, it is clear that these, too, are radically different from the western, liberal-individualist model. Contemporary Japanese civil society cannot be sharply distinguished from the activities of the state at many levels, from the local to the national, and shows little sign of converging with western civil society. If one of the two is to be selected for export, surely Japanese ideas, with their combination of various levels of community, family relationships and state responsibility, have rather more to offer the rest of the world than western individualism?

POLITICAL ANTHROPOLOGY BETWEEN UNIVERSALISM AND RELATIVISM

We have seen that the term civil society has a specific currency in the history of western ideas. It is less obvious that this term is a helpful one in understanding social realities, particularly in circumstances that are radically altered from those in which it was first used. We have seen examples of such unhelpful usage in Eastern Europe, where civil society has itself been cast as a homogenised and unified realm, mirroring the homogenising and unifying state to which it ostensibly stands opposed. Paradoxically, local uses of the term have ended up far removed from the 'classical' liberal-individualist model that the anti-totalitarian theorists wish to endorse. When we come to consider societies more remote from the western tradition, the case for using the term civil society may be even weaker. A basic and familiar tension between universalist and relativist approaches comes into play here: by addressing this, we may be able to clarify the distinctive elements of an anthropological contribution to current debates.

The would-be universalists are those who adhere to a relatively 'hard', analytic definition of civil society and believe it is useful to apply this definition cross-culturally. The only plausible candidate for this core definition is the liberal-individualist understanding that has emerged in the modern west. Universalists tend to see this civil society as a concrete and quantifiable thing, usually with the implication that a large dose is indispensable in the general quest for good government. They often confuse their analysis of what *is* with what they think *ought to be*, according to the specifications of their model. Adam Seligman tends to a universalist approach, though as we have noted he is far from sanguine about the contemporary prospects for implementing ideals that received their most cogent formulation several centuries ago. More optimistic is John Hall, a universalist who explicitly celebrates civil society as the unique accomplishment of the west (1995). Among the 'enemies' of civil society, he lists cultural factors in regions such as South Asia and the Islamic world. For him, civil society cannot be multicultural, and what Jenny White and Annika Rabo might see as the 'informal' empowering of Muslim women is not to be confused with an expansion of civil society. Ernest Gellner is similarly confident in the superiority of the west. There is almost gloating in his celebration of what 'we' have accomplished (though, as I have noted, his is a traditionalist 'mixed-economy' model of civil society, which differs from that of many contemporary neo-liberals). These authors share some common ground with Francis Fukuyama (1992), whose arguments about a universal 'end of history' are rooted in highly selective interpretations of a small number of western philosophers.

In the other camp are the relativists – basically, those who recognise that other societies have organised their social and political life in terms of different, often incommensurable ideals. Some societies may reject modern western notions of what is intrinsically good, as when a Brahmin rejects equality and upholds the hierarchy of caste, or a Mollah defends the sacred truths of Islam against secular pluralism. As Leo Schmit shows in this volume, Indonesian power-holders have consciously rejected the dominant western model and promoted their own 'authentic' alternative. Most anthropologists, striving to avoid ethnocentricity, will wish to grasp local concepts and culturally specific qualifications to individualism, rather than join Gellner's 'we' and impose western ideas. Relativists are therefore likely to highlight issues of bias and to deny the possibility of any genuinely universalist standpoint. They may be inclined to view civil society, along with other terms such as market economy and rule of law, as more or less efficacious myths. However, sometimes relativists, too, confuse what they see with what they would like to see: in describing unique, incommensurable cultures, they fail to notice those elements of social behaviour and aspirations that closely resemble patterns in other societies, including key elements of modern western societies.

The choice between universalism and relativism need not be posed starkly, and anthropologists, like other people, can negotiate an intermediary path. Some of those who sympathise with the egalitarianism and individualism of the 'universalist' definition of civil society may shift towards the relativist camp when they appreciate the steps required by the west to realise these aspirations, for example, in terms of the World Bank's 'structural adjustment policies'. On the other hand, when international agencies make concessions to alternative, culturally specific models, they may end up reinforcing existing power-holders and suppressing many forms of civic expression. It seems to me that anthropologists inclined to the relativist stance should be prepared to go along with the generalisation of the term civil society, up to a point. After all, the term clearly is being widely utilised in the real world, whether the relativists like this or not, and we cannot ignore the common elements in local refractions. There is deliberate ambiguity in the subtitle of this collection: the dominant western models of civil society are ones we wish to challenge, but we must also recognise that they are *challenging* models that have great appeal throughout the world. When students under some repressive regime take up the call for 'civil society' and make this central to their struggles for 'democratisation', is the anthropologist to advise such youth that their models of democracy and civil society are flawed, due to their western bias?

This might be dismissed as the 'slogan' usage. But a better response would be to enquire more closely into local political traditions. For example, some Chinese intellectuals have made great sacrifices in recent years for ideals that appear to resemble those of western liberal democracy. Unlike East European dissidents they have not, in fact, made much use of the term civil society. But there are precedents in the Chinese past, not just in the modern period but under earlier dynasties as well, for the kind of pluralist and contractual social arrangements that are central to the universalists' core definition of civil society (see Goody forthcoming). Sometimes these will be expressed in ways that strike westerners as strange. As John Flower and Pamela Leonard show in this volume, the lines between public and private will be drawn differently, or they may not, by western criteria, be drawn at all. The space of Chinese civil society may, in one sense, be encompassed within space claimed by the state. But before we rush to classify such a polity as an Oriental Despotism, we should look very carefully at the realities of power and accountability in concrete situations. The crucial point here is that 'civil society' in the hard, analytic sense of the universalists is not the unique product of the west after all: others have developed important elements of it, before and after the impact of the European enlightenment. It is therefore possible to retain the core of a universalist definition, whilst endorsing Goody's condemnation of the 'myopia' that ties this definition of civil society solely to the modern west.

If agreement can be reached on a core definition, might the term civil society be expected to enter other languages, and perhaps to take its place in anthropological dictionaries alongside such terms as caste or clan, or others like *mana* or *taboo* that originate in non-western languages? This seems unlikely. True, the demand for something like the modern western ideal of liberal individualism may be found increasingly in other societies. Older notions of personhood and social accountability have been widely undermined, and new organisations have come into existence that owe more to foreign example than to any indigenous model. Nevertheless, as many have pointed out, globalisation is by no means inimical to the persistence of cultural difference and in many ways it actually promotes new forms of difference. Universalists will need always to recognise the influences of local traditions, institutions and practices; in short, to enter the symbolic worlds of particular communities and their cultures. Goody himself (*ibid*.) takes an important further step towards expanding the definition of civil society when he points out that even political formations in West Africa lacking any consolidated form of the state reveal 'some space for manoeuvre between the personal and the public'. They, too, have specific practices and normative codes through which people are made accountable and responsible to other members of society. This is the broader meaning of civil society, and it can be fruitfully explored in *all* types of human society.

We are now in a position to open up a positive agenda for political anthropology. We may, for some limited purposes, wish to apply a core definition of civil society and use this for comparative analysis. But, instead of searching for the replication of one particular western model around the world, we should also be prepared to abandon this universal yardstick, and to understand civil society to refer more loosely to the moral community, to the problems of accountability, trust and co-operation that all groups face. In this sense, all human communities are concerned with establishing their own version of a civil society, or *civilisation*. When we begin to examine how this is accomplished, we find tremendous variation in ideas about good government, virtue and responsibility. In terms of the institutional implementation of these ideas we might, following the usage of David Anderson in this volume, identify a bewildering variety of 'citizenship regimes'. Civil society in the usual, more narrow specification, building on pluralism and the liberal individualism of Tocqueville, is the discourse of one type of regime. Much may be gained from the systematic investigation and comparison of such discourses. They are not static, and their relations to changing social and political realities are complex. The late-twentieth-century linking of civil society with non-governmental organisations in a context of deregulated and increasingly globalised economies is but one highly specific instance.

CONCLUSIONS

I began this introduction by suggesting that civil society is a topic that offers opportunities to political anthropology. This subdiscipline has traditionally been concerned with the evolutionary emergence of states, and with the classification of forms of political organisation (the main classification offered has been that of state versus stateless). It has ostensibly rejected western political theory, and yet this very emphasis on the state betrays the weight of that European tradition (Fortes and Evans-Pritchard 1940; Geertz 1980; Kuklick 1993).

Civil society is a term that hails from this same tradition. Anthropologists may be tempted to use it within the dominant modern framework, in which it has come to refer to a wide range of associational activity outside of, and usually opposed to, the state. There is no denying the force of the state–society dichotomy in many parts of the contemporary world. It seems likely that an essentially similar classification has existed throughout the history of centralised polities. Several contributors to this volume report an aversion to various levels of the modern state among the people they have studied, typically formulated in terms of the rejection of dependency and 'handouts' (see the chapters by Flower and Leonard, Dunn and Knight). However, the authors all move beyond this simple dichotomy in their analysis. They explore the complexity of the institutions that mediate between self and society, and the social relationships that underpin the functioning of both states and markets. Several contributors call for greater precision in distinguishing different levels of the state and different state ideologies. Others highlight the need for more careful specification of the social relations, for example, along the lines of ethnicity, gender and age. The emphasis in several chapters falls on the contradictory nature of people's attitudes towards the state, expecting it to guarantee social services and employment, but at the same time hoping that it will not seek to regulate and interfere.

Taken together, the studies in this volume argue for a more *in-*

clusive usage of civil society, in which it is not defined *negatively*, in opposition to the state, but *positively* in the context of the ideas and practices through which cooperation and trust are established in social life. There are few places in the late-twentieth-century world where the policies of the state and the actions of its agents in implementing them do not play a central role in these processes. These people, and the very idea of the state, should therefore be integrated into the analysis rather than bracketed outside it. In this way, the binary opposition that has been so dominant in western political theory and in the early development of political anthropology, might one day be left behind.

Political anthropologists have also experimented with approaches such as 'game theory' and various versions of rational-choice models, which leave little room for the integration of cultural diversity. A few have, more fruitfully, sought to correct western bias through studying the role played by language and by symbols, but the subdiscipline has struggled in recent years to sustain a coherent identity.[3] Civil society may offer a focus to reconstitute this specialisation or, better, to ensure that the political element receives due emphasis in all anthropological work. It is true that, like the term for state, the term civil society derives from western theorising. It is undeniable that it has been used in simplistic ways, notably as a unified realm in opposition to the state, and that its recent reduction by governments and aid agencies to the world of non-governmental organisations (NGOs) represents an impoverished view of social life. But political anthropology could adapt the term civil society to open up a kind of comparative political philosophy, concerned with all the diverse ideas and moralities that inspire cohesion and trust in human communities. This would involve addressing ideas such as the modern western idea of civil society in the context of analogues and parallels in other, non-western discourses. This political anthropology should not, of course, be confined to the investigation of ideas and moral discourses, and certainly not just to the textual discourses of élite groups. The ideas must be connected to actions and institutions: all fields of sociability imply a context of power, and practices that might appear at first sight trivial should not be excluded from the investigations. The anthropologist can expect to uncover rival, conflicting ideas, less fully articulated but perhaps more influential among larger numbers of people. Only through ethnographic research can we assess the extent to which a dominant discourse turns out to be a smokescreen, and the freqency with which moral norms are honoured in the breach. The narrow, western liberal-individualist idea of civil society has long been in need of such ethnographic investigation. The emphasis placed on this idea has intensified in modern societies as the actual qualities of civility and trust have been ever more dissipated. The contributors to this volume demonstrate that this theoretical emphasis on the individual does not take us very far in understanding everyday actions and practices, whether in western countries such as Britain, in the post-communist countries of Eastern Europe, or anywhere else in the world.

So, in terms of directing attention simultaneously to ideal codes and to the messy practical worlds in which people actually live their everyday lives, civil society can be a vital subject for political anthropology, An alternative juxtaposition will allow me to bring out two final points. The first is to distinguish two senses of *political society*. Political society in the narrow sense is that element in the model of Tocqueville which constitutes a necessary supplement to dualist models that contrast the state and its people, the private citizens. Examples such as that provided by Poland in recent years show the inadequacy of this dualist model. Though Buchowski's chapter implies a rather different view, the socialist state was not in fact opposed in any consistent, active way by the mass of its citizenry. Rather, opposition developed through the mobilisation of élite groups, small but highly articulate groups of intellectuals, and even smaller numbers of workers (Pelczynski 1988). Political society in this sense is unlikely in modern conditions to comprise more than a fraction of the total population (the fraction was somewhat larger in most socialist societies than is normally the case in stable, multiparty democracies). Much of the difficulty in managing the 'transition to democracy', not only in the ex-socialist countries but in many other parts of the world as well, stems from the inability of political society in this sense to speak for or represent the mass of the citizens. It emerged in opposition to an alien state, but often it has no more intrinsic legitimacy in the eyes of the citizenry than the displaced powerholders of the *ancien régime*. Political society in this sense is intensively studied by political scientists, and should not be confused with civil society.

Political society in the broader sense (and the main sense for anthropology) corresponds to the broader, looser notion of civil society outlined above. All human communities are held together by shared values and ideals. This makes them all inherently political. In this sense it was naive of some Eastern European dissidents to imagine civil society as a sphere free from politics. It is equally mistaken to diagnose changes in the global patterns of states and markets in terms of depoliticisation. It is certainly an obfuscation and an evasion of the political realities for the leaders of modern western states to pretend that they are strengthening civil society when they transfer responsibilities and functions away from elected bodies to so-called 'expert' groups. (Britain now has many thousands of these 'quangos', and they are responsible for a very considerable slice of public expenditure.) Such shifts are far from anti-statist in reality, and they are certainly not anti-political.

Unlike the theologians and political theorists who have also studied the moralities of civil society, anthropologists ground their contribution in ethnographic research. So long as humans remain culturally diverse these moralities will retain particular characteristics: western models of civil society may be extremely suggestive and may in some quarters evoke direct emulation, but they are very far from being plausible as a universal template. The western philosophers' model of civil society has itself undergone major changes. Some versions are no doubt more attractive than others, but the dominant contemporary model does not seem to have much to offer in resolving the practical problems of late-twentieth-century societies. Alternative discourses and practices may have more to offer.

Rather than pursue a universalist chimera by generalising one, narrow western blueprint of a civil society, it may be more appropriate to define our subject as *civil anthropology*. This would avoid the extremes of both universalist and relativist positions (I do not claim that it resolves the dilemmas of the philosophers). Many anthropologists are likely, as individuals, to be sympathetic to universalist notions of human rights, including laws that offer protection to individual human subjects. They should be aware that this universalism is itself the product of highly complex historical processes and that many of its elements are by no means unique to 'the west'. At the same time they seek, as anthropologists, empathetic understanding of the moral codes that provide the bases for solidarity and social control among the particular people they are studying. They are interested in tensions that exist *within* those communities. They may wish to compare the ideal codes with others, including that associated with western, pluralist models of civil society. The empirical investigation of real societies, western and non-western, pervaded by values and moralities that are culturally distinct, but all concerned in their own ways with standards of decent social behaviour, with human dignity, with what some people in Italy still refer to as *civiltà*, is a vast field. Civil anthropology will accord alternative moralities equal respect, and recoil from imposing western liberal-individualist conceptions where they have no place.[4]

NOTES

1 This is a good case for going back much further: the key terms of these debates – civil/civic, society, politics, community – all originate in the ancient Mediterranean world. The point has more than etymological interest. As John Corbin has pointed out to me, understandings of these key terms have followed different paths and, given their persistence in local languages, Southern Europeans have particular cause to resent the imposition upon them of a 'state versus society' debate that crystallised in Northwest Europe.
2 Lech Wałęsa had made essentially the same point a few years before this, substituting fish soup for the antique furniture – the different metaphors highlight the contrast between the high culture of the Czech and the populism of the Pole!
3 An introductory survey of the development of political anthropology is provided by Lewellen (1992). A more stimulating and adventurous approach is outlined by Gledhill (1994).
4 My thanks to John Corbin and Elizabeth Dunn for helpful comments on an earlier draft of this introduction.

REFERENCES

Cohen, J. L. and Arato, A. (1992) *Civil Society and Political Theory*, Cambridge, Mass.: MIT Press.

Fortes, M. and Evans-Pritchard, E. (eds) (1940) *African Political Systems*, London: Oxford University Press.

Fukuyama, F. (1992) *The End of History and the Last Man*, London: Hamish Hamilton.

Geertz, C. (1980) *Negara: The Theatre State in Nineteenth Century Bali*, Princeton, NJ: Princeton University Press.

Gellner, E. (1994) *Conditions of Liberty: Civil Society and its Rivals*, London: Hamish Hamilton.

Gledhill, J. (1994) *Power and Its Disguises*, London: Pluto.

Goody, J. (forthcoming) 'Civil society in an extra-European perspective', in S. Khilnani (ed.), *Civil Society*, Cambridge: Cambridge University Press.

Hall, J. A. (1995) 'In search of civil society', in J. A. Hall (ed.), *Civil Society: Theory, History, Comparison*, Cambridge: Polity Press, pp. 1–31.

Hann, C. (ed.) (1990) *Market Economy and Civil Society in Hungary*, London: Frank Cass.

Havel, V. (1993) 'The post-communist nightmare', *New York Review of Books*, 27 May.

Keane, J. (ed.) (1988) *Civil Society and the State: New European Perspectives*, London: Verso.

Konrád, Gy. (1984) *Antipolitics*, London: Quartet.

Kuklick, H. (1993) *The Savage Within: The Social History of British Anthropology, 1885–1945*, Cambridge: Cambridge University Press.

Kumar, K. (1993) 'Civil society: an enquiry into the usefulness of an historical term', *British Journal of Sociology* 44(3): 375–95.

——— (1994) 'Civil society again: a reply to Christopher Bryant's "Social self-organisation, civility and sociology"', *British Journal of Sociology* 45(1): 127–31.

Kuper, A. (ed.) (1992) *Conceptualizing Society*, London: Routledge.

Lewellen, T. (1992) *Political Anthropology: An Introduction*, 2nd edition, London: Bergin and Garvey.

Pelczynski, Z. (1988) 'Solidarity and "the rebirth of civil society"', in J. Keane (ed.), *Civil Society and the State: New European Perspectives*, London: Verso, pp. 361–80.

Seligman, A. (1992) *The Idea of Civil Society*, New York: The Free Press.

Tester, K. (1992) *Civil Society*, London: Routledge.

Wedel, J. R. (ed.) (1992) *The Unplanned Society: Poland During and After Communism*, New York: Columbia University Press.

—— (1994) 'US aid to Central and Eastern Europe, 1990–1994: an analysis of aid models and responses', in *East-Central European Economies in Transition: Study Papers submitted to Joint Economic Committee*, Congress of the United States, Washington: US Government Printing Office, pp. 299–335.

Chapter 1

Money, morality and modes of civil society among American Mormons

Elizabeth Dunn

Civil society is broadly regarded as the domain of relationships which falls between the private realm of the family on the one hand and the state on the other. A more specific definition of civil society sees it as 'the social relationships which involve the voluntary association and participation of individuals acting in their private capacities. In a simple and simplistic formula, civil society can be said to equal the milieu of private contractual relationships' (Tester 1992: 8). As such, civil society has been seen as the underpinning of capitalism and bourgeois democracy. However, as recent anthropological work (including White and Rabo, this volume) shows, civil society does not necessarily operate from the premise of liberal individualism. A broader definition of civil society is that of Charles Taylor: 'a web of autonomous associations independent of the state, which bind citizens together in matters of common concern, and by their existence or actions could have an effect on public policy' (cited in Kligman 1990: 420). If civil society is more like this, then a much wider range of non-state organisations needs to be included. Organisations which are based on the family or on residence, and which are based neither on contractual relations between unbound individuals nor on self-interest, must also be considered.

Arguments against universal individualism (e.g. Strathern 1988) tend to rest on a dichotomy between 'the west' and 'the rest'. The west, in this sense, provides a useful rhetorical device, which highlights the existence of non-individualistic, non-bourgeois forms of civil society. However, this is an incomplete picture of personhood and of civil society in 'the west'. In this chapter, I take the example of the Mormon church, a religious group founded and based in the United States, in order to complicate and enrich arguments about civil society.[1] Although American Mormons are people who participate in a capitalist, individualist society, they have created a form of 'civil society' that looks much more like those described for 'non-western' societies. I argue that through their moral doctrines on the family and on gift-giving, Mormons create a milieu where, in certain contexts, self-interest is denied and individuals are made less relevant as social actors. In doing so, they create a space which is not only apart from the American state, but which rejects state action. Through the gift, and its powers of social reproduction, Mormons make a civil society which is not based on private individuals, but rather on a moral system of community interaction.

CANNING THE GIFT

I had been sorting white beans for four hours. Over and over I reached out, swept a handful of beans across the stainless-steel table, and examined them. I picked out the dirt, the small grey stones, and the broken beans, and threw them into a bucket. Then, with a sweep of my hand, I brushed all the good beans into a plastic garbage can. The can had been emptied several times: I had sorted 200 pounds of beans, and had 200 more to go. As I sorted, other members of the work team would come by and help me sort for a moment or two between their other tasks. 'Have you counted all the beans, Sister Dunn?' Brother Richards joked, 'You know we need an accurate count!'

The beans I sorted were to become part of a beef stew, which would be cooked, canned, shipped and distributed by the church of Jesus Christ of Latter Day Saints (LDS or Mormons). Along with women from the Baltimore First Ward Relief Society,[2] I had volunteered to spend an evening transforming the food tithed by LDS farmers into cooked and preserved food. Other volunteers were using the huge machines in the factory (which is wholly owned by the LDS church, and used only for charitable production) to put the stew in metal cans. Later on, other volunteers would label the cans, and then ship them to 'bishops' storehouses', or the local church welfare distribution centres. The cans would be stocked with other food canned by other branches of the church in rooms like supermarkets, inside the bishop's storehouse. Local church leaders would then be able to collect bags of groceries and distribute them to church members in need. Throughout this whole process, all the inputs to the stew – the raw materials, the machinery used to can, the labour involved in growing, shipping, canning and distributing, the money used to buy vegetables not grown by Mormon farmers – were donated by church members. In essence, the stew was not just a gift in itself, but the product of a long series of gifts made within the context of the church. It was an integral part of the enormous Mormon welfare system, which includes not only gifts of food, but also donated clothing, help with bills and mortgage payments, an employment bureau, child-care assistance, and spiritual, financial and emotional counselling.

The LDS church discourages its members from accepting government welfare cheques. It preaches financial self-sufficiency, and to that end, encourages its members to save money and to store a year's worth of canned food and bottled water in their homes in case of natural disasters, social upheaval or financial need. However, the church recognises that unforeseeable circumstances sometimes force people to rely on others for assistance in meeting basic needs. Both the church welfare system and the Relief Society were developed to help church members meet those needs. Active church members, both men and women, are assigned three or four families to visit every month. Both a pair of men (home teachers) and a pair of women (visiting teachers) visit every family in the ward each month.[3] Sometimes they enquire after the spiritual needs of the family, ministering to them or providing a lesson or bible study for spiritual enrichment. At other times, if they see the family is in need of material things, they attempt to find out the extent of the need and report it to either the bishop or the Relief Society president.

Allocating funds or goods from the LDS charity programme is entirely up to the bishop. He prays, and if he receives 'divine guidance' that the person or family in question should be helped, he can allocate whatever amount he feels is necessary. The only requirement is that the potential recipient be 'judged worthy'. There are no hard and fast guidelines as to what being 'worthy' means, but LDS people I talked to suggested that, in general, the recipient should be an active member of the church.[4] Recipients should be actively searching for ways to improve their situations, whether by job hunting, re-examining their budgets, or getting more education or training in order to get a job later (the church has programmes for all of these things, and welfare recipients are encouraged to take advantage of them). The church sees its welfare programmes as short-term solutions to temporarily bad times, not as long-term subsidy programmes.

Recipients, no matter how poor, are also expected to be giving. They, too, are expected to tithe 10 per cent of their income, no matter how meagre, and to give of their time and work to others. If they are the recipients of material goods from the church, they are expected to donate time and work to the cannery or the bishop's storehouse. One man who was bedridden with diabetes was asked to become the bishop's 'secretary'. It was a task especially created for this man; one that allowed him to 'give' even though he could not get out of bed (Carlson 1992: 25).

The giving that welfare recipients do is not seen as payment or an exchange of labour for the charity of the church. Rather, it is seen as a morally necessary exercise which keeps welfare (the unreciprocated gift) from corroding the souls of recipients. As one official church publication puts it, 'Needy members are given the opportunity to work for the goods and services they receive, thus allowing them to maintain their dignity and make a meaningful contribution to others despite their untoward circumstances' (Ballard 1993: 112). One informant said that welfare recipients are expected to 'Give back, yes. Pay for, no.' Exact repayment (except on interest-free short-term loans to pay bills) is not expected, either during the time recipients are helped by the church or afterwards. Recipients are also expected to give to others when they are 'back on their feet', and to the extent that they are able, just as others gave to them. This, too, is not repayment or reciprocation of the original gift, but a second gift which likewise does not demand repayment.

TYPES OF VALUE

What is the value of the goods given by the Mormon welfare system? This is a question which is difficult to answer and may not even be meaningful in the context of the church. Within the space of the church, value has a very different meaning from the monetary value which is in use in domains more closely connected to the state.

I discovered this at one point during my shift on the canning line, when Brother Richards, who had been 'called' by the church to run the factory full time, came with another man to help me sort the beans. I asked Brother Richards what he thought was the aggregate value of the goods distributed from this particular bishop's storehouse. He refused to tell me, saying that the church did not divulge such information. I asked him if he would confirm a range: 'Is it over 100,000 dollars a year?' I asked. 'Let's just say "a lot"', he answered. Brother Richards was then called away, and I sat puzzling over his refusal to place a value on the gifts being given by and through the church. The other man, whom I had not met before, quietly asked me, 'Do you want to know how much the church gives away?' I nodded. He said, 'Well, how much money do you spend a week on groceries?' 'About 40 dollars', I responded. 'And how many members of the church are there?' 'About 4 million', I answered.[5] 'So,' he said, 'If 1 per cent of the church's members get groceries every week for a year, how much is that?' I sat, stupidly, trying to do the sum in my head. 'It's between 80 and a 100 million dollars a year?' I was really surprised. He said, 'And that's just groceries. That's why I laughed when you guessed 100,000.'

The whole incident, both Brother Richards's refusal and the other man's indirect way of telling me the amount, was confusing to me. Why did the men avoid quantifying the value of the gifts being given? After all, I knew that the LDS church had no prohibition about specifying the value of gifts to the church, that is, the 10 per cent tithe. Yet, in every instance that I asked, LDS people refused to specify the value of gifts given by the church, or by themselves acting for the church.

For Mormon volunteer workers, time given in the service of the church is likewise not easily broken apart and reaggregated to form a quantifiable total. This is the direct opposite of time and labour which is exchanged for wages. In the ideal typical case of wage labour, time is broken down into increasingly minute quantities, so that the employer can get labour value out of every minute he has purchased. But work-time given in the service of the church cannot be infinitely fragmented and reaggregated. For this reason, no monetary value is ever assigned to time or work given. This bears some striking parallels to both Brother Richards's joke about 'counting the beans' and his refusal to quantify the value of the church's charity. Like the beans once they were in the stew, the gifts given by church members to others are whole and integral things; they cannot be easily broken down into commensurable units.

The contrast between work-time exchanged for wages and the work-time given by church members was shown in a joke made by Sean Moore, a young man who came as part of the second shift at the cannery. When he relieved me at my job (which by that time was chopping onions), I said 'I can't believe you're working from midnight to 8 a.m. after working a full day at your job!' He laughed and said, 'Yeah, but you get more blessings that way!' 'Oh yeah,' I said, 'It's like getting overtime pay, time-and-a-half, right?' He replied, 'Exactly, I'm getting more blessings than you.' One might take this at face value, assuming that Mormons believe they are getting 'paid' in blessings from God for their work. In some senses this is true – every person that I asked said that they believed that because they were charitable, God would bless them. These blessings, however, are not a payment. Mormons do not believe there is a 'blessings-per-hour' rate of exchange, and they do not believe that God incurs a debt to them or is obligated to bless them because they work. In this way, Sean Moore's joking equivalence of blessings and wages was meant to underscore their fundamental *dissimilarity*.

We cannot repay God for his blessings. We cannot purchase his blessings by our service and our obedience. He cannot be placed under contract to us. What he wants from us is this acknowledgment of which I have spoken – that we see our relationship to him, that we acknowledge the ties that bind us to him, and that we accept his generous gifts with a loving heart.

(Okazaki 1993: 32)

Just as wage labour and donated work are dissimilar, so are tithes (in cash or in kind) and donated work-time. Tithes in cash or in kind are measured as they enter the church. The beans, for example, were weighed and assigned an equivalent monetary value when they were tithed by the farmer. Similarly, when people pay their tithe in cash, they fill out a form which details the amount of the payment and the amount of the income it was based on. Work-time, however, is never quantified. Even in the cannery, a quasi-industrial setting, time was not easily quantified: although each of us knew we were supposed to work about eight hours, from 4 p.m. until midnight, people arrived and left at different times. At midnight, people did not leave exactly on time, but worked until they reached some sort of a natural break in their tasks (e.g. finishing sorting one bag of beans). Church members do not 'watch the clock' while they are working for the church. They do not measure or keep track of the time they give or the work they do, nor do they ever assign it an equivalent cash value. Work-time and tithing cannot be substituted for one another: even if a person pays an extra tithe, he or she is still expected to volunteer to work. Likewise, working extra hours does not excuse a person from paying the full 10 per cent tithe. In the church, the capitalist truism that time is money does not apply. Because of the spiritual, moral and social virtues that Mormons believe service to others has, a Mormon cannot 'buy' his or her way out of serving in the church.

This suggests that time and work are the categories which transform the wages earned in the world outside the church into the gifts given and shared by church members. Volunteer work cooked the beans (which were individual, countable and separable), and turned them into a stew from which they were not separable. In the same way and at the same time, donated work-time 'cooks' money from outside the church which is given in tithes and fast offerings, and transforms it into food which does not have a cash equivalent. The essential value of money and commodities is converted, making them into gifts which are incommensurable with cash. In Mormonism, this conversion of quantifiable inputs (wages, commodities) into unmeasurable gifts reinforces the border between the social life of the church and the world outside it. Clear distinctions are made about the behaviour appropriate to each venue. For example, in the world outside the church, it is acceptable to charge money for one's work, but inside the church, all work is a gift. Outside the church, it is all right to act in one's self-interest (within limits), but inside the church, one should strive to be selfless and to act in the service of others.

THE CONCEPT OF THE FAMILY

The gift in Mormonism effaces some boundaries, and at the same time it creates others. This process is mediated through the concept of family, which is at the heart of the Mormon religion. At Sunday meetings in the Mormon church, speakers rarely refer to individuals except in the context of families. In Sacrament Meeting, for example, I often heard exhortations to young men and women to marry and form families. Individual behaviour, in this case adherence to a moral code which prohibits sexual activity, was explained to single adults in terms of the effects that premarital sex would have on their present (natal) and future (marital) families. Even physical health, which was said to be the responsibility of each individual, was related to families: the speaker said that you have to take care of yourself in order to be in good physical and spiritual health so you can fulfil your responsibilities to your family. The ideal type of the family as seen in church rhetoric is, of course, the nuclear family. Ideally, the father of the family earns a wage, while the mother takes care of the children and the home. Ideally, too, the nuclear family is set in the context of a large extended family which lives nearby. Women who are housewives have a large number of female kin nearby to help with child care, to teach home-making skills, and to help on larger chores such as quilting and home canning.[6] Labour is a gift that is given 'for free' by female relatives to one another and to their families, with only vague expectations that it will be returned in kind some day. Within the family, either nuclear or extended, gifts are not expected to be repaid to the giver; rather, each member is expected to contribute to the family to the best of his or her ability.

Baltimore Mormon women and their families differ markedly from the ideal nuclear and/or extended family. A few of the women, mostly those who are from Utah and who have come to Baltimore with spouses who are attached to Johns Hopkins Medical School, live in nuclear families with children. These women, however, are cut off from the larger extended families that they left behind in Utah. As Anne Brown, a Utah-born woman, said, 'Most young mothers here don't have family around.

It gets isolated here. I think society isolates mothers, because it doesn't value people who don't make money.' For Sister Brown, like several other young mothers I spoke to, the church has taken the place of the extended family she left behind. She talked about forming baby-sitting cooperatives with other mothers, and calling older women in the Relief Society for motherly advice. Although the women rarely get together for collective work, they do exchange child-care services, home-made dinners, and small home-made gifts, as well as talk, gossip and emotional support. The point is not that each individual woman is desperate for the help, but rather that the exchanges of gifts and work unify the women into a quasi-family, replacing the companionship and community spirit of the extended families left behind. Work-time again converts parts (isolated women) into wholes (pseudo-extended families).

Other women in the ward do not have nuclear families like Sister Brown's, much less large extended families. In the Baltimore ward, most of the members (about 95 per cent) are converts, not born-Mormons. Many of the members are from foreign countries or from inner-city Baltimore. Few of them have extensive experience with what the Baltimore Mormons call 'Utah culture', which is based on the extended family. Often, these converts are alone in some sense: either they are single and without either marital or natal families (in the case of the many foreign nannies in the ward), or they are the only Mormons in their families. The ward makes special efforts to incorporate these women in the 'extended family' of the church. They are invited to dinner in the homes of church members, they are visited regularly by home teachers or visiting teachers, and they are strongly encouraged to participate in the many weekly activities in the church.

When I asked Sister Brown about the role of families in the church, she told me that 'when you get away from Salt Lake City [Utah], you have fewer nuclear families'. She said that in the last several years, the church had become increasingly sensitive to the changing nature of families, and to the diversity of family types in wards. One way that this sensitivity is expressed is in the way that wards and the church as a whole take over some of the responsibilities and functions once assigned to the nuclear family, becoming 'like' a family. In an article from the church's official magazine, Virginia Pearce begins by explicitly equating wards and families. The piece is entitled 'Ward . . . families: part of Heavenly Father's plan for us'. She writes:

> I believe that Heavenly Father recognized that even though our relationship with him and our accountability to him are intensely

personal, we gather strength when we meet in groups ... Learning in groups is so important that Heavenly Father planned for us to be born into a group – the most basic, most hallowed, and most powerful group on earth: the family. Wards are not designed to replace the family unit, but to support the family and its righteous teachings. A ward is another place where there is enough commitment and energy to form a sort of 'safety net' family for each of us when our families cannot or do not provide all the teaching and growing experiences we need to return to Heavenly Father.[7]

(Pearce 1993: 79)

Pearce defines the ward-as-family functionally, illustrating six things that ward families provide members. All of these functions are phrased in terms of gifts, giving and receiving, but nowhere in the article does Pearce say that the relationship between a member and the ward is contractual, or that a member must give particular things in order to belong. In fact, in her first 'function', she explicitly says the opposite. She quotes Robert Frost:

Home is the place where, when you have to go there
They have to take you in.
I should have called it
Something you somehow haven't to deserve
        (Robert Frost, cited in Pearce 1993: 79)

She goes on to say, 'A ward is something you somehow haven't to deserve', and to equate the ward also to a body. She quotes the apostle Paul: 'For by one Spirit are we all baptized into one body, whether we be Jews or Gentiles, whether we be bond or free ... For the body is not one member, but many' (1 Corinthians 12:13–14). This equivalence between church, family and body/self is an aspect of the boundary drawing and crossing that is marked by the generalised reciprocity of the gift. Pearce talks about all the ways that the ward family is made stronger by gifts which pass among its members: gifts of listening and encouragement, prayer and fasting, and tangible gifts of aid in times of crisis. Even the act of receiving is explained as a gift: Pearce says that '[w]ard families provide ways for us to contribute' (1993: 80). She sees receiving as a gift which allows others to transcend individual selfishness, to 'quit thinking about yourself'. Pearce explains that this gives comfort and confidence to the giver: 'Paradoxically, as we concentrate on the needs of others, our own needs become less controlling' (*ibid.*).

The way in which giving within the church expands the boundaries of the self and the family was particularly clear in the case of Sister Diaz. In Sacrament Meeting one Sunday, the man leading the service asked the members to pray for Sister Diaz's daughter, who was missing. Later, in Relief Society, Sister Diaz stood and thanked the women for all the food they had brought to her home, and for all the time they had spent in comforting her as she cried, talking to the police, and caring for her other children. She also mentioned that several of the men in the bishopric (the ward leadership) had come to pray for her daughter and to ask God for her safe return. After church, I asked several of the Relief Society women about Sister Diaz. The women in the ward spoke of how difficult it was for Sister Diaz as a single mother and a recent immigrant; someone who was 'alone' in Baltimore. They told me that they could not imagine a greater pain than losing a child, and they spoke of how they, as church members, had to fill in for the family that was absent or that was non-Mormon. This 'filling in' was accomplished by giving gifts of food, of time, of blessings (from the men) and prayer, and of emotional support. In her thanks, Sister Diaz acknowledged this role, saying to the women, 'You are all truly my sisters.'

At the largest level, the church as a whole is a family, and all its members are brothers and sisters in Christ. As members of this family, they give to other members without expectations of recompense – even to those they do not know. At the cannery, we were giving to people we did not know, but who, as we canned, we could imagine. They, too, were part of the family of the church. In fact, they were imagined explicitly as such.

Giving, as Marcel Mauss (1990) pointed out, creates unity. The gift in the Mormon church creates a unity of a particular sort because it serves to transcend the boundaries of the individual. Because gifts of things, money or work within the family are not expected to be reciprocated, but instead go to the good of the whole unit, the boundaries of the individual are blurred. The goodness of the gift is for the entire family, and although its individual members partake of the gift and contribute gifts, there is no accounting kept. The individual ceases to be the relevant unit of analysis. In a strange sense, the family becomes the self under consideration: what one member gets, all receive. In a parallel way, the ward is also a 'self'. When a member gives to the ward, he or she receives at the same time. The gift is not seen as something that is alienated from the giver, or which creates a boundary between the self who gives and the other who receives. Rather, the process of giving incorporates both giver and receiver into a larger self. Giving to the collective is not imagined imagined as impoverishing the individual, but as creating a sum of abundance which is greater than the separate gifts and in which all will share.

The way in which the Mormon gift creates ties among individuals and makes communities echoes Mauss's analysis of 'archaic' societies. Mauss stresses that the gift always entails an obligation to reciprocate. Because gifts create these obligations, they create social ties, and therefore serve to unify communities (Mauss 1990: 12, 35, 46). But Mauss stresses that in addition to unifying individuals, tribes or families, the gift also creates divisions. In the process of transferring the gift, which contains something of the giver, both giver and recipient recognise that they are distinct and opposed. This is how the gift can come to form the basis of hierarchy: the gift that is too big or too lavish to be reciprocated in kind abases the receiver (Mauss 1990: 13, 24, 37). In contrast, Mormon giving, either personally or through the medium of church-sponsored charity, is not about creating distinctions and hierarchies among individuals, but about effacing them. The gift is given to incorporate the receiver into the collective self, whether that is the family or the ward or the church.

The way in which the Mormon gift blurs the boundaries between individuals and makes them parts of larger wholes is much more like what Strathern (1988) describes for Melanesia than what she describes for the west. Strathern asserts that in Melanesian thought, the western dichotomy between society and the bounded individual does not apply. Rather, the Melanesian person is a *dividual*, the 'plural and composite site of the relationships that produced' him or her, rather than an *a priori* unit which must be socialised (Strathern 1988: 13, 131; cf. Marriott 1976). Mormons see themselves in a similar way, as long as they are in the confines of the family/church. They view themselves as embedded in, and inseparable from, webs of relationships between men and women ('marriage'), among siblings or members of the same gender ('brotherhood' or 'sisterhood'), between parents and children ('parenthood' and 'family') and between self and God (a relationship which transcends and subsumes all the above relationships). Baltimore Mormons contrast this with the city outside the boundaries of the church, which they refer to as a place where people act as individuals and engage in transitory relationships for personal gain.

This is not to say that Mormons in Baltimore dispense with a concept of the individual. On the contrary, Mormon theology has an explicit doctrine of 'free agency', which means that individuals have the God-given ability to make choices. These choices can be about individual behaviour: the choice to obey or not obey the dictates of the Lord. They can also be about individual belief: the choice to accept or not accept Christ. However, the choices to accept Christ and to obey the word of the Lord inevitably lead the individual into a network of relationships, further blurring the boundaries of the self and converting the individual into a dividual. It is not the case that Mormons lack a concept of the self (such an assertion would be patently ridiculous), but that *within the domain of the church, the individual is made less relevant either as actor or as object of action.*

THE CHURCH, 'AMERICAN SOCIETY' AND THE STATE

The obvious corollary of the blurring of boundaries between self and other in the context of the church is that the boundary between the domain of the church and the 'outside world' is drawn at the same time. The members of the Baltimore First Ward often described the city of Baltimore (outside the church) as a place where there was a war of all against all. They mentioned the problems that they and other members faced: poverty and violence first among them. Stories about the disappearance of Sister Diaz's (non-member) daughter, or of Sister Sutcliffe, who was bludgeoned to death by her (non-member) son, were whispered before and after meetings. Church members used these cases as illustrations of 'American society' and 'Baltimore', which they portrayed as dangerous places made up of individuals solely in pursuit of their own gratification. These individuals stole, committed acts of violence, and engaged in immoral sexual acts without regard for the effects of their actions on others. The most common condemnation of these imagined people was that they were 'irresponsible' – that is, that they acted without regard for, or ties to, others. Sister Anne Brown drew a line between the church and 'American society' when she talked about the role of the gift and the Gospel in Mormon theology. She said that the Gospel teaches us to ask what we can do for one another, and creates a give and take between people. Giving can include letting other people help us. But, she added, the Gospel teaches that we should be self-sufficient. The church teaches self-sufficiency, but American society – and especially the American government's welfare programme – does not.

What is this paradox? How can the church claim to teach the value of giving and proclaim the need for self-sufficiency at the same time? Why is a lack of 'self-sufficiency' blamed for poverty and violence? Brother Sean Moore explained that the doctrine of self-sufficiency means that you should do your best to provide for yourself. When trouble arises, you should rely on yourself (and the preparations you have made) first; your family second; and the church third.[8] He said that you should not rely on government handouts, because that violates the doctrine of self-sufficiency. From this, I infer that while church, family and self are all parts of the 'self' in 'self-sufficiency', the state is not.

These points are underscored by Brother Moore's assertion that accepting welfare is one of the root causes of violence, illegitimacy and other ills of the inner city. Because people who accept welfare are not obligated to contribute anything to the collective, they are simultaneously dependent and unbound: the money that they rely on makes them into individuals, who do not (and cannot) free themselves from welfare to become responsible members of the collective. As Constance Horner, the former Deputy Secretary of Health and Human Services, said, 'People in need want to be connected to family and community. The Mormon church recognizes these ordinary human facts. Our governmental welfare systems, which isolate those in need and reinforce dependence, do not' (cited in Carlson 1992: 30).

Baltimore Mormons' talk about 'gentile' society echoes both Simmel's comments about 'freedom' in a monetised society and Mauss's comments about the destructive nature of government welfare. Simmel argues that in a monetised society, people can join many different associations just by giving money to them or getting money from them. They are not required to be part of a 'living community' with ties based on residence, religion, kin, politics or work. These people are only bound together by money:

> Since the interest of the individual participant in an association is expressible only in money, directly or indirectly, money has slipped like an insulating layer between the objective totality of the association and the subjective totality of the personality, just as it has come between owner and property. . . . This brings into existence a community of action of those individuals and groups who stress their separation and reserve at all other points.

> (Simmel 1990: 18–19)

This strange sort of 'freedom', a freedom from having one's life entwined with others, is what Mauss sees as the danger in welfare systems that do not require the recipient to give (or to work) in return. He sees such systems as creating egoism, individualism, isolation and stagnation as well as systems of inequality and hierarchy (1990: 69–74). Mauss, following Durkheim's lead, advocates the formation of *corporations*, solidarity groups based on shared occupation. The solidarity in these groups, Mauss suggests, would be based on mutual giving, including charity for the aged and sick.

Through their welfare policies, Mormons seek to create the kind of living community described by Simmel, or a religious community analogous to the corporations of Mauss and Durkheim. In insisting that church-welfare recipients give both work-time and tithes, and in making it impossible to substitute work-time and money for one another, Mormons seek to eliminate the 'insulating layer' between individuals and thereby make them parts of a greater self. It is for precisely this reason that they see state welfare, individualism and urban malaise as mutually reinforcing. This is the antithesis of Mormon communities and Mormon charity.

Many Mormons also believe that the government welfare system also encourages a dependence on the government which might infringe on their religious liberty, not only as individuals but as a group. Brother Adrian Scott told me that the church's welfare system

> grows out of a historical desire to take care of one's own, not to be dependent on the government . . . I think that the fault most Mormons find with the federal system is that it tends to breed dependency on the welfare system . . . the church is wary of receiving government funds in any form because they usually are offered with strings attached. The strings, in effect, could give the government the right to intervene in affairs that the church views as its responsibility.

This comment was echoed by many other Mormons. Most of them told me about the church's history of persecution and migration as a way of explaining both the welfare system and the distrust of the federal government. The Mormon church was founded in upstate New York in the 1830s, but was forced by mob violence to emigrate westward. Church members settled first in Kirtland, Ohio, and then were forced to move to Nauvoo, Illinois, where Prophet Joseph Smith and other church leaders were assassinated by an angry mob. Brigham Young then led the surviving church members on an arduous trek west, to discover a 'Zion' where they could worship free from persecution. They founded their Zion in the Salt Lake Valley, in what they called the state of Deseret, but which became the state of Utah. As another informant, Brother Milan Dilworth, told me, 'The Mormons have had a number of occasions in our history where the government would not insure our rights as citizens of the United States. When they moved to the Utah Territory wilderness it was to gain freedom.'

The first Mormon welfare system was started when Joseph Smith and the first converts left upstate New York and moved to Kirtland. There, church leaders proposed that all members of the church should give all their belongings, including farmland, to the church. These belongings would then be redistributed to all the members, so that each family would have enough to subsist. This plan, called the Law of Consecration came to Joseph Smith in a revelation received on 9 February 1831 (Mangum and Blumell 1993: 21). It promised that in the new Zion, all property would be made into one (the property of the church), and all the people would also be made into one. It was designed as a way for the church to incorporate all the homeless, landless converts who had found their way to Kirtland. Kirtland was never the communitarian Utopia that was envisioned by the church leadership. Few of the members signed over their property, and finally, in 1835, the Law of Consecration was reformulated so that members were only required to turn over that which was surplus to subsistence needs (Mangum and Blumell 1993: 26; see Doctrine and Covenants 42: 30–2). This is the basis of the law of tithing.

Mormons often bring up this history: the Law of Consecration, the Kirtland experiment, and the migration westward. They see it not only as the historical basis for the current Mormon welfare system, but as a lesson about the need to depend on one another in order to be independent from the government. Brother Tom Bingham wrote to me:

Why would Mormons want their own welfare system when the federal government was filling the void? . . . The history I just told [of the Law of Consecration] shows how the concept of self-sufficiency in Mormonism is engrained not only at the individual level, but at the social level. We feel an obligation to ourselves as a body. Also, I think that Mormons, historically, have been wary of the federal government's motives. I mean, Brigham Young led them westward to find a place to worship in peace, in large part because they didn't receive the support of the federal government in maintaining civil liberties guaranteed them under the Constitution. This might explain why . . . the church 'provided for itself' by forming its own welfare system. Today, however, Mormons pride themselves on being model citizens. . . . So why do we still have a welfare system and not rely totally on 'external' sources? Probably for three reasons: 1) Mormons remember history, 2) Mormons believe that at some future date we will be asked to live the Law of Consecration again, and perhaps 3) the system works; emphasis is placed on welfare services as being temporary services that aid a person and not a permanent lifestyle.

Baltimore Mormons depict the world inside the church as one of generalised reciprocity, indivisible work and indivisible gifts, morality, and intense personal connections between members of the church community. They value their liberty, as a religious group. In contrast, they portray the world outside the church as a realm of unfettered individuals, wage labour in which time and money are divisible, immorality, isolation and danger. They see the American federal government, with its welfare programmes which encourage this 'dependent individualism', as a potential threat. Yet, even with this negative characterisation of the potentials of the American state, and of 'society' as a whole, Baltimore Mormons continue to live quite happily in the wider world. The church tells its members to 'obey the law of the land', which includes paying taxes. The church asks most of its members to work for money, and it encourages many of its members to become successful business-owners.[9] The church itself runs several commercial businesses, including the ZCMI department stores and the Deseret publishing company. Official church publications even state that religious devotion will help in the capitalist business world: Ballard (1993: 85–6) tells the story of how, when he was a Ford dealer, he was offered a franchise for a new line of Ford cars. He says he felt the Holy Ghost clearly telling him, 'Do not sign the franchise.' He chose to ignore the words of this member of the Godhead, and signed the deal. It made him the first – and last – Edsel dealer in Salt Lake City.

How is it that Mormons can believe in the value of the gift, in some ways condemn individualism and the pursuit of self-interest, and draw a distinct boundary between themselves and the state, while at the same time being active participants in a federal system of government and a capitalist economy? The answer has to do with the boundaries that are drawn between the church and the outside world, and the way in which people and things can cross these boundaries.

CONVERSION

In her discussion of the transformation of value among Melanesians, Marilyn Strathern says that she will not call the movement of things and people between the domains of subsistence wealth and prestige wealth 'conversion', because the two domains are incomparable, and in fact do not simply comprise two different domains of exchange. She prefers the term 'transformation', because as domestic products pass into the realm of male prestige exchanges, 'the concept of wealth is freshly constituted' (1988: 159). Among Baltimore Mormons, the term conversion is much more appropriate, because in fact, the domains of church and 'the outside' are comparable, are explicitly compared, and are mutually constituted.

The term conversion, as it is used by Mormons themselves, refers to the missionary activities of the church, and to the process that people of any faith undergo when they are baptised into the church.[10] Most converts are baptised within several weeks of their first meeting with the missionaries. They are then considered to be full members of the church. However, as Sister Brown explained, the ties that bind them to the church are tenuous. Many of the converts do not know exactly what being a Mormon entails. Since the drop-out rate for converts is quite high, the process of binding the new convert to the church community begins right after the baptism. Church members visit the new convert at home, and try to provide 'support' for them and the decision that they have made. Sister Brown said that the pressures that take new members away from the church (including their non-member families) can be intense, so it is important that other church members give a lot of time and energy to this support. Support might include gifts of time spent teaching, listening and praying with the new member. It also includes the 'gift' of allowing the new member to give. New members can be assigned all sorts of responsibilities in the church, including piano-playing, song-leading, grounds maintenance and the like. Church members believe that giving the new member the opportunity to give is an important part of creating ties between the new member and the rest of the community.

The conversion of things, a process which brings them into the body of the church, is a process that is intertwined with the conversion of people. Like the boundary between members and 'gentiles', there is a boundary between objects of the world outside and those of the church. Because Mormons are not opposed to the capitalist world, both people and things regularly cross this border. For example, the wages and profits they earn are converted into meeting houses and canned goods and fundamentally changed in kind.

An interesting parallel to the Mormon case can be found in Carsten's (1989) article on the ways that Malays 'cook money', thereby transforming the wages and profits earned by men into domestic goods controlled by women. Most Malay men earn either wages (as migrant workers or boat hands) or profits (as fishermen). These wages and profits are viewed by Malays as divisive: a boat owner who hires his relatives as crew members must divide the catch or the profits from the fish among them according to their rank and tasks on the boat, and this creates familial tensions, hostility and resentment. The individualising, conflict-producing aspect of money is transformed, however, by the fact that men give all their wages or profits to the women of the household. The women of the household, often wives of siblings or mothers-in-law and daughters-in-law, pool a portion of the money they hold and use it for domestic expenses. In this system of pooled income, whoever has money spends it on household necessities: no accounting is kept and no direct reciprocity is expected. Because money is mediated by women, who represent the collective character of the family, the individualising, competitive, commercial relations that the money represents are changed into the collective, harmonious relations of the house and kin group. Carsten writes:

> When money enters the house, it is first transferred from men to women, and secondly, it is de-individualized, becoming the property of the married couple. Thirdly, this de-individualization is pushed further in the way that money is spent by women on household expenses. Division within the [multicouple] household is deliberately played down; there is one hearth and to the house and its running expenses are, at least in theory, met by all adult household members collectively. . . . Earnings may be tainted by ideas opposed to kinship, by commercial and individualistic values, but in their passage through the house, the central symbol of kin unity, and through the hands of women, they become imbued with the ideals of kinship and thus 'socialized'. The negative, antisocial power of money is thus neutralized through the action of women associated with the house.
>
> (Carsten 1989: 132)

Among Baltimore Mormons, the money which is earned outside the house and outside the church is similarly 'cooked' or 'socialised'. Wages and profits earned outside the church are quantifiable, as is the time spent earning them. These wages first pass through the household, where they are made the property of both the husband and the wife, and where the 10 per cent tithe is taken off. With the remainder of the wages, the wife converts her husband's wages into food by shopping and cooking. Her work is not quantified, and the food is seen as a gift to the children which does not demand reciprocation. The work of the wife/mother is the transformative act: she 'cooks' the money and changes it into a gift.

When money goes to the church in the form of tithes and fast offerings, it is similarly converted. The money that comes in is quantified and individualised. But as the tithes and fast offerings are used to purchase raw foods or machinery, which are used to make canned goods, money is turned into food. The food is unquantifiable, indivisible, and does not demand exact or direct reciprocity: it is a gift from the collective (church/family) to the individual. Because the food is a gift, it strengthens enduring social ties between members and the church. Again, the transformative category is the work that goes into the 'cooking', work-time which is not quantifiable or divisible and which is not remunerated. Work-time (as opposed to wage labour) is a category which converts both people and things. Missionary work brings people to the church, and gifts made with donated work-time bind them to the church. (These gifts can be spiritual as well as material, but the need for donated work-time – to teach and pray for spiritual gifts as well as to produce material gifts – remains the same.) 'Responsibilities', or the opportunity to give, and 'help' or 'service', or the opportunity to receive, convert individuals of different backgrounds into parts of a larger self, the body of the church. The system of giving is therefore not just about production, but about reproduction. As things and people are absorbed into the system of tithing and fast offerings, and converted into gifts and dividuals, the church reproduces itself and expands. Just as a wife/mother's cooking nourishes the bodies of the family, and allows her to make more children, the Mormon gift system nourishes the bodies of the faithful and adds more bodies to the church (cf. Strathern 1988: 144–5). In both processes, what is produced is not just individuals, but collective wholes: the family and the church.

This 'cooking system', taken to its limits, is what Mormons refer to as the Law of Consecration. Although the Law of Consecration, in its strict form, is no longer a commandment of the church, many devout Mormons see the society it describes as an ideal and a future, not a past, Utopia. Some Baltimore Mormons described it as the society that would exist after the second coming of Christ. Yet, Baltimore Mormons are comfortable with the fact that a communitarian social system does not exist now. They say that the Law of Consecration is an unrealisable ideal at this time, and they support the idea of a capitalist, market-based society (even in the Law of Consecration, the phrase 'thou shalt pay for that thou shall receive of thy brother' suggests that a market system of exchanges is never entirely phased out). However, they do see tithing and fast offerings, as well as the entire Mormon welfare system, as steps in the direction of the ideal, and as factors which mitigate the negative effects of the capitalist economy. Inasmuch as the current welfare system makes the 'people of the covenant' into 'one' in some ways, and inasmuch as it collects some of their property, LDS charity disrupts and mitigates what they see as the individualising, anti-family and anti-community effects of the capitalist system. This may be what Baltimore Mormons meant when they said that the Mormon system of 'family values' was the answer to 'problems of the inner city'.

Can we take Mormons' creation of an internal gift economy, one which is partitioned from the capitalist economy, as a critique of capitalism? This is a knotty problem. Certainly, Mormon charity, through a system of negations (volunteer labour implying its opposite, wage labour; giving as opposed to selling; charity as opposed to commodities, and so on) implies a recognition of some of the deleterious effects of capitalism. However, the welfare system is designed as a stopgap, and as a means of getting people back into the capitalist system as productive workers and wage-earners. It is viewed as complementary to, not opposed to, capitalism. Similarly, the domain inside the church is seen as complementary to, rather than directly opposed to, the world outside. Mormons comfortably cross the boundaries between the church and 'society' every day.

Along the same lines, the Mormons seek to expand their 'civil society' (although this is not a term they would use) not by opposing the state, but by creating an alternative domain to that of the state. As Brother Sam Freed told me,

> In my opinion, the church has its own welfare system because it believes in taking care of its own, and encourages independence and self-reliance. Ideally, the church organisation is the only type of government or organisation that would be needed. No big bureaucratic government, no taxes, et cetera. But of course, in an imperfect world, this is only an ideal.

The Mormons' attempts at changing society are focused not on undermining or revolutionising either the government or the world outside the church, but on drawing more and more individuals into the body/self/family of the church and on expanding the domain of the church's action. They do this via the gift and its powers of social reproduction.

CONCLUSION: BEEHIVES AND CIVIL SOCIETY

When Brigham Young founded Deseret as a Mormon community, he chose the beehive as its symbol. The beehive remains the insignia for the state of Utah today, and is said to represent two virtues: work and community. Work and community are at the heart of Mormon civil society. Work is the transformative category which brings individuals into the community and makes them part of the greater whole. Neither work nor community are neutral categories. They are explicitly *virtues*;

that is, aspects of a moral system. In many ways, that moral quality is what makes Mormon charity a realm of action distinct from the state. By using moral rules, the Mormons create a space where goods are valued differently than they are in the outside world. In doing so, the primary mode of state interaction with its citizens – money – is partially disabled. This, too, creates a boundary between Mormons and the state. Because in this context Mormons give (taxes) but do not take (welfare), there is an unreciprocated gift which accentuates the social distance between church members and the state.

What does all of this say about civil society as an analytic concept? It shows that there are many different premises on which civil societies or groups within a civil society can be built. There are many means through which groups can be formed and cohere. Voluntary contractual relations between discrete individuals are just one such arrangement. Altruistic relations between group members is another. This variety of 'civil societies' holds both for western and non-western societies. The same people may use different means of forming groups outside the state as they move from context to context. We might think of repertoires of civil society building, in a manner analogous to the repertoires of exchange recently outlined by Davis (1992). The range of these social formations and the way in which they are created and maintained are matters for ethnographic investigation.

NOTES

1 Many thanks to the members of the Baltimore First Ward, who gave me both a warm welcome and their time and energy to answer my questions, to DeeAnna Knotts and Connie Dunn for their help on questions of Mormon theology, and to Olive Dunn, who exemplifies the true spirit of the gift. All of these people stressed that their views are their own and do not represent the official views of the church. My views, similarly, do not represent official church doctrine and have not received official church approval.

2 Some relevant definitions: a ward is the equivalent of a Protestant congregation, or a Catholic parish. It is the smallest local grouping. A stake is an aggregation of several wards. The Relief Society is a ladies' benevolent organisation, which concerns itself with the material and spiritual well-being of its members and the members of the ward.

3 At the local level, the Mormon church has a completely lay organisation. Even the bishop of the ward is a volunteer. Almost all adult men who are active in the Church hold the priesthood and can perform a limited range of church rituals. 'Tithing' refers to the 10 per cent of pre-tax income, payable to the local bishop every month, that the church asks its members to donate. The church also asks members to fast on the first Sunday of every month. On that day, the members are to calculate the value of the meals that they

did not eat, and give the money to the bishop in order to support LDS charity efforts.

4   There was some disagreement on this point. One woman, a former Relief Society president, told me that LDS welfare was only for Mormons, but Brother Richards (the head of all the canneries on the East Coast) told me that it was up to the bishop to decide whether non-Mormons could be helped.

5   This estimate may be grossly inaccurate. Official estimates of the size of the church place it at about 8 million members, but this includes inactive Mormons who may not have attended church for years.

6   This may seem like a stereotype of the Mormon pioneer woman, but in fact, many jobs such as canning and quilting are carried out by groups of female relatives in Utah even today. I learned how to quilt when my grandmother, aunts and female cousins offered to make me a quilt for my new house. When I showed my quilts to one of my informants in Baltimore, a convert, she was amazed. 'You're more Mormon than I am', she joked, knowing that I am a 'jack' (inactive or lapsed) Mormon.

7   Mormons rarely refer to God as 'God', or even as 'Lord', but most often as 'Heavenly Father'. The use of the kin term reinforces ideas of the church as a family.

8   This statement was repeated nearly verbatim by many other informants.

9   The injunction to work for money holds only for the male half of the membership. Some Mormons have become very successful capitalists: Bill Marriott, the owner of Marriott hotels, is a Mormon, as is Kay Whitmore, the former chief executive officer of Kodak. Stephen Covey, who wrote the business best seller, *The Seven Habits of Highly Effective People*, is a Mormon. So is Hyrum Smith, the founder of the Franklin Planner Company, which produces a version of the 'Filofax' books often seen in business circles. In regard to the last two people, it is interesting to note that both Covey and Smith emphasise that bringing morality back into business will make both individuals and firms more successful.

10 The term conversion does not apply when the person being baptised is the child of a church member. Even though Mormons do not baptise children until they are 8 years old ('the age of accountabilty', or the age at which children can accept responsibility for their own behaviour), a child born into the church is in some sense a member even before baptism.

REFERENCES

Ballard, M. R. (1993) *Our Search for Happiness: An Invitation to Understand the Church of Jesus Christ of Latter Day Saints*, Salt Lake City, UT. Deseret Books.

Carlson, T. (1992) 'Holy dolers: the secular lessons of Mormon charity', *Policy Review* 59: 25–31.

Carsten, J. (1989) 'Cooking money', in M. Bloch and J. Parry (eds), *Money and the Morality of Exchange*, Cambridge: Cambridge University Press, pp. 000–000.

Covey, S. (1989) *The Seven Habits of Highly Effective People: Powerful Lessons in Personal Change*, New York: Simon and Schuster.

Davis, J. (1992) *Exchange*, Minneapolis: University of Minnesota Press.

Doctrines and Covenants (1984) Salt Lake City, UT: Church of Latter Day Saints Publishers.

hooks, b. (1993) 'Renewing feminism', *Found Object* 2: 1–19.

Kligman, G. (1990) 'Reclaiming the public: a reflection on recreating civil society in Romania', *Eastern European Politics and Societies* 4 (3): 393–438.

Mangum, G. and Blumell, B. (1993) *The Mormons' War on Poverty: A History of LDS Welfare 1830–1990*, Salt Lake City, UT: University of Utah Press.

Marriott, M. (1976) 'Hindu transactions: diversity without dualism', in B. Kapferer (ed.), *Transaction and Meaning: Directions in the Anthropology of Exchange and Symbolic Behavior*, Philadelphia: Institute for the Study of Human Issues.

Mauss, M. (1990) *The Gift: The Form and Reason for Exchange in Archaic Societies*, New York: Norton.

Okazaki, C. (1993) *Lighten Up!*, Salt Lake City, UT: Deseret Books.

Pearce, V. (1993). 'Ward and branch families: part of Heavenly Father's plan for us', *Ensign* 11: 79–80.

Simmel, G. (1991) 'Money in modern culture', *Theory, Culture & Society* 8 (3): 17–31.

Strathern, M. (1988) *The Gender of the Gift*, Berkeley and Los Angeles: University of California Press.

Tester, K. (1992) *Civil Society*, London: Routledge.

Chapter 2

How Ernest Gellner got mugged on the streets of London

Or: civil society, the media and the quality of life

Peter Loizos

How does an ordinary citizen answer with certainty questions about the quality of civic life, questions which go beyond how far his or her particular pay cheque will stretch? If each citizen necessarily has a slightly different view of what has been going on, does this have implications for the coherence of political debate in civil society? Do liberal democracies need zones of shared perceptions of the recent past, in order that their debates about governance may be more informed, and more coherent? And how far is a free press not only politically necessary for civil society, but, due to the difficulty of making good 'quality of life' assessments, sociologically necessary, too? These are some of the questions addressed in this chapter.

Civil society, a term from European political thought, has recently enjoyed a new vogue. The question of how far it is a term best treated as highly specific to particular (European) times and places, I leave to others. But even if its specificity is admitted, resonant concepts can diffuse very rapidly, in one form or another: the French and American Revolutions clearly acted as solvents for ancient modes of political domination, and their backwash effects are still being felt, from Lhasa and Beijing to Lagos, Berne and Papeete. I approach civil society as an idea which points to a complex of influential associations which may create themselves within the framework of liberal states. These assocations are not creatures of the state but serve to comment on it and modify it. Civil society can exist only while the state tolerates its existence. The associations in question should be non-trivial (bridge clubs, philatelists, and the like are not included) and are concerned with questions of governance. They inevitably include political parties, the communications media, and organisations of citizens interested in the quality of civic life.

I write simultaneously as an anthropologist interested in evidence and research methods, and as a citizen of Britain. But before starting on the particularities of the British case, it is worth remembering that anthropologists have been involved in debates about civil society not as cheer leaders for the concept, but as critics. In 1958, Edward C. Banfield, an American political scientist, authored *The Moral Basis of a Backward Society*, the central concerns of which were the relationships between development, associational life and political action. With the help of his Italian-speaking wife, he had studied at first hand a small town in Potenza, South Italy, with a population of 3,400 people. It had no newspaper, and nor had the 13 other small towns in sight of it. Church attendance was about 10 per cent of the population, and the only association was that involving 25 of the wealthier men, who met to play cards and chat. Banfield described in contrast the town of St George, Utah (population: 4,562) which in its weekly newspaper reported a rich associational life – Parent Teacher Association, Future Farmers of America, Red Cross, and a Business Womens' Club were all meeting, and a church was raising money for a children's hospital 250 miles away. The contrast was striking: a flourishing civil society in one town, and its remarkable absence in the other.

Banfield propelled his argument with a quote from Tocqueville: 'In democratic countries the science of association is the mother of science; the progress of all the rest depends upon the progress it has made' (1958: 7). He wondered if a rich associational life was one engine of economic development, how far it was a North European and North American special trait, and how far it would be found in the rest of the world. Banfield thought his South Italians could be understood as if they followed a simple rule: 'Maximise the material, short-run advantage of the nuclear family; assume that all others will do likewise.' This rule effectively killed off most forms of civic cooperation. Citizens had no faith in officials, and no appetite for political activism to improve their desperate poverty. Banfield was materialist enough to explain this 'ethos' of 'amoral familism' by three specific regional historical factors: high death rates, short-term tenancies for agricultural labour, and the absence of the extended family.

Once Banfield had published his book, every anthropologist who had worked in South Italy, or similar sorts of societies, had to take a position on 'amoral familism' (cf. Davis 1970). Most agreed that something had been described which was diagnostic, but they disagreed over its explanatory powers, and indeed, its causes. People found evidence of forms of association which Banfield had missed, and subtleties of behaviour which had escaped him. This was a debate about the implications of the absence of civil society which has marked resonances with post-Soviet debates.

Banfield certainly dramatised the issues: the book also had on its frontispiece that famous quotation from Hobbes about life without a sovereign, in a 'state of nature'. It is not usually quoted in full:

> In such condition, there is no place for industry; because the fruit thereof is uncertain: and consequently no culture of the earth; no navigation, nor use of the commodities that may be imported by sea; no commodious building; no instruments of moving, and removing, such things as require much force; no knowledge of the face of the earth; no account of time; no arts; no letters, no society; and which is worst of all, continual fear, and danger of violent death; and the life of man, solitary, poor, nasty, brutish, and short.

Since Potenza was close to the world which had given rise to Mafia and Camorra, forms of entrepreneurial criminality which still continue to flourish, Banfield could not be blamed for wanting to get to the bottom of the problem. Since the post-Soviet world is also witnessing the invention of Mafia-like enterprises, perhaps it is time for a more general re-evaluation of Banfield's arguments?

THE QUALITY OF LIFE IN BRITAIN

In Britain, and presumably in most other countries, citizens argue in ways Tocqueville would have approved of about the merits of particular policies, governments and systems. Those arguments often take the form of attempts to decide whether policies are making things better or worse, not simply in financial terms but also in terms of the whole quality and direction of social life. While it is easy to do this in a superficial manner, when we make flip judgements our peers will usually challenge us. We face a problem – to understand how the quality of life has altered, for ourselves and our fellow citizens. I argue that, although we all need to do this, we cannot do it rigorously, and in some technical senses it is difficult.

The quality of life problem has several aspects. Not only can it be hard to weigh up how much your own quality of life has been decisively affected; it is hard also to see what is happening to others. To add up all these differences and come to some informed overall conclusion is really tricky, so most of us rely in everyday life on gross, 'lumpy' judgements, which simply aggregate, leave out inconvenient exceptions, and lose sight of key relativities. How could it be otherwise? We have not developed any cognitive schema for thinking about such complex problems 'all at once'. We can tell if a person is out of work, divorced, injured, rich or poor. But judgements on more embracing quality of life packages do not lend themselves to analysis which is at the same time rigorous, yet easy to grasp.

How well equipped are we as individuals, and as citizens, to work out what is going on? In democracies, politicians spend energy second-guessing how far the electorate will be swayed at any given time by 'feel-good' factors, and pollsters make their livings by the ingenuity with which they can render versions of our perceptions. But understanding where we are is not easy: a modern economy, beset with creeping inflation confuses our attempts to compare the purchasing power of a pay-packet twenty years ago (when one's life-style was different) with one today. Such calculations are skilled and technical and are usually left to economists and economic journalists. Many citizens cannot follow the technicalities, and so remain at a loss to know what to make of such expert arguments. I remember a poll of 600 professional economists over whether or not Britain would benefit by joining the European Community, the economists were split 50/50. An ordinary citizen could have been forgiven for perplexity, and doing nothing more demanding than tossing a coin.

Because we have no agreed overarching criteria, we operate much of the time with three kinds of data which do not fit together very coherently. Our understandings of change are therefore liable to further difficulties of coherent aggregation. I shall discuss each at some length – the statistical trend; the analytic overview; and personal memories. They clearly need not be kept distinct – each can partake of information presented by the other two. But there is a tendency to keep them separate on grounds of clarity and consistency of method, which is only gradually being challenged. I shall conclude by arguing that, although we have classically defended a free press on political grounds, there may be equally compelling sociological grounds for valuing it and other communications media, because the technical difficulties raised by quality of life questions make us more dependent than we realise on insightful commentators. These problems have been particularly important in postwar Britain, during the slow growth of the welfare state, and more recently, during the Conservative attack on the state as employer. But these problems are not unique to Britain – they are currently being worked through in all industrial societies which have expanded their provision of social services. The British case, then, may be interesting not so much for its own sake as for its more far-reaching implications.

It seems to me that the British debate about civil society has been phrased in somewhat different idioms from those used in, and addressed to, post-communist Europe. The followers of former British Conservative prime minister, Margaret Thatcher, wanted to reduce the role played by the state and its employees, and allow 'the market' a greater role. They were keen to have private businesses do as much as possible of the work previously done by public employees. Their arguments turned on cost-effectiveness. They claimed they were mobilising the energies of committed people, energies which would be dissipated in strongly unionised, state employment contexts. These issues have been debated in some form in many households, canteens, building sites and common rooms throughout Britain, and for all except partisan hardliners the jury will be out for some time. But in addition to the attack on the state-as-employer, and its fiscal implications, there were two other attacks: one was upon the impartiality of the civil service, by increasing interference in its outputs – for example, when related to issues of employment trends – and another was on the freedom of the press, particularly upon the British Broadcasting Corporation (BBC) as a provider of news and current affairs programmes. In the case of the BBC, there were definite attempts to prevent too much criticism of the government. However, although this was an attempt at changing the margins of how the British political system works, few serious commentators believe that the basic freedoms of expression and political participation in Britain have been significantly eroded by government interventions. Due to the nature of the British 'first-past-the-post, winner-takes-all' electoral system, at most recent elections fewer than 40 per cent of the British electorate have voted for Conservative governments. The majority of Britons do not fear for the erosion of their basic freedoms, but they perhaps do have a sense that in all kinds of ways the quality of civic life in Britain has worsened: more crime; more corruption in high places; more ruthlessness in corporate life; more unemployment. Many people are better off financially, but are less secure in the workplace. Material standards continue to rise, but more people seem to be living rough on the streets, and young beggars are now visible in our major cities. How do we weigh up so many different processes, pointing in several different directions?

THREE MODES OF UNDERSTANDING THE QUALITY OF LIFE

If it is important for citizens to make informed assessments about how the quality of life is changing, for themselves, and for the wider polity, how do they do it? There seem to be three basic ways: through facts and figures; through expert overviews; and through personal experiences. Each has strengths and weaknesses, and their combination raises problems.

Statistical trends

Some arguments depend on statistical indicators – one in every three-and-a-half marriages will end in divorce; only 10 per cent of households in the United Kingdom are simple nuclear; the unemployment rate in the north-east of Britain is nearly 40 per cent for those aged under 30. Unemployment among young Blacks in London is more than twice the rate among young Whites. We encounter a great deal of this sort of thing, and we are rightly sceptical about putting too much trust in raw figures, but we cannot shake off the suspicion that well-researched analyses, with tables which aggregate life chances and life problems, are important sources of understanding. We worry over the implications of abstractions and percentages, and we know that vulnerable people exist who have been the raw material on which they are based.

Newspapers feed into our perceptions of the quality of life with quasi-statistical articles on social problems, such as divorce, 'unmarried mothers', crime, drugs and housing. The articles may include individual case histories, to give the numbers a persuasive realism. Take the crime rates, which have for the last twenty years been cross-fertilised, in the non-Conservative press, with analyses which seek to link the increase in specific crimes to unemployment. This strategy has two obvious weaknesses. First, as Conservatives are quick to point out, large numbers of unemployed people do not seem to commit the crimes supposedly 'explained' by unemployment. Second, although lack of jobs can help explain burglary, mugging, and some armed robbery, it is less obviously helpful in explaining concurrent rises in reported woundings and rape. And longer time series tend to reveal an upward trend in, for example, armed robberies, which extends back into periods of much fuller employment.[1]

Clearly, political bias can enter into statistical analysis, and the Conservative governments which flourished under Margaret Thatcher were notorious for their manipulation of statistical data, particularly that concerning unemployment. Experts have testified that there have been so many technical changes made to the way in which the unemployed are counted that it is a full-time expert job simply to keep track of them. This can only have served to undermine the confidence of the public in government pronouncements, as happened in communist states; but it has perhaps also contributed to a more general mistrust of the civil servants and of statistics more widely.[2] It has been persuasively argued that many Conservative policies were adopted without the research that should have informed them (Rosenhead 1992). The Thatcherite attack on the state as employer has led to consequences largely unforeseen by the people who led it, and unwanted by those who voted for the Conservative party.

Authoritative qualitative overviews

A second source of information with which we try to assess the implications of social change comes in overview articles and books – attempts by professional historians to pilot us intellectually through the uncertainties of contemporary history. These will often cite some statistical data to reinforce their arguments. Equally important, though shorter and more accessible, is the work of weekly columnists in newspapers and periodicals, trying to create coherent narratives from the flux of information available to them. They have access to more, and to more sensitive information than do most citizens, and we rely on them not so much for their end-of-article summings-up but for partial insights, emphases, the identification of issues, crises and predicaments. It is clear that if a particular commentator has authority and credibility for us, this person may come to influence us significantly. Are we then, in this context, merely choosing our preferred biases, rather than having them imposed on us by official statistics? Many of us read a particular columnist not because we agree with everything said, but to be challenged, and thus reassess our own biases. We read thoughtfully, and actively, as the letters columns in newspapers make clear. And we can read more than one 'source'.

Personal experience

A third important source is our own experiences, first hand, second hand, what we see and hear, and hear about from people we trust. The title of this chapter comes from various conversations with Ernest Gellner, a British scholar who has held chairs by turns in Sociology, Philosophy and Social Anthropology. Gellner's early work in the area of social theory was concerned with theories of social change, and although he has been sharply critical of Marxist states, he was also in the 1970s engaged in sustained dialogue with British Marxist scholars. On one occasion, in discussing the extent of violent crime in America, Gellner said he preferred to live in democracies even though they failed to control street crime as well as authoritarian states. His sound-bite conclusion was, 'I'll take my chances on the streets of New York.' About ten years later, he was thoughtful enough to describe to me having been mugged on the streets of London, something which we both regarded as an unpleasant innovation. I did not then remind him of the earlier conversation, although he surely remembered it, but it seems appropriate to recall it now. I am confident it did not alter his preference for democratic government, but in this he is, perhaps, a little unusual: many of us seem to be decisively influenced by unpleasant personal experiences.

But here a technical difficulty creeps into the problem of judging from one's own personal memories and experiences, which should undermine any simple reliance upon these exclusive modes of understanding. Consider those unhelpful comparisons produced by old people of how much more money was 'worth' in their youth. We can usually stop such narratives by saying 'Yes, but wages were lower then, weren't they? How much were you paid a week?' When I observe the surprisingly helpful young waiters and waitresses in inner London, how clear is my perception? I'm comparing my experience as an uncertain youth, dealing with older waiters, with my experience now, as a middle-aged prosperous professional. The waiters (like the policemen) are younger, and that can be partly explained as an objective fact by the restructuring of the national economy, and the distortions of the London labour market – the employment needs of young Australians and New Zealanders making their grand tours, and the hopes of unemployed actors and actresses. London is a magnet to the young. There are jobs in the London service sector, boosted by tourists from the countries which have driven British industries out of the market. That is part of the measurable world. But how the waiters treat me is influenced by their perceptions of my age, status and power to tip. That will be vary from customer to customer. So we have grounds for many differing perceptions of the quality of life in contemporary London, and, by implication, of the country as a whole, and of other countries. I believe this also relates to whether citizens regard their society as well governed. I shall now illustrate this at more length.

BIOGRAPHIES, APATHY AND INVOLVEMENT

My next-door neighbour and I have quite different understandings of the Thatcher period in Britain, 1979–90. This is a little surprising because we both started life as supporters of the main opposition, the Labour party and have never voted Conservative. We joined the Social Democrats, who broke away from the Labour Party in 1981, and we have similar social origins, and professional trainings. Our disagreements are about the old question of agency. To Jack Skipton, the Thatcher Conservatives have attacked a sane, caring and well-founded society out of ideological malice and free-booting profit-motivated greed. In the process, they have turned a safe, positive and fairly cohesive society into a divided and embittered one.

To me, the difficulties started well before the election of Margaret Thatcher, and although I concede the ideological malice, in my view, the Conservatives after 1979 gave a determined push to a vehicle which was already moving downhill. Britain's internal peace and order in the 1950s and 1960s were inertial, a carry-over from the national coalitions and solidarities of the war effort. The peace was internal only – British troops fought a series of colonial disengagement actions throughout my youth in Palestine, Kenya, Cyprus, Malaya, Suez and Aden, and I witnessed the British army relieve the Catholics of Londonderry from a seige by the Protestant B Specials in 1969. Britain's internal order was somehow related to its external role, but it was a Janus-like situation.

In discussion we have narrowed the differences which might have moulded our perceptions to the following factors: Jack grew up in a happy family which was economically and professionally rising. I grew up with a rather overworked, downwardly mobile mother, who worried about money a lot. I am six years older and can remember something of the war and rationing. Jack was born in 1943, and things seemed to get better, steadily, throughout his childhood. He spent two years in Kenya in 1973–5, which was in many ways a frightening and violent society with very little going for it on the civic level. While there, he missed a decisive moment in Britain, a period when most of the country worked only a three-day week because of fuel shortages and the miners' strike. In 1975, some 48 per cent of GDP was spent by the government (Halsey 1988). Jack, returning to Britain, felt he was coming back to a country with good institutions and civic traditions; I was already wondering if we were on the edge of major political breakdown. If people as socially alike as my neighbour and I can have such different perceptions about where we are, and why we are there, and the meaning of the social and economic indicators invoked by government and opposition, then this problem, magnified many thousands of times, may have wider consequences in a pluralist society. How can disagreement be constructive, if there is no agreed point of intellectual departure, in terms of some sketch of what is and has been going on in society more widely? There are too many discrepancies for easy agreement. This can lead to political incoherence, and deadlock, the politics of factional opposition, rather than rational bargaining.[3]

Another way to approach civil society is through the relationship between the individual citizen and political parties and the issues of activism and apathy. Political parties are machines which aggregate citizens' interests, and seek to get these interests represented within the political system. Citizens hope that these party machines are run well and have good ideas for improving the condition of society, but they differ in how much time they wish to devote to the political system. Political leaders and academics sometimes worry about how few people are prepared to give up their time for campaigns. Words like 'apathy' are invoked, and poll results are cited which purport to show that significant numbers of citizens do not know which party is in power, cannot name three ministers, and insist that the most important issue facing the nation is whether or not Britain will win the World Cup.[4] Clearly there has been a fear that Thatcher's drive to restructure the economy would drive us all into similar attitudes, that we would become atomised greedy individualists, apparently in the image of her city cronies. When she famously declared that there was no such thing as society, any final year social studies student who had read Young and Wilmott (1957) could have told her that people have wider kinship, friendship and neighbour-hood relationships than her market-driven individualism allowed for.

This is why one of the issues which always comes up after certain kinds of violent assaults is the failure of people who 'must have seen or heard what was going on' to prevent it. Citizens are shocked by a nightmare of the ripped-up social fabric. The Jamie Bulger case of 1994, when two young boys in the city of Birkenhead killed a younger child and none of the people who saw them leading their unhappy victim to his death intervened, was treated by the media as a symptom of collective pathology. However, some media sources pointed out the statistical rarity of murders by children in Britain, which did something to keep the issue in perspective. It was rarely suggested that a less pessimistic explanation of the 'indifference' of passers-by was the apparent normality of two older 'siblings' in charge of an unhappy younger one, an unkindness of a routine nature, to which our more violent society has accustomed us. After all, a society in which 95,000 woundings reach the attention of the police in a year is not exactly trouble-free. This is where we live. It comes home to us: my son attends a rock concert in our local park and reports that two drunken men had a knife fight, and that there were woundings. They finally had to be restrained by security staff. My son reports this calmly. He is not surprised. I am distressed, but also unsurprised. These things are in our local paper every week. This is London in the 1990s. A friend in a nearby suburb says her son has been mugged so many times they've lost count.

Where the nightmare of Albert Camus's hero in the 1950s was of a man who thought he should have jumped into a river at night to save someone from drowning, 1990s' nightmares involve imagining dealing with street violence without dishonour. In our fantasies, we may heroically intervene to protect a fellow citizen from assault. In practice, many of us are hoping not to be put to the test.

CONSENSUS, SYLLABUSES AND THE REBIRTH OF CIVIL SOCIETY

One further problem in determining the quality of our collective life is the relative weakness of our models for causal and contextual under-standing, both as offered in the press and, as far as I can discern, in our secondary educational system. Although many a journalist on quality newspapers appreciates that 'correlation is not causation', and that causes of increases in crime may be complex rather than simple, it is uncommon for us to be taken through that complexity in any very illuminating way. In this sense even our quality press needs to take us further. When Fidel Castro first came to power he would take many hours to explain the problems of the Cuban economy to his fellow citizens. These marathon speeches may have been boring but they took the economy seriously, and did not insult the intelligence of the listeners. It is clear that in authoritarian regimes, particularly if nationalist, Marxist or Confucian, the state makes serious, if interested, sometimes perverse attempts to create consensus among the citizens. In liberal democratic societies we are inclined to reject such near-monopolistic shaping of the citizens' mind-sets. But as we in Britain struggle daily to make sense of our predicaments, family by family, on a piecemeal basis, reading various papers, watching different programmes, one could wish that amidst all this liberal diversity we had, as a baseline from which to disagree, a good shared sense of recent British and world history, and some rigorous but memorable models of social causation to fall back on. If we had a more clear basis for our agreements, our disagreements might be both easier to tolerate and to transcend. The lack of a consensual baseline makes for intellectual incoherence which inevitably aids extremists, whose simple messages become the more attractive. Thatcher's election rhetoric was unsubtle, if perceptive about the anxieties of the day. An electorate better educated about economic history, German and Japanese postwar reconstruction and the violent foundations of Empire might have thought twice before voting for 'Britain Great Again'.[5]

The issue of a reasoned consensus has exercised those who determine English secondary-school history. Although some conservative voices call for greater emphasis on a handful of authentic British heroes, design of recent history syllabuses reveals attempts to see our recent past more truthfully. The syllabus on Europe and the United States in this century, for example, treats the harshness of the Treaty of Versailles as a major cause of political humiliation and the subsequent rise of the National Socialists in Germany. In other centuries the British role in the slave trade is described with more critical honesty than ever before. How England reacted to the Irish Famine is left less obscure than it was, and thus our ability to understand the passions of Irish nationalists is enhanced. We see the recent past just a little more clearly, but we still have to work hard for models with which to understand the present. Here is a project with some long-term pay-offs, if as a nation we can find the intellectual energies to embrace it.

In the last thirty-five years, London (and Britain more generally) has seen a tendency towards disillusionment with professional politicians, with citizens more ready to support activist groups, arguably a move away from élite-led politics towards a more participatory society. While few of us wish to give up on the parliamentary system, and we take for granted the legal framework which Parliament provides, there is a growing sense that concerned citizens should not wait for parliamentarians, tied into aggregating corporate parties, to get things working. It is often more satisfying to work through such pressure groups as Greenpeace, Shelter (aid for the homeless), Release (aid for drug users), Oxfam, the Consumers' Association, Stonewall (homosexual rights), Mind (the mentally ill), and hundreds of others. Through them, things can still be done. By membership, subscription, identification and other forms of support, we can feel direct involvement. This is akin to reading the same political commentator on a regular basis, when gradually a feeling of personal trust is created. Both the journalists and the charities function sociologically as if they are known to us personally. For me, at least, when my favourite political columnist died it was like losing a wise friend. For anthropologists, it is the media-related social closeness of columnists, charities, even political parties, which puts them in an influential role between the personally known, and the socially distant and impersonal state. They can earn our loyalty, and we do not need to go to war to feel this bond. The only 'war' they inspire is a competition over values, which can be conducted peacefully and imaginatively. Here is a notion of civil society that is media-mediated, and it has not yet been much examined.

At the same time as the incidence of interpersonal violence continues to increase, other aspects of our social relations seem to change in more encouraging ways. The campaigns to create sympathy for the physically handicapped, and for people who have been mentally ill are good examples, and the increasing concern of young people for suffering in less developed countries is another. This leads to the following conclusion: if the Third Estate is an effective element in civil society which helps us make sense of our worlds, then the liberal defence of free media makes good sociological sense, on top of the political sense usually claimed, for we really need all the help we can get to understand the society we live in.

Does Britain today have weaker kinship ties than it did 100 years ago? Do high divorce rates mean 'the decline of the family' or, more plausibly, the appearance of more complex family relations (cf. Simpson 1994)? What do such changes imply for civil society, governance, social order and the quality of our lives? Does the greater involvement of women in the labour force leave fewer look-outs to curb delinquency in urban neighbourhoods, and fewer carers for elderly relatives? How are we to trade off the benefits and costs in this equation (cf. Finch 1989: 237–43)? Is the shift to an activist, do-it-yourself citizenry (including anti-crime networks, some authorised by the police and some unauthorised) one of the particular effects of the decline in deference? Or, is it the 'culture in contraflow' modishly conjured by Perry Anderson (1990), a phoenix arising from the nutritious compost of burned-out socialisms? Did Margaret Thatcher, in spite of all her efforts, end up by unwittingly strengthening the Labour Party? She declared imperiously that there was 'no alternative' to capitalism. But there are certainly alternatives to Conservative rule, and all kinds of social developments have ensured that the market will not be able to determine our lives without challenge. For persistent democrats, socialists, anthropologists and reformers of all kinds, there is an open-ended project of stopping our society rolling back towards the brutalities of the early Industrial Revolution. The task requires comparisons with regimes and solutions in other states, and the concept of civil society, when grounded in rigorous attempts to take stock of the quality of all our lives, may help us concentrate more effectively.

In such tasks anthropologists should have distinctive contributions to make. The contribution of this chapter has, I hope, been to suggest how the fact that the quality of life is conceptually difficult to describe in a way which does justice to the complexity of the issues, links up with the issue of why the nurturing of free media is important for civil society in ways perhaps not intended by seventeenth-century political theorists.[6]

NOTES

1   The evidence cited in Halsey (1988: table 15.8) suggests, for example, that there has been a serious rise in woundings since 1920. At first they doubled every ten years, but between 1950 and 1960 (years of high employment) they trebled. They have more than doubled each decade till 1990. There is no obvious reason to suppose that this is an artefact of reporting changes.

2   It is possible to argue, of course, that numerical data are always presented from a point of view, but to go from there to a justification of gross manipulation, massaging and deliberate confusion of the electorate, is indefensible.

3   Neither Jack nor I are economists. A second neighbour, Mary Campbell, an economic journalist, would trace the difficulties which paved the way for the Thatcher government, to patterns of employment practices, the strength of some trade unions, the uncompetitiveness of British industry and the country's weakness in international financial markets. Mary has never supported the Conservatives, or the Labour Party. Her enthusiasms have been for the Liberals and the Owen wing, in the early 1980s, of the Social Democrats.

4   The global passion for soccer is one in the eye for that fashionable relativist catch-phrase, incommensurability.

5   I do not for a moment believe that we should buy the authoritarian package in order to obtain a consensus. We have to build the consensus federally, through determined consultative work with grass-roots units, or their elected representatives.

6   My thanks to Mary Campbell, Gill Shepherd, Elizabeth Dunn and Chris Hann for their helpful comments on earlier drafts of this chapter.

REFERENCES

Anderson, P. (1990) 'A culture in contraflow', pts 1 and 2, *New Left Review* 180: 41–78, 182: 85–137.

Banfield, E. C. (1958) *The Moral Basis of a Backward Society*, Glencoe: Free Press.

Davis, J. (1970) 'Morals and backwardness: a comment on the moral basis of a backward society', *Comparative Studies in Society and History* 12: 340–53.

Finch, J. (1989) *Family Obligations and Social Change*, Cambridge: Polity Press.

Halsey, A. H. (1988) *British Social Trends since 1900*, Basingstoke: Macmillan.

Rosenhead, J. (1992) 'Into the swamp: the analysis of social issues', *Journal of the Operational Research Society* 43(4): 293–305.

Simpson, R. (1994) 'Bringing the "unclear" family into focus: divorce and re-marriage in contemporary Britain', *Man* 29(4): 831–51.

Young, M. and Willmott, P. (1957) *Family and Kinship in East London*, London: Routledge and Kegan Paul.

Chapter 3

Anti-semitism and fear of the public sphere in a post-totalitarian society

East Germany

Susanne Spülbeck

In May 1991 I started sixteen months of anthropological fieldwork in the village of Schopflach in Thuringia, which was formerly part of the German Democratic Republic (GDR).[1] Some months prior to my arrival, the state authorities had placed some seventy Jews in a hostel there, ostensibly as a temporary measure.[2] The main subject of my research was the interaction of villagers and Soviet-Jewish refugees.

Whenever strangers show up in a community, they initially constitute a challenge to the social order – the consensus – of the members of that community on the nature of the world. Georg Simmel describes the threat that a stranger may pose to the locals as follows:

> This freedom which enables the stranger to experience and deal with even a close relationship as if he had a bird's-eye view of it certainly entails quite a few dangerous possibilities. From time immemorial rebellions of all kinds have been attributed by the party under attack to outside incitement by foreign agents and agitators.
>
> (1922: 510)

In order to be able to cope with this threat, social reality in the village has to be renegotiated, giving rise to a discourse which assigns the stranger a place in the social order. This discourse may take very diverse forms. Interaction between the locals and the foreigners in Schopflach was based on the same communication patterns that had determined interaction between the locals prior to the arrival of the strangers. For the purpose of analysing the different spheres of communication, I have applied Habermas's (1990) concept of the public and the private sphere, as well as his theories on the formation of private and public opinion. The formation of opinions in the village and the manner in which these spread from the private sphere of the family or close friends to the public sphere of the village, before finally finding their way into the institutionalised public sphere, for example, local council meetings or the local press, were patterned processes.

The village of Schopflach is situated in the northern foothills of the Thuringian Forest. It has 1,600 inhabitants, its own local council and mayor, a Protestant parish priest, a kindergarten and a primary school. Until quite recently, the area was one of the poorest in Germany. The harsh climate, poor soil and the existence of only very small strips of arable land on the hills made it impossible for most Schopflachers to make a living exclusively from the land. Outwork, including the manufacturing of carnival masks and primitive forms of glass-blowing, was common from the beginnings of industrialisation down to the 1950s. During the first half of the twentieth century the village economy was characterised by a combination of small-scale farming and low-paid outwork for the two small local factories. In the early 1950s, after the communist administration of the GDR had established a firm grip on the economy, the two local factories closed down. Most members of the local élite had left the village during the Second World War. By 1991, not one of the former élite or their descendants held any important position.

In the GDR period most people from Schopflach turned to the neighbouring town to find jobs in the glass industry there. Agriculture was abandoned. The economic position of most villagers improved substantially, aided by the promotion of the village as a resort by the tourism authorities. As in many other parts of the former GDR, the guaranteed-employment structure collapsed after reunification. In 1991 the unemployment rate in the region had reached 21.5 per cent.[3] Unemployment was the main topic of conversation during the entire period of my fieldwork.

Many Schopflachers depicted the political history of the village as a history of passivity and apathy. If, however, you questioned the older people more persistently about the period prior to totalitarian rule, that is, before the electoral victory of the Nazis in 1933, some of them invoked a picture of vivid political debate and open controversy in the village. During the entire period from 1919 until 1945, Schopflach had just one mayor. He is remembered as a rather authoritarian figure. In the late 1950s his successor was arrested and charged with political conspiracy. After that incident no villager was willing to take up the post, and so it was held by strangers. This situation lasted for more than ten years. Today, although the political system has become a more liberal one and the office of mayor itself has been turned into a well-paid position, it is still very difficult to fill the post. This crisis of political representation is not untypical of small villages in Eastern Germany.

THE EFFECTS OF STATE SURVEILLANCE

In the course of my fieldwork I came to realise that communication in the public sphere was characterised by much mutual fear. A basic fear of the other also had its effects on relations with the foreigners, and hence it became central to my research. The work got off to a good start. I made friends quickly, and some of the friendships have lasted to this day. The numerous interviews I conducted were based on the method of person-centred communication (Rogers 1951). Almost all the interviews, which concentrated on topics pertaining to the life histories of the interviewees, were accompanied by strong emotional outbursts and tears. All the same I noticed that, without exception, the interviewees never forgot that they were being recorded. That was an early indication of controlled speech.

My initial approach was to compile family biographies for the purpose of examining the transmission of anti-Semitic stereotypes. When I asked individuals for interviews, no one turned me down. But as soon as I started to ask other members of the same family to participate, they found all sorts of excuses. No one refused openly to cooperate. Nevertheless, it was obvious that my desire to speak with the whole family was unwelcome. The points in fieldwork when we meet with such resistance can be particularly revealing, providing valuable clues to understanding the culture under investigation (cf. Erdheim 1988). Therefore I asked the Anti-Semitism Research Centre in Berlin, the body sponsoring my research, to extend my period in the field. I then focused my work on this refusal to allow a stranger to enter the private sphere, that is, the family.

After the German Democratic Republic had joined the Federal Republic of Germany, former GDR citizens were granted access to any files the Stasi, the State Security police, had kept on them. One case received wide media attention: Vera Wollenberger, a GDR dissident, had been spied on for years by her own husband. It was revealed that Stasi observation had penetrated the private sphere and that Frau Wollenberger was not the only victim. Up to that point, it had been very difficult for me to talk about the intricate network of state surveillance on the level of personal experience. Whenever I had raised this topic, the interviewees would put up massive resistance. Eventually I learned to avoid the word Stasi and use a special code of allusions, which at least made it possible to communicate, albeit vaguely. Before the media exposure of the Vera Wollenberger case, however, the possibility of talking about the Stasi in the context of everyday life in the GDR remained limited.

I had already had numerous, extensive conversations with Kurt Kühn, who from 1979 to 1989 was a local councillor.[4] He was in his early sixties and having worked in the village as a postman was able to provide me with a great deal of basic data on the households in the village. One day, when I visited him on a chilly winter afternoon, he appeared quite agitated. He had just read about Vera Wollenberger in the newspaper and seen relevant television reports. Up until then he had described his life in the GDR as uncomplicated, despite constant frustration over the scarcity of consumer goods. His political function, so he kept telling me, had never really caused him any difficulties. The whole story about the Stasi was being exaggerated in West Germany: it had never been of any significance to his daily life. 'As if people were preoccupied with this – what a load of baloney! Everyone would say whatever occurred to them; you didn't constantly ask yourself whether someone belonged to them or not', he had told me only a few weeks earlier, cutting short any further discussion of the topic.

But now he seemed to see the whole matter differently: 'How should a person react? What must it be like for the woman? Her own husband!' Kurt Kühn seemed to be upset and in a pensive mood. 'How could they get the husband to spy on his wife and pass on the information?', he wondered. The two of us speculated about the vicious circle in which Knud Wollenberger must have been trapped to be capable of spying on his wife – with whom he had raised three children – for ten years. We tried to find excuses for him. 'Who knows what kind of abyss we will be confronted with,' he mused, 'as all these things now become public? Well, I wanted my files, too ... but I'm not sure I want to know. Imagine them being married for years, with children and all ...'. He continued his speculations about the Wollenbergers, who were now getting divorced, and a little later he said to me:

> When you get down to it, you can't trust anyone at all. Let's be honest, what do I know? – Let's just assume – after all, how do I know what you are going to do with your recordings. There is simply no guarantee; what if you happen to be with that bunch too? After all, it can happen anywhere; who would be in a position to know? You wouldn't know, you just couldn't.[5]

In this conversation Kurt Kühn was preoccupied with the potential consequences of the Wollenberger case for his own life. Previously, he had described state surveillance as something irrelevant to him person- ally. Now it had become something incalculable, which threatened the intimacy of even his closest relationships. He tried to imagine what he would do if he were in Vera Wollenberger's shoes, and his own wife an informer. He suggested I might be a Stasi agent, merely claiming to be conducting a scientific survey. Such speculations, where the distinction between reality and paranoia blurred, provided a brief glimpse into the deep state of confusion and anxiety caused by the disclosure of what had happened to Vera Wollenberger. This reaction completely contradicted everything I had heard from him and from everyone else in Schopflach in the preceding eight months. Never before had the topic of state surveillance been raised with such openness and personal involvement. Apparently the private sphere of the family had been presumed to be a safe domain, in which it was possible to speak one's mind freely without having to fear adverse consequences.

Kurt Kühn was not the only one to be disillusioned by the new disclosures, which continued to receive plenty of attention, especially in the tabloid press. In the following days I repeatedly experienced situations in which the Wollenberger case prompted people to discuss the subject of the Stasi fairly candidly on a personal level. A deep uncertainty about the information-gathering activities not only of one's own family, but also of neighbours and acquaintances became suddenly apparent. Over and over I realised that the people I was talking to had only the vaguest clues as to whether or not other villagers had been active as Stasi informers.

Frau Kellner, who had settled in Schopflach shortly after the war, while still a teenager, soon became very important to me. Although she was now in her early sixties and had earned herself the respect of the village, she still viewed life in this village from the perspective of a newcomer. Her father had been arrested for political reasons at the beginning of the 1960s. She herself had had to give up her old profession, because as a teacher she would not have been permitted to travel to West Germany, where part of her family lived. From the perspective of this somewhat marginal position, Frau Kellner told me her life story and recounted everyday experiences with the Stasi:

Here in the village no one knows who has that kind of a background. People assume that Frau F. does, because she was Red alright, and, as far as her husband is concerned, that's certainly what everyone claims. I asked him straight out once, straight out I asked him, when he was here because of an electrical problem. I said, 'Heinz, now tell me, is it true: do you have something to do with it or not? Everyone says you do.' He was speechless. No one ever asked him about it just like that. Then he said, 'No, no.' He actually seemed grateful to me for bringing it up. It certainly was strange. But who knows . . .?

The other theme to surface in the conversation with Kurt Kühn about

Stasi surveillance concerned my role as a fieldworker. Kühn drew an analogy between my work and the activities of the Stasi. He was not the only one:

> Field notes, January 1991: I had a discussion with Babsi, which lasted late into the night. She is accusing me of doing the same thing the Stasi used to do. I walked around, listened to the things people said and wrote everything down. Who, after all, could check up on what I did with my notes? I tried to justify myself, pointing out that the Stasi had been disbanded – a statement which apparently seemed ridiculous to her. Just like H. (another village friend), she believed that the only reason so few people in the village were turning down my request for an interview was that people simply did not dare to say no. They had never learned how. In the end, they could not be sure about my real background (that is, whether I did not have Stasi connections after all) and what the consequences would be, if they declined an interview. Babsi left at two-thirty. I'm pretty confused.

A few weeks earlier a village teacher had showed up at my landlady's house in a very distressed state. I had conducted two interviews with her, which my landlady had arranged and in the course of which Frau K. had made no secret of her communist convictions. As a teacher she was still subject to a series of background checks, the outcome of which was uncertain. These would determine whether or not she could go on teaching. The checks were primarily of a political nature. Mrs K. now had second thoughts and was worried that the interviews might not only be used for my Ph.D. thesis but also be passed on to 'other authorities', who would take account of the ideological aspects of the conversations when deciding the future of her career. She asked my landlady to put in a good word for her. The three of us attempted to resolve the matter by talking about it together. My landlady and I tried to convince Frau K. that I was indeed an anthropologist and that I did not spy on people 'on the side'. I can only speculate about the extent to which we succeeded, although further contacts were quite cordial.

These details exemplify the atmosphere in Schopflach in the winter of 1991–2, towards the end of my first year of fieldwork. Throughout this project I had regular psychological supervision, in an attempt to meet the requirement for critical self-reflection during fieldwork. Within the framework of this supervision, my own growing resistance against the conduct of research under the prevailing conditions, as well as the resistance put up by my informants, were both analysed by an ex-perienced psychotherapist. With this support I was able to explore the reasons for the anxiety I observed during interaction in different situations.

I found more and more indications that it was not only my presence in the village as a researcher which was being experienced as something threatening: rather, I realised that communication among the locals themselves was influenced by a subconscious perception of the other as a potential threat. As the taboo on the Stasi discourse was slowly lifted in the course of media coverage of the Vera Wollenberger case, it turned out that many of the people I talked to in Schopflach actually *continued* to feel threatened by state surveillance. In their dealings with people who did not belong to their private sphere, that is, the circle of their closest relatives and friends, the villagers proceeded in such a way that the possibility of the other's being an informer could never be excluded from the frame of reference of this interaction.

For consciousness of the self to emerge, an attitude to the other must be part of one's system, as a controlling authority for one's own actions. Mead (1934) refers to this phenomenon as the 'generalized other'. For the villagers of Schopfloch the Stasi remained an essential part of that generalised other, even after the GDR ceased to exist. Encounters with other people still implied the possibility of the other passing on what was being said. The 'attitude of the other' to which Mead refers always included the informer.

During a working breakfast in the museum of local history in the nearby town a staff member insisted, 'We always said what we wanted, without thinking much about who we were talking to. The press is now making much too much of a fuss about it.' Several minutes later she said, 'Of course, we always thought about what we were saying, and to whom. After all, all of us, for example at the university, knew there was one Stasi informer in every seminar group.' The subconscious effect of state surveillance can be felt in the tension that lies within this contradiction.

In the months after the dismantling of the GDR regime, what I encountered were not the traces of totalitarian dictatorship described by C. J. Friedrich (1956), that is, of a system which relies on diffuse terror. Rather, what struck me was the deep-seated feeling of insecurity that had been instilled by the experience of fifty years of unpredictable state surveillance. For insecurity to be instilled permanently and remain effective, however, terror is needed as a 'socialization shock' (Habermas 1990: 354). The system of constant threat, with its destruction of the public sphere, is then able to build on this traumatic experience, by making every encounter outside the private sphere appear potentially dangerous. Few of the interviewees were able to put this situation into words. Only the shock of discovering that the refuge of the private sphere, previously considered safe, was also subject to surveillance and control, temporarily led to an articulation of personal anxieties. The taboo was momentarily lifted under the pressure of media debate, but it was reimposed shortly afterwards.

FEAR OF WITCHES IN THE CONTEXT OF SOCIAL RELATIONS

I stumbled fairly quickly across another taboo subject in Schopflach: witchcraft. It was talked about in a subtle pattern of denial and affirmation. Thus, for example, one informant told me, 'There are no witches, there are only bad people.' Shortly afterwards she said that a woman known to be a witch had walked past her house and that she had felt it safer to close the window – especially because it was a Tuesday, and witches were supposed to appear on Tuesdays and Fridays. Generally, a witch arrived unexpectedly and left an object behind. If this object was not recognised, the witch might cause misfortune. If the object was recognised it could be removed, causing the witch to suffer some adversity or another, for example, to fall ill. A witch was never a member of one's own household and never bewitched anyone belonging to the same household, according to my understanding of the beliefs prevailing in Schopflach. A witch might be from the same neighbourhood, or might be a stranger to the village.

It was always difficult to talk about instances of witchcraft in Schopflach. In fact, it seemed to me that the mere mention of the topic made the interviewees feel uneasy. For the most part, people would tell me about cases from the past, the protagonists of which (the witch and the victim) were already dead. The informants were mostly elderly men and women, or sometimes newcomers who had established enough contacts in the village to warrant occasional warnings about a female or male witch, and lessons in the rules of protective magic. Many of the interviewees declared that witchcraft had played an important role in the village in the first years after the Second World War, but was of little significance nowadays. Not until shortly before I left did I find out from a good friend that her mother-in-law lived in mortal fear of a neighbour, regularly protecting the entrance to the house with magic and blaming her frequent illnesses on witchcraft attacks by her neighbour.

I cannot judge to what extent the fear of witchcraft had an important influence on the relations of the villagers. However, there was a discourse on witchcraft and this discourse included a specific repertoire of protective magic – which essentially amounted to people distancing themselves from the person who was feared as a witch.[6] The important point here is that a pattern of collective paranoia coming from another tradition, one much older than the State Security Service, affected relationships and patterns of communication in the village. And again, the family was, in theory, the only place where one could not possibly be confronted by a witch.

What happens, then, with the arrival into this 'social drama' (Goffman 1959) of a group of strangers – to be more precise, a group of Soviet Jews? To understand the reactions to the refugees, one further tradition is important: stereotyped anti-Semitic prejudices. There was no manifest aggressive rejection. Nevertheless, when the refugees first arrived, a consensus emerged in the village that they were running some obscure but flourishing black market: 'They are Jews, and Jews trade and cheat. They have always been doing that. They don't work, and they are cunning business people.' Stories from before 1933 about Jewish tradespeople who passed through the village were retold in order to stress the point.

The people who talked about the refugees along these lines were obviously indignant, but they were not overtly aggressive. The refugees came from big cities in the former Soviet Union (notably Moscow and Kiev) and had brought with them an obviously urban life-style, expressed in their style of dress. The villagers, who had a long experience of regional poverty and who were threatened by a new wave of joblessness, commented with an old anti-Semitic prejudice: Jews are rich and cunning businessmen. During the first months, this old prejudice enabled the villagers to assign the Jews to a familiar social place. The stranger, as we know from Simmel (1922), is always part of the group and each group has its place for strangers. During these first months the patterns of discourse in Schopflach showed villagers representing the refugees in the village as 'Jews' with an anti-Semitic connotation. In this sense the Jewish strangers were a part of the village, and Simmel's concept is useful for understanding the situation.

For some time, the refugees were a topic of daily gossip. But after several months had passed, loudly voiced indignation disappeared, and the discourse on the refugees gradually gave way to public silence. At this point, one might conclude that people had simply become used to the fact that a few Jewish foreigners were living in their village and that the locals had turned back to their own problems. But there are some indicators that point in another direction. For example, in the course of a quarrel between two factions of the refugees, shots were fired into the air in the middle of the night. Such things simply do not happen in a peaceful little village in the Thuringian Forest! Nevertheless, no one talked about this incident – deafness was feigned.

PATTERNS OF COMMUNICATION

For a study of the public sphere and communication, the structural similarities between Stasi paranoia, an obsessive belief in witches and the discourse on the Soviet-Jewish refugees can be illuminating. That is not to say that Stasi paranoia, a fear of witches and anti-Semitic xenophobia are comparable in the sense that there are structural similarities between these realms as such. But there are similarities between the communication strategies for dealing with the perceived threats.

It is possible to discern three coping strategies to which people resorted in the three different realms: ignoring, implying and isolating. The main pattern of coping with collective paranoia, whether witches or the Stasi, was to *ignore* it, to pretend it did not exist and not to talk about it. The same was done with the refugees after a while. This silence went together with a style of communicating by allusions, so as to avoid the danger of referring to things by their actual name. Thus the second communication strategy for dealing with threatening situations was *implication*. It was dangerous to talk about witches, and people only did so by invoking cases of witchcraft from the past and talking about witches who were already dead. Even then the cases were prefaced with phrases like: 'I don't know, but it was very strange.' Talking about the Stasi was also perceived to be dangerous. When I tried to ask people about their personal experience with the Stasi and the involvement of certain people, I always came up against a brick wall. As soon as I mentioned the word Stasi, the interviewee withdrew, changed the subject and gave me the feeling that I had said something offensive, that I had used an almost obscene word. I had to learn a certain code of allusions and special terms to be able to talk about it. Only after the first shock of Vera Wollenberger did it become possible to talk about the Stasi for a short period of time. The silence about the Soviet-Jewish refugees went hand in hand with whispers, rarely explicitly formulated and presented without dramatisation. These whispers were about Jews who dealt in drugs and arms. The speaker could not prove anything, although he or she always claimed to be firmly convinced that it was true. Here, it was implied that the underlying wish was for the police to pursue the matter, arrest the Jews and get them out of the village, as the Nazi regime had dealt with the one Jewish inhabitant of the village.

The third similarity in coping strategies is the *isolation* and separation of families in order to prevent them from getting too close either to a witch or to a Stasi informer. The only place that appeared safe from persecution or witchcraft was the private sphere. An expectation of persecution as soon as people came out of their private niches did not make for curiosity toward strangers, or as a 60-year-old woman from Schopflach phrased it: 'Just think about it – if you no longer have any dealings with the people in your village, then what's it going to be like towards strangers? You won't have any [dealings with them] whatsoever!'

From this perspective, the concept of the village community, with all its imagery of genuine identity and solidarity, proves to be a romantic ideal which is very remote indeed from the reality of this village. Much more important for interaction in this village were the conditions of social isolation. In sharp contrast to the common image of a German village, Schopflach had hardly any stable associations, such as a regulars' table at the pub, groups of friends meeting regularly, social clubs, societies or sports clubs. At the same time the political culture was devoid of local party organisations or other political groupings.

The old élite had vanished, but no new groups appeared to have taken its place. The contradiction between the different versions of the political history of the village in the repertoire of the villagers' recollections can be interpreted in the context of this development. While most of my informants described the history of the village as a history of power-lessness and disinterest in politics, others remembered heated political debates.

An elderly glass-blower told me that in 1920 several communists from the area had hidden out in the woods for a few weeks to escape arrest. He himself had been sent into the woods repeatedly by his mother to supply the men with basic necessities. If this story is true, then there was a public sphere in the history of the village before totalitarian structures were established – one which met the conditions set out by C. W. Mills for an integral public sphere, namely where 'public communications are so organized that there is a chance immediately and effectively to answer back any opinion expressed in public' and 'such discussion readily finds an outlet in effective action, even against – if necessary – the prevailing system of authorities' (Mills 1956: 303). It seems that, until the 1930s, associations occupied a prominent place in village life; for instance, there were several choral societies and gym clubs in Schopflach, whose activities followed the annual festive cycle. In the 1950s these associ-ations were dissolved and replaced by mass organisations set up by the state.

Memories of a time when there was still an effective public sphere in the village suggest that later conditions of state control, threat and surveillance, were characterised by cognitive dissonance (see Festinger 1964). People had the nagging feeling that social reality had not always been as they experienced it under totalitarian conditions, and that it did not necessarily have to be that way. But, as the local people say, 'impossible things must not happen', which might explain why the dominant version of the village's history described Schopflach as a place which had forever been characterised both by poverty and by power-lessness. Such recollections referred to the long experience of bitter need, which did not end until the beginning of the 1950s, when the economic restructuring of the GDR was carried out. In this discourse the reason for political apathy was economic deprivation. In the present period of economic change with all the accompanying insecurity, this was a prominent local theme. This version of the village's history suggests that there had never been an interest in participating in the public sphere, that the villagers had always been excluded from shaping public opinion, and that 'everyone just did their own thing'. In other words, communication outside the limited sphere of the family had always been poor and the social setting in the village always characterised by isolation.

As Hannah Arendt (1962: 485) points out, under conditions of totalitarian rule, friendship and any other type of social relationship arouse suspicion. The basis for an ideologically legitimised totalitarian order and its 'loyalty' (the recognition of its validity by all) can only be provided by completely isolated individuals, whose ties to family and friends have failed to secure them a place in the world (Arendt 1962: 486). It is this isolation which prevents participation in the public sphere. From the perspective of isolation, which makes the public sphere appear to be a threat and declares quiescence to be local history, the development of a collective civil consciousness is not only difficult but dangerous. This consciousness, the knowledge that one lives in a community and is responsible for the conditions in that community, together with the ability to combine this knowledge with a corresponding set of values, is the prerequisite for shouldering political responsibility and actively particip-ating in the political process. These characteristics of a *polites*, a citizen, which are derived from the Greek *polis*, have remained the basis of concepts of civil society. If individuals are to shoulder responsibility and exercise their rights as citizens, however, they must be able to express their opinion in the public sphere (Habermas 1990: 356).

During the analysis of the communication structures observed in Schopflach I also made use of Habermas's definition of public and private opinion. In modern society with its mass media, Habermas differentiates between informal, personal opinion within the private sphere and formal, institutionalised and authorised opinion in the public sphere (Habermas 1990: 355). Public opinion in the full sense is only formed to the degree that critical expression mediates between the two spheres of communication (1990: 357). In other words, participating in political life as a responsible citizen is only possible if individuals have the opportunity to express their opinion in the public sphere. Similarly, Hannah Arendt emphasises the opportunity to organise in groups and to have the discussions taking place within these groups represented in the public sphere as prerequisites for political participation. Democratic freedoms, so she argues, are based on the equality of all citizens before the law, but this equality only makes sense and can only work when the citizens belong to distinct groups that can be represented, or when they are part of a social or political hierarchy (Arendt 1962: 465).

In his analysis of mass society, Moscovici gives a plausible description of the state of insecurity which results from the isolation of the individual. The individual 'lives like a stranger in a machinery made up of other individuals, to which he only has mechanical and impersonal relations. Hence the uncertainty, the diffuse anxiety in every person, who feels like the puppet of hostile forces unknown to him' (Moscovici 1984: 14). In Schopflach the fear of such hostile and anonymous forces finds its symbolic expression in the anxiety caused by state surveillance, the fear of being bewitched, or xenophobia and anti-Semitic reactions. Isolation and the anxiety it causes make individuals easy to control, placing them at the disposal of the state. The totalitarian order needs the mass.[7] For it to maintain its control, it must permanently prevent the private sphere of communication from participating in shaping public opinion, while controlling the latter. To do this it must keep the individual in a state of isolation and anxiety. This strategy succeeded so thoroughly in Schopflach that remnants of this isolation and anxiety were still effective and discernible even after the collapse of the GDR.

CONCLUSIONS

1 If you take a closer look at the discourse on the native and the stranger which circulates in the public sphere of an East German community, the frequently cited xenophobia seems to be but a special manifestation of a much broader phenomenon, namely a fundamental fear of the other, an implicit assumption that your partner in a dialogue can pose

a serious threat to you. This is an attitude which seems to dominate the public sphere in general.

2 From this point of view, feeling like a stranger is characteristic of any interaction in the public sphere. The public sphere is itself threatening. It is occupied by witches, Stasi informers and all kinds of menacing people, who all have to be kept at arm's length – at least conceptually.

3 Accordingly, there is a tendency to avoid the public sphere altogether, rather than actively occupying it and claiming it as one's own. Public communication is an important factor in dealing with strangers. The breakdown of important parts of public communication leads to an inability to cope with xenophobia.

4 In the public sphere characterised by a fear of the other, where the surveillance system of a once all-powerful state is still widely thought to be at work, the concept of the citizen as an active and politically responsible person is difficult to realise.

An old factory worker from Schopflach summed it all up as follows: 'They have picked people up, under Hitler, in GDR times and, don't you believe, young lady, that this is going to change now.'

NOTES

1 This chapter was translated by Monka Guarino. The name of the village and also all personal names have been changed.

2 The Government of the GDR decided on 11 July 1990, to 'give permission to stay, for humanitarian reasons, to foreigners who are persecuted and discriminated against' (*Deutscher Bundestag*, Drucksache 11/8439, 14 November 1990, p. 1). The government of the Federal Republic modified this decision to allow Jews from the Commonwealth of Independent States (CIS) to come to Germany, if they could prove their Jewish identity at a German embassy in the CIS. They would then have the unlimited right to stay in Germany as a *Kontingentflüchtling*, including the right to state support.

3 *Statistisches Landesamt Thüringen* [Statistical Office of Thuringia], Referat Öffentlichkeitsarbeit, Monatszahlen Heft 4/1991, p. 22.

4 He was a member of one of the so-called 'bloc parties' allowed in the GDR, under communist control. From the 1949 local elections in the GDR until 1989 this party held a majority in Schopflach.

5 The greater part of my conversations with Kurt Kühn have been recorded on tape.

6 In this context, an elderly woman in Schopflach told me that her mother once declined to accept a basket of strawberries offered to her during the harvest season by a neighbour suspected of being a witch. Ever since, these two neighbours have severed all relations, according to my informant.

7 I use the terms 'totalitarian order' and 'totalitarian rule' in Arendt's sense (1962: 489). She describes a form of government which, although it may

78 Susanne Spülbeck

legitimise itself with different ideologies, essentially depends on something which, as she puts it, no state and no mere coercive apparatus can achieve: only a movement kept in constant motion is capable of constantly controlling each individual in all aspects of life. In this sense the term is useful not only for describing the Stalinist and Nazi regimes, but also any other dictatorship which pursues the goal of controlling all areas of life (cf. Bracher 1995).

REFERENCES

Arendt, H. (1962) *Elemente und Ursprünge totalitärer Herrschaft*, Frankfurt am Main: Europäische Verlagsgemeinschaft.
Bracher, K. D. (1995) *Wendezeiten der Geschichte: Historisch-politische Essays*, Munich: Deutscher Taschenbuch Verlag.
Erdheim, M. (1988) *Psychoanalyse und Unbewußtheit in der Kultur*, Frankfurt am Main: Suhrkamp.
Festinger, L. (1964) *A Theory of Cognitive Dissonance*, Stanford, Calif.: Stanford University Press.
Friedrich, C. J. and Brzezinski, Z. (1956) *Totalitarian Dictatorship and Autocracy*, Cambridge: Cambridge University Press.
Goffman, E. (1959) *The Presentation of Self in Everday Life*, Garden City, NY: Doubleday, Inc.
Habermas, J. (1990) *Strukturwandel der Öffentlichkeit*, Frankfurt am Main: Suhrkamp.
Mead, G. H. (1934) *Mind, Self, and Society*, Chicago: Chicago University Press.
Mills, C. W. (1956) *The Power Elite*, New York: Oxford University Press.
Moscovici, S. (1984) *Das Zeitalter der Massen*, trans. E. Moldenhauer, Munich: Hanser Anthropologie.
Rogers, C. R. (1951) *Client-Centered Therapy*, Boston: Houghton Mifflin.
Simmel, G. (1922) 'Exkurs über den Fremden', in G. Simmel, *Soziologie: Untersuchungen über Formen der Vergesellschaftung*, Munich and Leipzig: Verlag Duncker and Humblot, pp. 509–12.

Chapter 4

The shifting meanings of civil and civic society in Poland

Michał Buchowski

ANTHROPOLOGICAL APPROACHES TO CIVIL SOCIETY

Chris Hann (1992, 1993, 1995) criticises the notion put forth by some western scholars and former Central European dissidents that there was no civil society in Central Europe during the communist period. Since scholars accepted the totalitarian model, the language of civil society appeared to be absent.[1] However, civil society itself continued to thrive at the grass-roots level, although western intellectuals could not possibly have been aware of it. By comparing philosophical ideals and desired western patterns with the communist reality (see Staniszkis 1989), Polish scholars also contributed to this image. As for the dissidents, they liked to imagine themselves as the 'heroic underdogs' opposing the totalitarian state. In effect, Hann asserts, scholars were mistaken in perceiving members of communist societies as atomised and unable to form an authentic civil society. This critique is entirely convincing. Hann also emphasises the many positive effects which the communist regime brought to the life of local Hungarian communities. Tázlár serves as an example of this wonderful story: 'It became well integrated into the national society and experienced unparalleled material prosperity as a result of reformist socialist policies' (Hann 1992: 163). He is well aware that all forms of association had to be licensed by the communist party, (see 1993: 78, 89), but this was of minor importance for ordinary people. Post-communist developments indicate little change at the village level as far as elections to the community or cooperative bodies are concerned (Hann 1993), and it was the parties associated with the new order that 'seemed to stand for the atomization of the society' (Hann 1992: 160). The results of recent elections, highly favourable for the post-communists, suggest that many people miss the old system. If this is so, why is it that Central European societies wanted to change and have in fact changed their political regimes? In Hann's opinion, the turbulence of the transition has brought home to people the benefits of the previous order and today's deficiencies can help us to discover the reality of communist civil society. I can agree with him on this, while not fully accepting his overall view on the advantages of communism. Like him I will argue against the conventional opinion that civil society was simply absent in Central Europe before 1989. However, I shall challenge the view that nothing has really changed 'for the better' in this respect after 1989.

Two crucial questions lie behind my argument. First, how should civil society be defined in a context different from that of western democracy where the concept originated? Second, what kind of civil society is emerging in Central Europe in the post-communist period, and how it is related to the past order? The concept of civil society must be contextualised and operationalised if it is to be useful in anthropological work. Hence I shall consider how the meaning of civil society and the rationality of governing underwent changes in Poland before 1989, and how they have changed again in recent years.

The central problem boils down to the connection between social reality and theoretical models of that reality. When philosophers write about civil society, they usually postulate an ideal, authentic democracy. Social scientists understand civil society rather differently, mostly in terms of the organisation of its contents. Various, sometimes contradictory, aspects of civil society are seen as germane to its functioning. Political science usually regards individualism, a market-oriented economy and pluralism as indispensable, and the essence of civil society can also be seen in increasing differentiation, or in pluralistic normative integration. As Rau has put it, '[a] precondition for the existence of civil society is a normative consensus of its members' (1991a: 6).[2] Individuals share some moral values and pursue their internalised goals via freely established institutions. These associations fill in the space between the family and the state. This creates two prototypical possibilities: either the interests of state and society converge, or they are in conflict.

A major discrepancy between anthropologists' and political scientists' understandings of civil society seems to turn on the range of activities which falls into this category. Hann writes that 'a focus upon the presence or absence of organized interest groups and autonomous associations is completely inadequate for a diagnosis of the condition of society' (1992: 160). Casual groups formed, for example, for physical exercise, also contribute to social cohesion. Moreover, even actions ensuring individual or family well-being are *social*, since for pursuing their goals 'men and women combine in groups with kin and neighbours'. This is 'another level of co-operation based upon informal networks deeply embedded in the local community' which 'must be taken into account' (Hann 1992: 161; see also White, this volume).

This view diverges significantly from the standard definition given by political science. Drawing on Hegel's comprehension of civil society as a 'free association between individuals' Scruton writes that, when contrasted with the state, a civil society denotes 'forms of association which are spontaneous, customary, and in general not dependent upon law' (1983: 66). This part of the definition easily accommodates an anthropological conception of civil society. However, Scruton goes on to insist that civil society be distinguished from society, 'the first denoting only those associations which also have a political aspect, the second accepting all association generally'. Many forms of association, such as self-help groups, sports' clubs, informal neighborhood groups, will fall outside this definition of civil society. My own experience exemplifies the point. As a teenager living in an agricultural research station in a small Polish village in the 1970s I was a member of the People's Sports' Clubs (*Ludowe Zespoły Sportowe*). Like many people of my age, I played soccer in a local league. Both the station and the nation-wide organisation financed our league, but no one much cared about the source of assistance. What mattered was the equipment we received and the possibility of travelling by van to our Sunday games. Our manager, both trainer and player, was a driver employed by the station. In other words, he was a perfectly ordinary person. I do not know if he was a member of any political party nor did it matter. Players never thought of their activities in political terms. Were we, as teenagers, building a civil society? I would maintain that we were, while most other social and political scientists would say we were not.

Anthropologists, as students of life in small communities, tend to favour the expanded view of civil society. For them, the rudiments of civil society lie in the fact that individuals form common-interest groups that are not necessarily overtly political. The meaning and range of the political domain cannot be precisely delineated. Heading in the same direction, Gellner claims that

> civil society . . . cannot simply be identified with the existence of plural institutions, capable of acting as a kind of countervailing force to the state . . . It certainly specifies one element necessary for the existence of civil society, but it is not sufficient.

> (1991: 498)

Foucault emphasises that every society 'exists within the state's unifying framework of legal regulations yet, at the same time, is a natural reality which is, in essential respects, inaccessible to centralized political power' (quoted in Burchell 1991: 140–1). He too maintains that attempts to define civil society and the state as two opposed, separate and timeless entities are misguided and schematic. Civil society is 'the correlate of a political technology of government'. It is a '"transactional reality"', existing at the mutable interface of political power and everything which permanently outstrips its reach. Its contours are thus inherently variable and open to constant modification' (Foucault, quoted in Burchell 1991: 141).

Following these thoughts, we may best understand civil society as a coin with political power on one side, and all that eludes it on the other. The discontinuity between the two sides is the effect of a dialectical tension, which will depend upon the historical and social context. *Civil society* is a means, a technology of governing and at the same time, a mode of exerting pressure on the power of state. I call this last aspect *civic society*: social institutions embedded within civil society capable of acting as a kind of countervailing force to the state.

It further follows that we must be ready to *relativise* the notion of civil society. Western theoretical concepts do not always fit different cultural contexts and there are limits to their usefulness. Politically oriented groups are not the only components of civil society, and western standards of what is or is not political do not apply everywhere. The meaning of civil society cannot be defined in terms of the opposition of society to the state, but should be seen as a dialectic of these two elements.

The traditional Aristotelian view of the relation between the state and society, partially inherited by modern times, assumes their ideal unity. Classical modern versions of this relation, like the Hegelian or liberal models, make a clear distinction between them (see Cohen and Arato 1987: 309). Anthropological research prompts reservations. A kind of Aristotelian consolidation of politics and society can be seen in the Durkheimian ideal-typical society ruled by mechanical solidarity, where by definition political and other institutions of social life converge. To be more precise, they are not differentiated at all; they are implicit in social life. Dispersed political functions are performed alongside other functions by every member of the community. A society characterised by mechanical solidarity would simultaneously be a civic society.

The communist states wanted to realise the Aristotelian ideal, but also the Hegelian ideal that the state would somehow overtake or merge with society. In theory, increasing democratisation should have eliminated the dichotomy. A Soviet-type system of 'institutional pluralism' (Hough and Fainsod 1979) was presented as one 'in which the leadership and various sections of society were almost harmoniously involved in macrosocial processes' (Rau 1991a: 1). In this model, the communist party controlled the situation in multifarious ways. It represented society's interests through its pervasive presence, ranging from the central administration and army officer corps to student groups. Society's interests were also to be represented in parliament. However, its composition was always decided by an official body, in Poland called the National Unity Front (*Front Jedności Narodu*), made up of various corporate groups and parties which were, again, overseen by the ubiquitous party. 'Democratic centralism' preserved the activists' obedience to their party. The *nomenklatura* system ensured that only loyal people could hold the most significant posts in the system. This projected integration of the state and society became fully fictional. In the political dimension people were alienated from public affairs, while politicians became detached from human affairs since they merely transmitted the decisions of the party to the masses. In this way, even supposedly non-political institutions were converted into administrative organs. The integration of state and society was not achieved from the bottom up by means of vigorous civic society, but from the top down by means of the heavy hand of bureaucracy.

This is a rough outline of the political situation in the communist period in Central Europe. The concept of civil society was predicated on this fundamental dualism between 'the authorities' and 'society'. With these theoretical and political constraints in mind, let us turn to the case of Poland.

CIVIC SOCIETY IN 'COMMUNIST POLAND'

People following their own interests and forming groups contributed to social cohesion during the communist period in various ways. I shall give several examples in order to provide a sense of the scope and character of civic society in the recent past.

First there were *official* associations, corporations, leagues, all created, and licensed by the state. They included many grassroots organisations, such as the Village Women Housekeepers' Association, people's sports' clubs, and volunteer fire brigades. Youth associations, the Polish Students' Association, Polish Scouts, and the Country Youth Association, as well as professional and liberal arts associations, also fall into this category. These organisations were supervised by the authorities and therefore had a political dimension. The political agendas of these groups had contradictory features. On the one hand, they were imposed by the state and all senior posts had to be approved by the party. On the other hand, local or ordinary members were supposed to show respect for the authorities. At some level, the apolitical character of every such organisation ended: they were all designed as part of the huge project of 'organised society'. One might say that these types of associations were political at the top and non-political at the bottom: for an anthropologist they are certainly part of *civil* society. I suggest that, even if the political scientist overlooks them completely, they are also part of *civic* society. Despite the grip of the party and restrictions on political expression within them, these groups provided a significant means for collective activity. Even though political aspects were ordinarily invisible or ignored, what mattered in subjective terms was the possibility of action and the promotion of private or group interests against the authorities. Many of these groups, especially professional organisations, transformed themselves into dissident bodies in the 1980s.

Unofficial civic society took various forms, including extended kin groups and informal interest groups. One of the goals of the Soviet state was to change human nature so that people would put their revolutionary obligations to the party above loyalty to their families or local groups (see Rau 1991b). However, *homo sovieticus* never fully developed. It proved impossible for any government in Central Europe to control every aspect of social life. Family life remained private and was not thoroughly subverted by the state. Now, for most scholars, the family is something opposed to civic society rather than a part of it. Participation in family life is not fully voluntary and social roles are ascribed and not freely chosen. However, I maintain that in the context of authoritarian states, the family often fulfilled functions that in other societies are assumed by institutions outside it. In Poland, the family has been perceived as a sanctuary in a hostile sea of social relations (see Podgórecki 1987: 603; Tarkowska and Tarkowski 1988: 44). Several studies show that Poles have always put the family at the top of a hierarchy of values (Dobrowolska 1975: 260; Bednarski 1987: 85; Buchowski 1993: 64; Tyszka 1982: 152). A similar attitude still holds.[3] In a context in which other forms of civility are reduced to the minimum, the family becomes a bulwark against totalitarianism.

The nuclear family could easily be consolidated in the extended family and this conviction shaped economic, social and cultural life. In the 1980s, the extended family often functioned as an economic unit, with its members lending and borrowing money, usually to subsidise the young, running small enterprises, and so on. The formation of such family-based groups was conditioned by, among other things, the economy of permanent shortage. A complicated network of mutual services, rooted in tradition, was a spontaneous means of helping people to protect their standards of living (see Wedel 1986). This 'family-centrism', in turn, influenced customs and everyday actions. Participation in a family-oriented social life strengthened existing ties and the focus on material interest: 'the pursuit of common economic goals required family solidarity, and this limited social contacts to family communities and extrafamilial interest groups' (Grad 1993: 88).

These familial interests are sometimes characterised as 'amoral familism' (Tarkowska and Tarkowski 1988, following Banfield (1979)). Several negative effects of this kind of familism are indicated: there is 'an atomism and egoism of small groups'; 'internal ties frequently degenerate because of the rivalry of consumers caused by the economic shortages'; competition between micro-groups creates 'aggression, social pathology and all features of an "unfriendly society"' (Tarkowska and Tarkowski 1991: 104). Ethical dualism is said to impose a rigid morality and loyalty towards persons from the inner circle, and extreme moral laxity towards everyone else. Moral relativity also meant double standards with regard to private versus state property.[4]

In the traditional village setting, familism was connected with neighbourhood mutual help and other traditional forms of local community cooperation (see Nagengast 1991: 175–96). In the 1980s, economic ties were often fortified by political factors, particularly in the cities. Martial law and the danger of persecution for unauthorised activity encouraged people to restrict their social ties to kin and close friends. Quite often this kind of extended family integration had a political aspect. All in all, one can imagine Polish society in the 1980s as a whole composed of cross-cutting units based on extended families. These microstructures formed a network of tightly knit interest groups. There is no doubt that in many respects this edifice of society presented something which may be described as amoral familism, but this is not a justification for excluding these family-oriented microstructures from the notion of civic society. Just as individuals are the key entities in civil and political-science models of civil society, so these informal groups were fundamental to civic society in Poland. As the Tarkowskis rightly noted (but overlooked in their analysis), under martial law these grass-roots 'direct ties constituted an alternative public sphere ... [T]his alternative sphere generated social integration. It served as a buffer against the economic crisis in Poland confronted during the 1980s' (Tarkowska and Tarkowski 1991: 104).

Religious organisations were official, but usually not fully controlled by the party. The position of the Catholic church in Poland was unique in the whole socialist camp. History showed that 'the Catholic Church, with its special position within the Polish nation' was an organisation that the communists 'could neither destroy ... nor use for their own purposes' (Piekalkiewicz 1991: 158). This church was in fact the only structure independent of official state institutions. The organisation itself presented a mighty power. At the end of the 1970s it consisted of 14,000 churches located in 7,000 parishes administered by about 20,000 priests (*Rocznik Statystyczny* 1980: 27). The Catholic University of Lublin (the only non-state university behind the Iron Curtain) and other theological institutes and seminaries were centres of independent thought. Various religious activities were sponsored by the church, ranging from rosary circles and youth preaching groups to social-assistance associations. There was even token Catholic representation in the communist parliament through *Znak* (see Micewski 1978). Should such an enormous self-governed organisation be considered an element of civic society? I think so. The church had a stimulating effect throughout society. Deeply embedded in the national tradition and local community life, it represented the interests of various groups at different levels. The church not only maintained religious freedom but preserved elements of freedom of speech through its preaching. After martial law was imposed on 13 December 1981, the church structures became 'safe havens' for secular dissidents and independent cultural activity (see Weigel 1992). In other words, the church was itself a major organisation of civic society, and at the same time it provided an infrastructure for other independent groups. When other forms of non-authorised civic society were suppressed, the church became the most natural and convenient venue for the expression of society's feelings and organised activity.

Finally, Poland also had politically independent organisations which engaged openly in social activity. The beginning of social protest in Poland can be traced back to June 1956 when workers in Poznań demanded 'freedom and bread'. A part of the ensuing 'October Thaw' was the development of workers' self-governments (*samorządy robot-nicze*) in the industrial plants. Although these workers' organisations were quickly curtailed, later years saw further protests and numerous attempts at forming independent trade unions and political parties (see Karpinski 1989; Raina 1982). In 1976, the Workers' Defence Committee (*Komitet Obrony Robotnikow,* or KOR) was established to provide help for families of detained workers and to defend those brought before the courts. KOR was in fact the first autonomous non-religious organisation to achieve notable social impact (Lipski 1985). It aimed to build up autonomous social bonds and saw grass-roots associations as the most viable form of civic defence against totalitarianism. Without aspiring to power or threatening the socialist principles of the state, it set out to protect individual rights. Its ideas were put into practice a few years later by *Solidarity*, an organisation which had 10 million members in 1981. Officially a trade union, *Solidarity* was a movement which at the same time played the multifaceted roles of political party and civic society structure (see Goodwyn 1991). Various organisations outside of party control were able to flourish under its umbrella. When the communists found out that attempts to control *Solidarity* were futile, they decided to crush it forcefully (see Holzer 1983). But defeating *Solidarity* was not an easy task, and the changes in the collective consciousness after 1980–1 were irreversible. They added up to a disenchantment of the communist world (Buchowski 1991: 431, 433). The communist regime's lack of legitimacy was finally revealed, and people became aware of the power of organised groups. An entire independent society, with an underground press and mechanisms for distributing aid to the persecuted and their families, was consolidated in the 1980s. Eventually, the communist élite came to the conclusion that it was not possible to govern the country without social endorsement, and they entered the 'round-table talks' that led to the election of a non-communist government in 1989.

These unauthorised political organisations meet most of the standard classical political definitions of civil society and they clearly meet my definition of civic society. Independent institutions arose to represent the interests of social groups towards the state. The legitimacy of the communists' power was openly challenged. Even when martial law was imposed, society was able to organise itself. While we should not overestimate the impact of anti-totalitarian groups on the entire society, neither should this be underestimated. If the social pressure had not been as strong as it was, the historical change would have never happened. Consequently, claims denying the existence of civic society in communist Poland cannot be sustained.

COMMUNIST GOVERNMENTALITY AND CIVIL SOCIETY

In a situation in which the party aspired to control every aspect of life, any activity that undermined official prerogatives was regarded as political. *Solidarity* was accused of trying to grab power, as distinct from simply strengthening civic society. Aware of the threat of external military intervention, moderate *Solidarity* leaders advocated a 'new evolutionism'. This was the idea that, even without changing political structures, it would still be possible to build an independent social edifice (see Michnik 1985). 'New evolutionists' dreamed of a society organised like villages in a feudal kingdom, in which localities paid taxes and tributes to the sovereign but remained independent in their internal affairs. They presupposed a 'reabsorption of state power by society', as in the Paris Commune (Gordon 1991: 30). Some thought thereby to establish 'socialism with a human face'. This goal proved to be unrealistic because it clashed with the communist notion of governmentality.

For Foucault, governmentality is:

> [t]he ensemble formed by the institutions, procedures, analyses and reflections, the calculations and tactics that allow the exercise of this very specific albeit complex form of power, which has as its target population, as its principal form of knowledge, political economy, and as its essential technical means apparatuses of security.
>
> (1991: 102)

This aspect of governmentality can be called a mode of governing or a *rationality of governing*. Communist governmentality can be characterised as a technique which relied on the state's power to control every possible aspect of life. Communists, as Leszek Nowak (1991) put it, wanted to become triple-lords, ruling over economics, politics and culture. In other words, they 'fused the political, ideological and productive hierarchies into one single unified *nomenklatura*' (Gellner 1991: 495). This governmentality was marked by an implicit disregard for democratic procedures and social initiatives. Private property was limited and economic activity was controlled by the state. Cultural institutions were supervised by the ideologists and society was controlled at as many levels as possible. Various forms of force became popular tools. This was the essence of communist 'governmentality', as understood in the original Foucauldian sense.

Here I would like to suggest another, derivative sense of governmentality. 'Governmentality' can be seen as a mentality of governing. Ruling élites devise and accustom themselves to a particular mode of governing. For several decades the Polish élites internalised the communist mode and made it a 'natural' form of political behaviour. For this reason, the abrupt attempt to change it shocked the beneficiaries of the system and provoked radical reaction. Military intervention was, in fact, a typical example of the party's governing mentality, a step they could always set in motion at times when their position was jeopardised.

Society's task was to change both the mode and the mentality of governing. By striving to expand a private sphere and its own independence, every society tries to 'discipline the state', as Foucault put it (Foucault 1972; cf. Gordon 1991: 27). The disciplining of the state varied considerably in each of the communist countries, but the most open and effective process of this kind took place in Poland. Eventually, as we have seen, a breakthrough to democratisation and the possibility of more developed forms of civic society was achieved.

The meaning of civil society in Poland in the 1980s changed as a result of these changes in the mode and mentality of governing. The use of force against civic society gave way to less rigid techniques (see Walicki 1991). In politics, the shift meant the recognition of independent social initiatives and of the necessity to cooperate with civic structures. Of course, *perestroika* helped in this process. As long as *Solidarity* claimed that it wanted only a limited revolution, the party practised controlled repression (see Smolar 1991: 178). However, the outcome went much further than anyone supposed. The party systematically withdrew from cultural and scientific life, and permitted pluralism in these domains. It shifted from a centralised state economy towards a free market with an increasing role for the private sector. Members of the *nomenklatura*, that is, those who had taken over state property in the late 1980s, were among the main beneficiaries of this process.[5]

These economic changes were not sufficient to allow the emergence of civil society in the political scientists' sense. Party control was still too pervasive. The core of the problem lay not in the articulation of group interests, but in the impossibility of forming groups united by economic, as distinct from merely symbolic, interests. The persistence of collective property and the revolutionary legitimacy of power prevented the formation of civil society in the true Hegelian sense (Staniszkis 1989: ch. 6). The ideology of the dissidents of this period may be called, following Piotr Ogrodzienski, an 'ethical civic society'. Its most conspicuous element was the focus on self-limiting revolution, and it emphasised the ethical values of human rights, dignity, truth and openness. This ethical code, together with a common interest in undermining the existing political order, brought together the church and dissidents tending towards the left. A widespread perception of the pathological quality of everyday life justified this ethos and enabled it to receive wide social approval (Ogrodzieński 1991: 71–2). We should keep in mind, however, that in many respects this support was mostly *symbolic*, focused as it was around national symbols and symbolic values. It was never rooted in economic interests. In the end, only the *nomenklatura* was allowed to form an economically based civil society group.

One could conclude that, by classical standards, a rather one-sided civil society existed in Poland. Most people, with the church and the *Solidarity* movement in the forefront, were interested in building civic society structures, while the party wanted to preserve the *status quo* and was not interested in changing the rationality of governing. There were no groups united by common economic interests, apart from a fragment of the *nomenklatura*. Most people used a simple binary classification: 'us', ordinary people, versus 'them', the rulers. However, this political science view needs to be supplemented by an anthropological perspective. Organised opposition to the authoritarian regime was a part of a larger whole. The vast range of social life which permanently eludes centralised political power continued to function. Family, extended family, informal groups, and various other forms of associations operated outside the reach of effective bureaucratic control. Although less visible and neglected by the regime, they constituted an integral part of the total social system. All of these forms too, along with dissident groups and the party, operated within a single political framework. The 'rulers' were necessarily influenced by society's behaviour. They may have been, in a sense, parasitic on the system, but in the end they too contributed to the vigorous expansion of a new civil society.

CIVIL SOCIETY TODAY: EVOLUTION AFTER THE REVOLUTION

After the peaceful collapse of communism, Poland embarked on a systemic transformation which affected most spheres of life, particularly the relation between the state and society. This meant a profound redefinition of the essence of civil society (see Smolar 1993). Politically, one form of ideological control was removed. No political party can now claim a right to control others. New areas of free activity and associational life have opened. These encompass charity, self-help and professional bodies, local self-government, religious organisations, and political parties.[6] Economically, Poland, like other countries in the region, began to establish a market economy. The state has withdrawn further from direct intervention in the economic decisions of companies, including state-owned enterprises. The ownership structure has already changed substantially, and a plentiful class of new private entrepreneurs has emerged. Culturally, the old ideological restraints have been removed. No political pressure is exerted on artists or cultural activists and censorship has disappeared. In all these respects, the new Poland contrasts with the old communist governmentality. The nature of the state and the make-up of civil society have been transformed. Democratic freedom has enabled new relations to be formed between the state and its citizens. In this context, Hann's assertions that previous bonds have been shattered and social cohesion ruptured are misleading. There is plenty of evidence to show that new forms of autonomous civic activity have emerged. Thus, 60 per cent of the workforce outside of agriculture now work in the private sector; employees are organised into around 1,500 trade unions, 200 of which are national in scope (Wrabec 1993). More than 2 million private entrepreneurs have emerged, most of them from scratch, with their own employers' associations and clubs. The number of registered political parties has grown from 3 to 250, and religious groups too are mushrooming (cf. Urban 1994). Non-governmental organisations currently number about 15,000.[7] Local government agencies combine with other initiatives to counteract the state administration and promote local self-government.

All this is only one side of the picture. The same problem can be approached from a different angle. First, one can point to the inertia of those accustomed to the welfare state. This is visible among farmers, state farm agricultural workers and the employees of large industrial plant. Trade unions and many political groups caught the changing wind in their sails and the results of the 1993 elections, much more favourable to the Left, demonstrate this inertia (see Buchowski 1994b). Signs of social apathy can be also seen at the grass-roots level. In the quarter of Poznań where I live, important decisions for local life are taken at general meetings. Attendance at these meetings in the communist past was minimal, but in 1989 my neighbours roused themselves. A group of the most active and wealthy among them took over control of the shopping centre from the nation-wide monopoly *Spolem*. Around 150 people would show up at meetings, fiercely discuss current affairs and contest for voluntary posts. In March 1994 I attended a meeting at which only thirty people were present. The atmosphere was nothing like that of five years before. According to survey data, in June 1992, 91 per cent of those questioned thought they could exercise no significant influence over the life of the country in general, while 79 per cent thought the same about local community problems, and 60 per cent concerning their place of employment (Tarkowska 1993: 100).

A similar point can be made about political activity, with less than half of the electorate demonstrating any interest in politics. Election turn-out has never surpassed the relatively low level of 62 per cent attained in the watershed elections of 4 June 1989.[8] After 1989 there was a rapid decline in the proportion of the population affiliated to a political party.

The fall of communism brought a number of former dissidents to the fore as national political leaders and state officials. This phenomenon led Mastnak and de Candole to claim that the state and civil society have merged (Mastnak 1990; de Candole 1991; cf. Cahalen's 1993 'government-in-waiting' theory).[9] According to these writers, the danger of a one-party state was looming again. These conjectures proved unfounded. Post-communist socialist parties are still active and in some countries, including Poland, they have won elections. Moreover, many of the grassroots associations which had previously appeared united under one banner did not in fact have a political agenda at all. Ecological issues, for example, had been politicised by the nature of the communist system. Now, these groups still exist, but outside the strictly political domain. They remain active in influencing state policy, but not through directly engaging the state (Cahalen 1993). Moreover, as movements split into diverging factions, many prominent dissidents failed to act as 'government-in-waiting' members. Currently, with post-communists forming a coalition government, most of the former dissidents are in opposition.

How should we interepret these conflicting tendencies, the democratisation of political structures and an expanding sphere of civic activity on the one hand; and signs of social passivity on the other? Do we have a more 'civil–ised' society in Poland than we did before? A more meaningful and neutral question might be: what is the nature of the new rationality of governing? The answer has to be multilayered. The most visible change has occurred at the political level, where decentralisation of state power and freedom of civic activity have become the main principles of social life. New problems, such as unemployment, have prompted new forms of civic action. In this way, we can speak of the proliferation and increased differentiation of organised activity. However, mental and behavioural patterns from the past remain powerful. In welfare expectations and job habits, a reluctance to accept new forms of organised activity can be explained by the working of three related ingredients inherited from the past. It may in part be a reaction to the 'organised' model of social life imposed by the communists. It may also relate to dissatisfaction with the performance of the new political élite. Third, there remains the conviction that the family is still the only sphere that counts in realising one's aspirations. In this new context, familism can indeed be viewed as an obstacle to the new 'western' forms of civil society.

The rejection of communism in 1989 did not imply support for a new order of the kind the post-*Solidarity* establishment had in mind. This massive endorsement was primarily symbolic (Ziółkowski 1993: 117). In other words, people's opposition to the old regime was built around symbolic national, civic and anti-communist values. Ethical civic society was anchored in the non-economic sphere. When communism had been defeated, the symbolic unifying factors quickly faded away. Simultaneously, shock therapy in the economy redefined or created social groups and differentiated their interests. The post-*Solidarity* political élite embarked upon a 'war at the top', and fragmented in a rather distasteful manner. The fragility of a purely symbolic society was exhibited in the most recent parliamentary elections, in which parties advocating strong anti-communist rhetoric were marginalised. However, this component has not disappeared completely, and now, when post-communist socialists are in power and social dissatisfaction continues, it may come to the fore again.

The dissolution of the major past principle of civil society and economic reform have created a new constellation of interest groups, but it is still too early to say where this process of systemic changes will lead. Civil society's condition depends on the larger social, economic and cultural context. One might say that the construction of a new civil society is in a state of becoming. This view corresponds to a widespread perception of Central Europe as undergoing a rite of passage, as being between socialism and capitalism, betwixt authoritarianism and democracy (Bauman 1992: 114–16; Buchowski 1994a: 140–1). Previous ethical principles consolidating society against state power have become obsolete and new interest groups have emerged, integrated according to new principles. However, state employees still comprise a large portion of the workforce and their interests collide with the state in complex ways. Symbolic values are no longer a moral sanction for protests, but new demands are being addressed directly to the state itself. Many people do not want the state to withdraw from its paternalistic role. They would like to enjoy political freedom in a country where the state continues to provide fully for social welfare. Current problems with moulding new state–society relations can be seen as a struggle between two very different mentalities, and changing the mental attitude of 'learned helplessness' (Koralewicz and Ziółkowski 1990: 157) will take a long time.

Post-*Solidarity* governments had a vision of civil society close to the western type, in which the role of the state is significantly reduced. However these politics clashed with an image of the function of the state as provider, coupled with the belief that the role of ordinary citizens is merely to demand, that had taken deep root under communisim. In other words, post-*Solidarity* leaders' rationality of governing did not fit deeper habits of social apathy, particularly strong among the working class and in the countryside.

The turbulence of the transition period caused discontent and further political upheavals. Its impact has been largely ignored by the wishful thinking of post-*Solidarity* politicians. Post-communist parties have gained votes with promises to implement more 'pro-social' economic policies, and there are signs that a more centralised rationality of governing is being restored. The state administration's prerogatives are being strengthened, a range of local government decisions is being restricted, and privatisation has been held back. The new authorities of the post-communist left are showing their old proclivity for strengthening central government administration.[10] As a result, all the existing, supposedly transitional structures are frozen. New social initiatives have been precipitated by economic and political developments, but many elements of the past persist and are being reinforced by the current authorities. In this sense, Poland, and maybe some other Central European countries, are no longer in a transition period. Poland sailed out on a journey but now finds itself adrift at sea. It commenced a rite of passage that will not now be consummated: the status predetermined by the 'western elders and wise men' will never be achieved. Perhaps Poland is crossing uncharted waters, and will eventually end up in some exciting new location. But its present form of civil society remains a hybrid of old and new elements which, like that of the recent past, fails to fit any philosopher's model.[11]

NOTES

1   The concept was not in circulation at that time, at least as far as areas outside Western Europe are concerned. In Polish political dictionaries, such as the Political Dictionary published in New York in 1980 and reprinted without censorship in Poland, or that published five years later in London (Karpinski 1985), there is no entry under 'civil society'. Local relations of power, leadership, and routine activities were not yet seen in a civil society perspective.

2   Rau's argument is misleading in that it reifies both state and society as monolithic units, rather than viewing them as assemblies of diverse or even conflicting interests in a continuous process of 'fission' and 'fusion'.

3   According to the Centre for Social Opinion Studies polls carried out in November 1993, 71 per cent of Poles declared that a happy family was the most important value in their life, well ahead of a professional career or wealth (*Tylko rodzina* 1993). These raw data need qualification. Family

happiness is often understood as family welfare that is strictly connected with individual career and financial success (cf. Buchowski 1993: 64–5, 69). Nevertheless the very high emphasis on the family as a source of values is significant in Poland.

4 I am describing several aspects of family ties in terms of 'amoral familism', but without wishing to endorse the moral overtones as laid down by political scientists. Perhaps all these relations should be viewed simply in terms of in-group versus out-group behaviour.

5 As Wojciech Jaruzelski, the Polish leader in the 1980s, said proudly in front of the State Tribunal on 9 March 1994, 'more than 90 out of 100 of the richest Poles from the list compiled by the weekly *Wprost* started their [private] economic activity in those years [1980s]' (WZ: 1994).

6 The case of ethnic-minority associations is instructive. Previously limited in their activity to a strictly controlled official cultural domain, they can now function more freely. The example of the pro-German minority in Silesia is probably the most conspicuous. In the past they were a politically sensitive group and therefore forced to remain silent. Now they have their own associations and representation in parliament (see Sakson 1991).

7 For example, one list of non-government and non-profit organisations compiled in 1993 totals 4,515 organisations, not including regional branches of nation-wide organisations (Zespół 1993). A directory of non-government organisations focusing on social work lists 1,793 organisations (Informator 1993).

8 In elections to local government in May 1990, voter turn-out was 42 per cent; in the first round of presidential elections in September 1990 it was 61 per cent and in the second round it was 53 per cent; in the second parliamentary elections in October 1991 it was 43 per cent. In the September 1993 parliamentary elections, the third held since 1989, voter turn-out was 51.5 per cent; and in the most recent local government elections, held on 19 June 1994, it was a mere 35.8 per cent.

9 Mastnak and de Candole's understanding of civil society is inadequate according to the criteria set forth here. The state and civic society are not two separate realities, and continuous relations develop between them.

10 One example of this pattern was the boycott of a programme designed to allow local governments to take over state schools (see Kaczmarek and Wyszyńska 1993). An administrative reform expected to confer many rights on local elected authorities (the so called *reforma powiatowa*), was planned for 1995, but was, in effect, postponed indefinitely (see Koral 1993). Most self-government activists are very dissatisfied with post-communist politics (see Koral 1994).

11 I would like to thank Deborah Cahalen, Elizabeth Dunn, Carole Nagengast and David Slattery for their help in editing this text in English and for helpful comments.

REFERENCES

Banfield, E. (1979) 'The moral basis of a backward society', in A. J. Heidenheimer (ed.), *Political Corruption: Readings in Comparative Analysis*, New Brunswick: Transaction Publishers.

Bauman, Z. (1992) 'The Polish predicament: a model in search of class interests', *Telos* 25(2): 113–30.

Bednarski, J. (1987) *Zroznicowanie rodzinnych srodowisk kulturowych* ('Differentiation of Family Cultural Environments'), Poznań: Wydawnictwo Naukowe UAM.

Buchowski, M. (1991) 'The magic of the king-priests of communism', *East European Quarterly*, 25(4): 425–36.

—— (1993) 'The family value system', *The Centennial Review* 37(1): 61–72.

—— (1994a) 'From anti-communist to post-communist ethos: the case of Poland', *Social Anthropology* 2(2): 133–48.

—— (1994b) 'Poland: an old society after new elections', *Anthropological Journal on European Cultures*, 3(1): 61–84.

Burchell, G. (1991) 'Peculiar interests: civil society and governing "the system of natural liberty"', in G. Burchell, C. Gordon and P. Miller (eds), *The Foucault Effect: Studies in Governmentality*, Chicago: University of Chicago Press, pp. 119–50.

Cahalen, D. (1993) 'A place to stand: social movements and civil society in Poland', paper presented at the 92nd American Anthropological Association Meetings, Washington, DC.

Cohen, J. and Arato, A. (1987) 'Spoleczenstwo obywatelskie a teoria spoleczna', trans. K. Kanliowska, in A. M. Kaniowski and A. Szahaj (eds), *Wokół teorii krytycznej Jurgena Habermasa* ('Concerning Jurgen Habermas's Critical Theory'), Warsaw: Kolegium Ortyckie; Polish translation of 'Social movements, civil society and the problem of sovereignty', *Praxis International* 4(3), 1984, pp. 307–45.

de Candole, J. (1991) *Czechoslovakia: Too Velvet Revolution?*, London: Alliance Publishers.

Dobrowolska, D. (1975) 'Wartosci zwiazane z zyciem rodzinnym' ('Values connected with family life'), in J. Komorowska (ed.), *Przemiany rodziny polskiej* ('Changes in the Polish Family'), Warsaw: Instytut Wydawniczy CRZZ, pp. 260–78.

Foucault, M. (1972) *Surveiller et punir: naissance de la prison*, Paris: Gallimard.

—— (1991) 'Governmentality', in G. Burchell, C. Gordon and P. Miller (eds), *The Foucault Effect: Studies in Governmentality*, Chicago: University of Chicago Press.

Gellner, E. (1991) 'Civil society in historical context', *International Social Science Review* 192: 495–510.

Goodwyn, L. (1991) *Breaking the Barrier: The Rise of Solidarity in Poland*, Oxford: Oxford University Press.

Gordon, C. (1991) 'Governmental rationality: an introduction', in G. Burchell, C. Gordon and P. Miller (eds), *The Foucault Effect: Studies in Governmentality*, Chicago: University of Chicago Press.

Grad, J. (1993) 'Customs and the decay of "real socialism"', *The Centennial Review* 37(1): 73–92

Hann, C. M. (1992) 'Civil society at the grassroots: a reactionary view', in P. G. Lewis (ed.), *Democracy and Civil Society in Eastern Europe*, London: St Martin's Press, pp. 152–65.

—— (1993) 'From comrades to lawyers: continuity and change in local political

culture in rural Hungary', *Anthropological Journal on European Cultures* 2(1): 75–104.
—— (1995) 'Philosophers' models on the Carpathian lowlands', in J. Hall (ed.), *Civil Society: History, Theory, Comparison*, Cambridge: Polity Press, pp. 158–82.
Holzer, J. (1983) *Solidarnosc 1980–1981: Geneza i historia* ('Solidarity 1980–1981: Genesis and History'), Warzaw: Krag.
Hough, J. F. and Fainsod, M. (1979) *How the Soviet Union is Governed*, Cambridge: Harvard University Press.
Informator (1993) *Informator o organizacjach pozarządowych działających na polu pomocy spotecznej* ('A Directory of Non-Governmental Organisations Working in the Field of Social Help'), Warsaw: Klon.
Kaczmarek, M. and Wyszyńska, M. (1993) 'Albo szkota, albo akwarium' ('Either school or aquarium'), *Gazeta Wielkopolska* 297 (12 December), pp. 000–000.
Karpinski, J. (1985) *Polska, Komunizm, Opozycja: Slownik* ('Poland, Communism, Opposition: A Dictionary'), London: Polonia.
—— (1989) Portrety lat: *Polska w odcinkach 1944–1988* ('Portraits of Years: Poland in a series 1944–1989'), London: Polonia.
Koral, J. (1993) 'Świat z niczego' ('A world from nothing'), *Gazeta Wyborcza* 238 (October).
—— (1994) 'Recydywa centralismu' ('A relapse of centralism'), *Gazeta Wyborcza* 112 (16 May).
Koralewicz, J. and Ziółkowski, M. (1990) *Mentalność Polaków* ('Mentality of Poles'), Poznań: Nakom.
Lipski, J. (1985) *KOR: A History of the Workers' Defence Committee in Poland*, Berkeley and Los Angeles: University of California Press.
Mastnak, T. (1990) 'Civil society in Slovenia: from opposition to power', *Studies in Comparative Communism* 23(3–4): 305–17.
Micewski, A. (1978) *Współrządzic czy nie kxamac? PAX i Znak w Polsce 1945–1976* ('Participate in Governing or Not Lie? PAX and Znak 1945–1976'), Paris: Libella.
Michnik, A. (1985) *Letters from Prison and Other Essays*, Berkeley and Los Angeles: University of California Press.
Nagengast, C. (1991) *Reluctant Socialists, Rural Entrepreneurs: Class, Culture and the Polish State*, Boulder, Colo.: Westview.
Nowak, L. (1991) *Własnosc i władza* ('Property and Power'), Poznań: Nakom.
Ogrodzieński, P. (1991) *Pięc szkiców o społeczenstwie obywatelskim* ('Five Essays on Civil Society'), Warsaw: Instytut Studiow Politycznych PAN.
Piekalkiewicz, J. (1991) 'Poland: nonviolent revolution in a socialist state', in J. A. Goldstone, T. R. Gurr and F. Moshiri (eds), *Revolutions in the Late Twentieth Century*, Boulder, Colo.: Westview, pp. 136–61.
Podgórecki, A. (1987) 'Całościowa analiza społeczenstwa polskiego' ('Global analysis of Polish society'), in E. Wnuk-Lipiński (ed.), *VII Ogólnopolski Zjazd Socjologiczny. Materials (7th All-Polish Sociological Congress)*, Warsaw: Polskie Towarzystwo Socjologiczne, pp. 576–612.
Raina, P. (1982) *Political Opposition in Poland: 1954–1977*, London: Poets and Painters Press.
Rau, Z. (1991a) 'Introduction', in Z. Rau (ed.), *The Reemergence of Civil Society in Eastern Europe and the Soviet Union*, Boulder, Colo.: Westview, pp. 1–23.

—— (1991b) 'Human nature, social engineering and the reemergence of civil society', in Z. Rau (ed.), *The Reemergence of Civil Society in Eastern Europe and the Soviet Union*, Boulder, Colo.: Westview, pp. 25–50.

Rocznik Statystyczny (1980) (Statistical Yearbook of Poland), Warsaw.

Sakson, A. (1991) 'Mniejszosc niemiecka a inne mniejszosci narodowe w Polsce' ('The German minority and other ethnic minorities in Poland'), *Przeglad Zachodni* 47(2): 1–23.

Scruton, R. (1983) 'Civil society', in R. Scruton, *A Dictionary of Political Thought*, London: Pan Books.

Smolar, A. (1991) 'The Polish opposition', in E. Feher and A. Arato (eds), *Crisis and Reform in Eastern Europe*, New Brunswick: Transaction Publishers, pp. 175–252.

—— (1993) 'Vom homo sovieticus zum Bürger', *Transit. Europäische Revue* 6: 51–62.

Staniszkis, J. (1989) *Ontologia socjalizmu* ('Ontology of Socialism'), Warsaw: Krytyka.

Tarkowska, E. (1993) 'A waiting society: the temporal dimension of transformation in Poland', *Polish Sociological Bulletin* 2: 93–102.

Tarkowska, E. and Tarkowski, J. (1988) '"Amoralny familizm" czyli o dezintegracji społecznej w Polsce lat osiemdziesiątych' ('"Amoral familism" or on social disintegration in 1980s Poland'), in E. Wnuk-Lipiński (ed.), *Grupy i więzi społeczne w systemie monocentrycznym* ('Social Groups and Ties in the Mono-Centric System'), Warsaw: IFIS PAN.

—— (1991) 'Social disintegration in Poland: civil society or amoral familism?', *Telos* 89(3): 103–9.

Tylko rodzina (1993) 'Tylko rodzina' ('Only family'), *Gazeta Wyborcza* 294 (17 December).

Tyszka, Z. (1982) *Rodziny współczesne w Polsce* ('Contemporary families in Poland'), Warsaw: Instytut Wydawniczy Związków Zawodowych.

Urban, K. (1994) *Mniejszości religijne w Polsce 1945–1991* ('Religious Minority Groups in Poland 1945–1991'), Cracow: Nomos.

Walicki, A. (1991) 'From Stalinism to post-communist pluralism: the case of Poland', *New Left Review* 185: 92–121.

Wasiutiński, W. (ed.) (1980) *Słownik Polityczny*, New York: Instytut Romana Dmowskiego.

Wedel, J. (1986) *The Private Poland*, New York: Facts on File.

Weigel, G. (1992) *The Final Revolution: The Resistance of the Church and the Collapse of Communism*, Oxford: Oxford University Press.

Wrabec, P. (1993) 'Nasze drogie związki' ('Our expensive trade unions'), *Gazeta Wyborcza* 217 (16 October).

WZ (1994) 'Dwa przedwojnia' ('Two pre-war times'), *Gazeta Wyborcza* 58 (10 March).

Zespół (1993) *Jawor 93: Informator o organisacjach pozarządowych w Polsce* ('Jawor 93: A Guidebook of Non-Governmental Organisations in Poland'), Warsaw: Fundusz Wspolpracy.

Ziółkowski, M. (1993) 'Group interest and group consciousness in the process of system transformation: the case of the Polish intellegentsia', *The Centennial Review* 37(1): 115–34.

Chapter 5

Bringing civil society to an uncivilised place

Citizenship regimes in Russia's Arctic frontier

David G. Anderson

There is a peculiar but revealing term for the European portion of Russia in the vocabulary of Russian settlers living in Siberia: the *materik*. Although the Siberian north can be distinguished geographically from other Arctic territories by the fact that it is composed of a vast and continuous continental mass, the term *materik* redundantly means 'the mainland'. With this term, in defiance of geography, Russian newcomers recall their cities of origin in a far-away heartland and allegorically place their adopted homes on islands – as if their life histories were those of colonists who had traversed wide and dangerous seas to reach a new land. While the theme of the relationship between the centre and the frontier is a rich one in the history of Russian state building (Bassin 1993), I will focus specifically upon the institutions, social rights and civic practices that the settlers saw themselves bringing to these remote islands and their aboriginal inhabitants. Although civic practices from the mainland are found to have varying degrees of usefulness, the mainland always remains in the minds of the settlers as the measure of civility and good government. This unusual and almost nostalgic view of the central civil institutions of Russian society provides a critical angle for those wishing to understand what foundation (if any) supports a post-socialist civil society in Russia.

How meaningful is it to write of civil society in post-Soviet Siberia? The term itself has next to no vernacular currency among natives and Russians alike. The few thousand Evenkis, Dolgans, Buriats and Russians of several remote villages who supported my anthropological field expeditions in 1989 and again in 1992 and 1993 are hardly a representative sample of Russian society.[1] Furthermore, the former Soviet Union and Siberia form mythical archetype in both popular thought and in social theory for the *complete absence* of any kind of autonomously managed or socially meaningful public sphere. The short answer to these challenges is that the unexpected and outlying example can prove the robustness of a concept. The longer answer will contradict each of these points in turn by establishing that, as good civic practice was extended to the allegorical islands of the Russian frontier, it came to be institutionalised in a socially meaningful manner. Unlike the coffee houses or political parties in Euro-American society, civil society in Siberia was harboured within different 'citizenship regimes' which formed restricted yet significant channels for economic and political practice. The past tense is deliberate: the assault on forms of civic entitlement and participation has never been greater than with the current politics of privatisation. My aim is to draw on complex case materials to expose certain mystifications in the theoretical literature on civil society. While there is a need for a theoretical language to debate the quality of participation in public life, there is at least an equal need to ensure that the western language of civility is not inappropriately applied to non-western legal settings.

Before turning to the argument about civil society in Siberia, I shall first introduce the people who shared with me their ideas on this subject and on their history.

NATIVES AND NEWCOMERS IN KHANTAISKOE OZERO

Khantaiskoe Ozero is a village of 612 people of primarily Evenki and Dolgan nationality packed within the narrow confines of an alluvial peninsula in the middle of an alpine lake. Lake Khantaiskoe is the third deepest in the former Soviet Union, achieving nearly a kilometre of depth due to the trenching of ancient volcanic activity. The most lucrative artefact of those ancient eruptions is the mineral composition of the surrounding mountains. The flat-topped front ranges of the Pultoran plateau, which compose a mesmerising reflection in the lake during the midnight summer daylight, are rich in cadmium, nickel and platinum. The metallic stores of the region are intensely mined and smelted at the city-state of Noril'sk just 140 kilometres north of the village. Noril'sk is the largest 'island' in this sector of Siberia. To reach Khantaiskoe, you take a Boeing aircraft to the mining city and then successively smaller craft until you finally reach the shores of the lake on a freight helicopter or a biplane with skiis. Despite the trouble that you must take to reach it, the village is definitely part of Noril'sk's archipelago. The profits from the mine are now helping to support some of the essential services of this village as well as others in the region. The precipitates from the furnaces also waft down upon the translucent waters of the lake when a north wind blows.

In the most recent letter I received from Khantaiskoe Ozero, the Evenki language teacher proudly reported that she and her students are assembling a history of the village in drawings and in pictures. To the anthropologist, the counterpoising of 'village' and 'history' is striking since the ensemble of buildings at Lake Khantaiskoe is a very recent social creation. The economy of this region was based upon a highly mobile combination of hunting, fishing and the use of harnessed reindeer which was unsuited to the intensive use of a fixed place. Although Soviet power brought a trading post to Lake Khantaiskoe in 1928, established the first *artel'* ('small cooperative') 'Red Hunter' in 1932, and built a school in the early 1940s, until the late 1960s most people travelled regularly living in dozens of homesites across this scenic but harsh landscape. There were structures on the site of the village from the mid-1940s built by conscripted German and Latvian carpenters. However, it was not until the great economic reforms of the early 1970s, the grouping together of smaller population points, and the construction of the hydroelectric plant on the Khantaika river, that the village came to be the central institution both spatially and socially in the lives of the local Evenkis. Due to the demographics of the area, this short history is experienced by local people as three generations. The indigenous Evenkis often contrast their 'cultured' manners and their fine knowledge of the Russian language to the *nekul'turnye* ('not cultured') manners of the Dolgans who were forcibly relocated to Khantaiskoe Ozero when their village was administratively liquidated in 1969. A central part of the identity of the Khantaiskoe Evenkis revolves around their village, their schools and their 'cultured' traditions. Hence, for the Evenkis, it is symbolically important for school children to write the history of this landscape and its peoples as the history of a village.

Despite the interest shown in the history of the village, the admirable civic consciousness of the Lake Khantaiskoe Evenkis did not arise spontaneously. As the collages of the school children will no doubt portray, many waves of 'newcomers' (*priezhie*) established the social and physical structures which would eventually become a village. The first newcomer was a Sel'kup intellectual who was seconded by the Taimyr district party association to head the original 'clan soviet'.[2] Following him came the deportees of the Great Patriotic War. Then, with the campaign's intensification and restructuring, came increasingly large waves of Ukrainians, White Russians and Great Russians seeking the security and wealth of subsidised salaries, guaranteed pensions, and the opportunity to trap a few furs informally for their relatives. The most recent arrivals are the Azerbaijani technicians and traders who, escaping war in Baku, have made a most lucrative business selling vodka in various dilutions, and used clothing. It is tempting to identify the reception and settlement of refugees as the main theme in the history of this cosmopolitan village. The forebears of the Evenkis and Dolgans were in their time themselves refugees from Imperial Russian tribute-takers and Bolshevik collectivisers. However, the local Evenkis do not interpret the history of the village in this way. For them, *priezhii* is an important category. It marks people who have been sent with a particular project or mission and is often bound up with an accusation of intrusiveness, acquisitiveness and an insensitivity to local ways. In the past, many newcomers have become locals.[3] The first teachers are now the most highly respected bearers of 'culture'. The German buildings are now the most coveted homesites. However, the latest cultural import of un-regulated speculation and trade is fiercely resented by Evenki villagers loyal to the state system of distribution.

Despite the best efforts of the village teachers, mechanics and accountants to portray a narrative of progress, it is immediately obvious that the new reforms have a high social cost. Drink has always been an important part of conviviality of life on the tundra, but since the liberalisation of the vodka trade, the number of deaths due to drowning and drink-associated violence has risen to unprecedented levels. More importantly, the inconsistent supply of trade goods and petrol of socialist times has become a mere trickle. The knowledge of how to live independently in the mountains, which the elder *tundraviki* (tundra-men) complain is slipping from the hands of the younger generation, is now desperately needed as both state and market distribution networks fail.

The future of the Lake Khantaiskoe Evenkis seems even more troubled. The change in the fortunes of the Lake Khantaiskoe Evenkis is due to the breaking-up of the complex social contract between the administrative state and its citizen-clients into the single dimension of the monopolistic market relation. In reflecting on the alcoholism and lack of trade goods in the village of Khantaiskoe Ozero, one wonders whether the root of the crisis is too much culture or too little; too strong a civic relation, or one that is too weak. Certainly the economic and political crisis in Russia, whether rural or urban, is a very *modern* one and thus one worthy of 'modern' tools such as concepts of democracy, state, market and civil society.

KUL'TURA, DEMOKRATIIA AND CIVIL SOCIETY

There are many definitions of civil society in the history of social and political thought and these have been extensively analysed and compared by political theorists and sociologists (Cohen and Arato 1992; Keane 1988; Kumar 1993). For this case I will select one controversy germane to Russian and Eastern European contexts, a particular ambiguity in the classic approaches of Hegel and Marx to the term civil society itself. In terms of political prescriptions, the debate concerns whether or not it is possible to distinguish an idea of civic practice independent of the rights claimed by bourgeois economic actors to freedom in the sphere of commerce. This ambiguity is given in the German term *bürgerliche Gesellschaft*, which can be translated both as citizen society and as bourgeois society. This gives the term a dual voice which (for example, in the Hungarian debates) allows political activists to express both a call for a liberal economy *and* a call to rights of association and political participation (see Cohen and Arato 1992: viii, 97; Hann 1995: 168).

I argue that the debate on the proper balance between *citoyen* and *bourgeois* is also at the centre of Russian political debates. At first glance, the terms do not express this. Unlike in Hungarian and German, the term civil society in Russian (*grazhdanskoe obshchestvo*) does not evoke creative ambiguity; rather it has very formal and bookish connotations. Although Soviet Marxist usage clearly marked the term as a component of bourgeois societies, lexically the first term is simply the adjectival form of the word 'citizen' (*grazhdanin*). Thus the *bürgerliche Gesell-schaft* of Marx and Hegel is literally rendered in Russian as citizen society.[4] Citizen society tends to connote the everyday world of social entitlements, such as civil law (*grazhdanskii kodeks*), the provision of passenger airline transport (*grazhdanskaia aviatsiia*), or civil work (*grazhdanskaia sluzhba*): aspects of everyday life which are important, as we shall see below, but not on the high ground of public discourse.

I would locate the analogous Russian debate to the distinction between civic rights and bourgeois rights in two unexpected words: *kul'tura* and *demokratiia*. The former became popular in Russian as late as the 1880s, accumulating connotations from German Romantic philosophers, Marx-ist activists, and several generations of evolutionary ethnology (cf. Grant 1995; Volkov forthcoming). The latter, ultimately Greek-based, but also much used in the nineteenth century, seems to have become swamped relatively recently with imported meanings from English linked with the market reforms.[5]

Kul'tura is usually translated by the word culture but in practice it tends to be used more like the English word civilisation.[6] The classic examples of *kul'tura* are courtly institutions such as the ballet, symphony or opera; fields in which Russia's achievements are world renowned. However in Russia the term clearly has a wider meaning embracing the everyday civic services which are supplied as a social right. On many occasions before flying from St Petersburg to Noril'sk, or from Dudinka to Khantaiskoe Ozero, and then again from Khantaiskoe Ozero to Number One Reindeer Brigade I was repeatedly warned away from the 'low level' or even 'complete absence' of *kul'tura* awaiting me at my destination. Highest on the list of concerns of my well-wishers was not so much my boredom at not being able to discuss critical philosophy but the physical condition of the built surroundings. *Kul'tura* embraces not merely the song and epic poetry of a people but their level of technology, the weatherproofness of their houses, and their success in managing imported systems of bookkeeping and running water. There is a direct connection between *kul'tura* and being 'scientific' (Humphrey 1983: 364). By far the most effective example of *kul'tura* as civilisation can be found in the title of a massive state campaign to develop the outlying rural areas of Siberia in the late 1950s: 'Measures to develop the economy and the culture of the peoples (*narodnostei*) of the north'.[7] It would be out of place here to develop the juridical detail of this legislative history and its uneven implementation. Suffice it to say that it had far-reaching effects on the lives of the native peoples of the north. Under the component parts of this resolution and its subsidiary acts massive capital funds were devoted to the construction of houses, schools, mechanised transport, and whole settlements complete with civic amenities such as stores, public baths, electric power, and water, as well as the enforcement apparatus to ensure that small-scale mobile producers kept their families in one place. For all of its shortcomings (such as the lack of a public sauna), Khantaiskoe Ozero was lauded over other villages in Taimyr for its 'culture' in the form of a bread bakery and electrical plant which continued to function in the face of economic collapse. For Russian newcomers, the state authorities and the native intelligentsia alike, the word *kul'tura* embraces both a certain collection of mundane social services and 'high culture' without diluting a judgemental and somewhat imperial scale of values.

Demokratiia, which nominally means democracy, takes most of its contemporary meaning from the reformers who spearheaded the market reforms under the leadership of President Yeltsin. The nuances of democratic theory may be discussed under this rubric within the corridors of the Academy of Sciences, but in the rural areas of Siberia the term seems to carry a pejorative meaning of chaos, or at best a kind of avaricious connotation of individualism which corresponds quite closely to the stereotypes of western society once exposed in the pages of the centrally controlled press. For the members of Number One Reindeer Brigade of the Khantaiskii state farm, a shining example of a 'democrat' was a young man who wished to withdraw from the state farm in order to establish a farm on a territory of his own. Other examples of *demokratiia* were seen to exist in the speculative trade in vodka or stolen petrol. In accordance with the whispered understandings of *demokratiia*, most of voters in the Taimyr Autonomous District voted against Yeltsin's economic reforms and his bid to overrule parliament in the referendum of 1993.

Given the scale and suddenness of the deregulation of public life within the Russian republic, it is not surprising that the appellation of reform is often shaded with derogatory meanings. Raised within a regime where a nationalist denunciation was a crime equal to the informal sale of an Arctic fox pelt or to the theft of a state reindeer, people do not instinctively find the exercise of free speech more inherently innocent than an act of informal exchange. It is tempting to read into such examples proof that no distinction between free speech and free trade existed and thus that civil society did not exist. However the contexts in which *demokratiia* was discussed shows that this conspicuous absence was more a product of emphasis than of confusion. In contrast to the way that intellectuals usually use the term, for the hunters and herders of Taimyr – a context where tacit and unspoken communication is given special respect – people were not interested in the aspects of the reform programme which supported rights to produce words. The most visible and immediately meaningful aspect of reform, and hence *demokratiia*, was the unjust nature of free-ranging economic activity, which was seen as parasitic upon the rights of others in the community to receive their due share of the goods consonant with their positions.

That *demokratiia* tends to be linked with profit-seeking bourgeois action is confirmed also by some Russian newcomers fresh from the mainland. To these young entrepreneurs, the *demokraticheskii* programme signalled mainly rights to unencumbered economic activity. Several Russian trappers (who carried out a furious trade in illicitly sold furs) described themselves proudly as 'self-made men'. Characteristically, autonomous economic agency and rights to be the master (*khoziain*) of a property were seen to be a fundamental part of the 'Russian soul'. In fact, the only freely formed association within the village Khantaiskoe Ozero in 1992 and 1993 was the Union of Hunters, whose express purpose was the defence of private property in land.[8] It is not at all surprising that these entrepreneurs supported the reformers and criticised the communist old guard (one complained often that the Taimyr district was a 'natural preserve for communists'). As if to confirm their radical support for bourgeois rights over civil rights, the final ringing statute of the 'code of honour' of the Union of Hunters was a vow of silence about the activities of their fellow members. The interest in limiting free speech was linked to the desire for a protective veil of secrecy. By limiting gossip between themselves, members of the Union saw themselves trading freely (and illegally) without alerting the gaze of jealous eyes.

Although the technical term *grazhdanskoe obshchestvo* rather poorly reflects the Polish and Hungarian debates about civil society, these examples show that there is no shortage of opinion about the place of the *citoyen* and the place of the *bourgeois* within contemporary Russian society. Under the rubric of *kul'tura* and *demokratiia* one can find repositories of vernacular meaning which, although not analytically rigorous, capture the tension between civic rights and rights to market activity inherent within the concept of civil society. However, in this specific case, the tension is not a passive one. *Demokratiia* is generally seen to be damaging the fabric of civil entitlements. This is the aspect that underwrites the resentment to the reforms and, as will be argued below, contributes to the struggles between allied groups under a nationalist banner.

CITIZENSHIP REGIMES

Before returning to the perceived chaos of *demokratiia*, I will explore how the belligerent provision of *kul'tura* has come to be associated with a type of citizen society. The development of *kul'tura* through the agency of state managers and immigrant newcomers is more than a simple extension of social services. Rather it is symptomatic of an extension of a civic infrastructure. On a symbolic level, the injection of 'culture' in the taigas and tundras of Siberia coincided with the issuing of passports which gave individuals rights to travel, to enrol in higher educational institutions, and to conduct financial transactions with the post office and the pension system. On a deeper social structural level, the reorganisation of production and indeed the spatial and institutional rearrangement of everyday life placed Siberian native peoples firmly within the bureau-cratically organised matrix of state socialist power, with its characteristic penchant for vertical command chains and paranoiac aversion to hori-zontal trade and organisation. It is quite clear that at the early stages of this institutional onslaught, these new 'citizens' were treated as clients, on whom the state wished to leave its imprint. However, thirty years of resistance and negotiation with a rigid yet segmental bureaucratic structure also formed a tradition of civic practice which came to be experienced as varied citizenship regimes.[9]

Beyond the building of villages, hospitals and opera theatres in the wake of the reforms of the 1960s, *kul'tura* became unevenly associated across occupational 'positions' (*mesta*). Until very recently there was no category for the unemployed in the state-run economy. Thus, just as the web of employment and administration was universal, so was the ranking of positions with respect to the overriding priorities of social and civic development. At the top of the hierarchy in Khantaiskoe Ozero, not surprisingly, were the teachers, administrators and civil leaders.[10] Towards the bottom were the settlement labourers and the hunters, herders and fishermen on the land. In terms of the meritocracy, the rules of entrance to one level or another were the state-set recruitment requirements of formal education (although informal contacts also played a major role).[11]

The positions in which Evenki employees work and socialise take on a natural coherence and solidarity in Khantaiskoe Ozero as in any other place. While co-workers clustered around similar positions might share a particular subsidy coefficient in their pay cheques, access to housing, rights to travel or for education, what is distinctive of the institutional legacy of the Soviet era in this sphere is a shared life history. The young teachers of the Khantaiskoe school were all educated in the Igarka Pedagogical Institute or in the Faculty of Northern Peoples in Leningrad. Specialists within the state farm *apparat* have a common history in agricultural institutes in Noril'sk and Krasnoiarsk. Party members often attend the same party schools and congresses. Even reindeer-herders, who otherwise have little formal education, would be selected to go the reindeer-herder congresses held yearly in Dudinka. Unlike other aboriginal institutions, such as extensive kinship, what is called the *kollektiv* builds solidarity between professionals (who may happen to be kinsfolk) vertically through an array of positions which are authorised by the state.[12] As Borneman (1992) argues in his study of East and West Berlin, the overlap of the life course with work units and residential units is an important element of a sense of belonging within Soviet-type societies.[13] I see this element more than any other as explaining the sentiment that many *khantaiskie* Evenkis feel for the school, the farm and the settlement itself. All of these buildings with their multitude of associated *kollektivy* have been lived in and built by kinsfolk; an aspect that makes them monuments to the succession of generations as well to the entitlements of *kul'tura*.

Although the formal requirements of occupations play a structuring role, informal understandings also colour the positions provided by the state. During the plague of alcoholism which coincided with most of my stays in the settlement, people were especially critical of the teachers and the settlement administrator appearing drunk in public ('Our children are already so [morally] weak [that they need a good example]!'). I should think that a large measure of resentment for the state farm director and his Azerbaijani entourage of engineers was connected with the mismatch of their passion for informal trade between their positions as state servants. The status connected with being a member of the administrative *apparat* was most visible in the fashion sense of the young women set into these positions. At an assembly of the rough-hewn fishermen where the director exhorted and pleaded for greater fidelity to production quotas, the Evenki state farm economist shone out with her elegantly pinned black hair, high heels, and imported Bic ballpoint pen (which she borrowed from me before the meeting). In a reversal of status, the young wife of Vitya (the eldest son in Number One Reindeer Brigade) philosophically recounted how she had her face unceremoniously dunked in the wash-stand when one day she appeared in her village flat wearing cosmetics.

It would be misleading to brand the *kollektiv* as either an alienating or a consolidating institution. It is sufficient to note that this social phenomenon took its place beside extensive kinship as a rubric under which people resided together, collected their remuneration, and built alliances (cf. Humphrey 1983: 300, 342). *Kollektivy*, formally defined by career posts and strengthened by the institutional direction of the life course, were a locus of social life with multifaceted social rights which may have been closer to a concept of citizenship than to a concept of status (Humphrey 1983: 433). The position into which one was 'set' (*ustroien*) included not only rights to a salary, but also included rights of *kul'tura* defined by access to housing, consumable goods, transport and 'communal services' (heat, water, bread, milk, light). The differential allocation of services and goods as *kul'tura* is marked with specific administrative tools, such as the internal passport, which makes it appropriate to speak of the existence of differing citizenship regimes.

Until the reforms of the 1960s, most people in rural collective farms did not possess passports of any description. With the extension of *kul'tura* to the frontier areas came the extension of the central civic document of Soviet life, the *propusk*. This document established a person's vital data (age, sex, birth date, photograph) as well as their nationality and permission to reside in a certain area (*propusk*).[14] In addition to the internal passport, a Soviet citizen might bear supplementary documents such as a 'labour book' (*trudovaia knizhka*), a 'military ticket' (*voienii bilet*), or a 'party ticket' (*partinii bilet*) with which finer distinctions of the citizenship regime might be established. It should also be noted that there were different varieties of passports. The internal passport was most common, but there are also differing grades of international passports (civilian, service (*sluzhebnii*), diplomatic). In the case of a 'service' passport, it is not uncommon for one person to have several passports from different enterprises. Although printed on similar paper, passports differed depending upon the district and agency (*ucherezhdenie*) which issued it. Autonomous districts, like Taimyr, have their 'own' passports. To extend a passport or to make a change in any one of its component parts, one would always have to return to the local agency that issued it. Thus, just as jet-setting academics in the Euro-American market may discuss which is the best passport to hold, within the borders of the former Soviet Union it was also possible to debate which was the most advantageous passport. Similarly, there are often stories told of 'marriages of convenience' arranged in order to obtain a *propusk* or to be eligible for a flat.

The intricate distinctions between different types of internal passports (let alone external passports) still do not worry residents of Khantaiskoe Ozero. The point that is important here is that just as positions within an institution conferred something more than what is commonly associated with status, the internal passport conferred discrete entitlements specific to particular communities. Thus, instead of identifying the bearer of a member of a common 'citizen society', the passport linked a person to one of many regulated societies within a hierarchical federation. This is something less than the ordinary definition of 'citizenship'.

Of special importance to the citizens of Khantaiskoe Ozero was the authorised nationality inscribed within the passport. Whereas before the 1960s, collective identities were used in a rather fluid manner, the passport administrators when gazing across southern Taimyr unambiguously ratified a division between two 'peoples': Evenki and Dolgany.[15] To lend weight behind this distinction, the redistributive state generally treated the Dolgans as an 'avant-garde people' (*peredovoi narod*) allotting to them preferential positions within farms and administrative posts. Nationality was not the only dimension of preferential redistribution. Women were eligible for maternity rights, family allowances, and in some cases the right to purchase special products.[16] Holders of particular residence permits (*propuski*) were the sole authorised recipients of coupons which in many places supplemented money as a medium of exchange. Married couples were given preferential places in the allocation of housing. Certain categories of pensioners or war veterans possessed differential rights to free transport or to go to the 'front of the queue' (*v pervuiu ocheredi*) or even to queue 'outside of the queue' (*vne ocheredi*). These varied rights of access were numerous in Soviet society as in other societies. What made these privileges more than social rights was the fact that they were stratified by the place that one occupied in a civic hierarchy. With a glance at a passport one could tell that a pregnant Evenki woman was not only entitled to free health care and paid maternity leave but would be automatically treated as a priority patient in the interests of the reproduction of her people.[17] A Russian hunter would be allowed to buy back his furs at cost from the state farm while the Evenki hunter would be allowed to legally use five furs for his 'national costume'. The same passport plus an education certificate (*gramota*) would allow a fresh arrival from the mainland a spacious new state farm flat while an indigenous Evenki widower would have to bed down with relatives in a cramped room.

When the passport was extended to the hunters, herders and fishermen of Taimyr, its validity remained anchored within the administrative structures peculiar to Taimyr. While these tools of administration were bluntly wielded at a very high level, symbolically they illustrate that both employment and citizenship were not social rights of a single dimension equally pressed on to each individual but instead facilitated the culturally appropriate triangulation of a person within a position, a *kollektiv*, and a citizenship regime. When asking the question 'Who are you by national- ity?' (*vy kto po natsional'nosti*) you can satisfy your ethnographic curiosity as well as assess the potential bundle of rights available to the man or woman standing before you.

The idea of a citizenship regime is useful in understanding the unsettled reaction of people to the crumbling of social institutions within the former Soviet Union generally and in the extensive settlement of Khantaiskoe Ozero in particular. It is curious that the stresses introduced into what Zaslavsky (1982, 1993) calls the Soviet social contract were not associated with collective action in defence of the civic infrastructure but instead the vociferous rhetoric of nationalism. The village Khan- taiskoe Ozero, like many civic spaces in the former Soviet Union, is riddled with nationalist accusations which occasionally erupt into drunk- en brawls of Evenkis versus Dolgans. Extrapolating from these local yet tragic events, it seems that nationalist outbursts do imply a very deep defence of what are usually thought of as 'social rights' but which may be better understood as rights within a citizenship regime. The central role of *kul'tura* in the legacy of social provisioning of the Siberian frontier after 1957 established a close link between nationality and lucrative positions within state institutions. Occupational positions came to be lucrative in more than a mere monetary sense, embracing moments from the quality of housing to the type of social community in which one lived. The step-by-step collapse of common access to land and communal services seems to have disturbed not only people's material well-being, but also their sense of collective entitlement. The nationalist sentiment evident in the use of terms such as *priezhii* ('newcomer'), *natsional* (native), *tongus* (Evenki) and *teho* (Dolgan) does not seem to evoke so much a racial attribute as the sentiment 'our own people deserve better'. This sentiment is paradoxical if one reflects (as many villagers do) that 'before we all lived in the same farm peacefully and now we are at war (*voiiuet*)'. Instead, it is more useful to reflect upon the plurality of *kollektivy* generated within one enterprise and one settlement by a centralised administrative system concerned with developing *kul'tura*. When the legacy of the Soviet citizen society is understood, the prospect of *demokratiia* seems much less emancipatory and desirable. Reforms which stress the bourgeois right to trade regardless of the tacit social contract have the effect of reducing a complex and nested system of citizenship regimes into a single dimension experienced, as one Evenki hunter said, as the 'right to argue'.[18] While the reforms may have expanded the right of producers to speak their mind within highly regulated social and political institutions, they have impoverished their position materially, socially, and also in terms of the capacity to participate in a wider division of labour. Although the internal passports of the Russian Federation still record nationality, residential permits and marital status, the rights accruing to these markers of citizenship have dissipated within the space of a few short years. There is no question that the varied citizenship regimes of the past were often manipulated to suit individual interests or were unequitable in their guarantees. However, the resentment behind the reforms in Khantaiskoe Ozero, like other parts of the former Soviet Union, reflects a claim that the hierarchical civic infrastructure of the recent past was less oppressive than the narrow guarantees of 'democratic citizenship' being enforced today.

CONCLUSION

The rising political tide of *demokratiia* in the Russian mainland, like the tide of *kul'tura* before it, is often associated with the début of a civil

society in civic islands like Khantaiskoe Ozero. This short exposition of
the rights once exercised by Evenkis has demonstrated that the debate on
what constitutes a civil society is not a new one even in Arctic Siberia.
It has been shown that among different citizenship regimes within the
village of Khantaiskoe Ozero there was a clear understanding of what it
meant to be a citizen in that place and in that state farm. Ideas of
citizenship are seen to be opposed to the entrepreneurial practice of the
bourgeois. These two elements in the local debate are part of the general
debate on civil society – and are indeed implied by the the term itself.
What is distinctive in the Khantaiskii debate is that the single-dimen-
sional rights to 'argue' and to own are perceived as an intrusive erosion
of professional solidarity, corporate property and social guarantees. On
the part of Evenkis, this has provoked a desperate and tragic strategy of
nationalist resistance rather than an openness to alternative forms of
democractic organisation.

The theoretical work that suggests how the two counterpoised meanings within the term civil society might be productively reconciled is that
of Cohen and Arato (1992). These two scholars have long advocated a
'three-part model' of social structure whereby the circulation of commodities and the administrative dictates of the state are strictly distinguished from a civil society which fosters a vibrant lifeworld of
symbols and solidarities. The relationship between these three parts is
critically measured by means of Habermas's concept of 'colonisation of
the lifeworld'. Cohen and Arato extend this concept to identify the
moment when either the state or the market become so prominent as to
turn their sibling institution into a passive satellite to the detriment of the
productive functioning of both institutions. The project of Cohen and
Arato is to advocate the institutionalisation of rights to association and
communication to ensure that autonomously organised social movements
can directly intervene to restrain either the state or the market from
dominating social life. Thus, their definition of civil society is 'a sphere
of social interaction between economy and state, composed above all of
the intimate sphere (especially the family), the sphere of associations
(especially voluntary associations), social movements, and forms of
public communication . . . institutionalized and generalized through
laws' (1992: ix). Conceptually, their model is creative. It not only avoids
the confusion of civil society being here the market and there a civic
right, but it also can be used to analyse the distinctive type of power
perfected in Soviet-type societies with the very same categories used
to examine the more familiar market relation in western societies.
Unlike many analyses where Soviet-type systems are branded simply as

inefficient or non-modern, their model allows one to identify exactly when the administrative state 'colonised' local markets or cultural institutions. Similarly, as in the current political context in Khantaiskoe Ozero, one can now speak of popular resistance to the colonisation by the market of state institutions and the citizenship regimes which have hitherto been nested within them.

The scholar who wishes to apply Cohen and Arato is well advised to do so sparingly. The book is excessively complex. With the dexterity of jugglers, Cohen and Arato toss between themselves three spheres, two realms, three societies, two subsystems and then an indeterminate number of 'mediations' which allow for the institutions of one or the other of the three societies to be coordinated from one of the spheres (most importantly, from the lifeworld). More telling, especially for this analysis of the legacy of multiple citizenship regimes in the former Soviet Union, is the firm and blind conviction of the necessity of 'differentiation' (differentiation of institutions, differentiation of spheres, differentiation of types of rights) *before* a proper social balance can be struck. Cohen and Arato prescribe the following for 'the East':

> We admit the necessity of first building differentiated subsystems: an expert administration and a self-regulating market economy. In this sense, there is no substitute for establishing an economic system of hard budgetary constraints based on free prices, demonopolization, and abolishing the paternalistic system of subsidies and bargaining. . . . Still, we cannot accept Kornai's [1990] claim that even those who want to establish mixed capitalist economies today must for an extended period promote yesterday's unregulated version. . . . Instead of copying solutions from the West's past or present, the new democracies would do well to understand the reasons why both liberal and welfare-state models are experiencing new problems today. This does not mean that one should look for a mythical third way between capitalism and socialism, West in East, in the manner of either market socialism or the various neopopulisms. If there are any solutions here, they lie in the experience of the West, pointing not to the West's past or present but to its future.
>
> (1992: 489–91)

For tidy scholarship, one can agree that one should be precise about the vision of civil society one is advocating – thus the issues of 'differentiation' certainly have their place when reading civil society in Hegel, Gramsci, Parsons, Foucault and Habermas. However, it is quite another matter selectively to prescribe political parties, press freedom and liberal markets as institutions which are 'differentiated', 'modern', 'non-ascriptive' or 'universal'. In the quote above, the obvious resemblance of such institutions to a generic Euro-American state is baldly stated. Is it not conceivable that the lines of 'differentiation' might be drawn differently in a place with different cultural and jural traditions?

The point emerges clearly when the model is applied to cases like the Siberian example described above. The state farm Khantaiskii in the Soviet period was clearly a highly differentiated institution when compared to the norms and world-view of the flexible social order which preceded it. It was also a complex and hierarchical institution whose goal was the production of primary products (or, at least, numbers representing these products). Formally, according to this model, it should be classed as an institution of economic society. Yet at the same time, the *kollektiv* to which one belonged within the farm made a great difference to a person's civic guarantees (pensions, wages, fringe benefits), participation in political matters (setting quotas, norms of production), and even to the more narrowly defined institutions of modern lifeworld maintenance (access to television, cultural clubs, films, festivals). Thus what may be formally seen as an economic institution upon concrete analysis was shot through with a multiple number of 'mediations' which allowed it to collect significant inputs and in fact organise large portions of 'civil and political societies'. Admittedly the employees of the state farm Khantaiskii were as often clients of the state as they were autonomously acting citizens. However, these 'clients' insist that they never felt as constrained, marginalised and impoverished in the days of their 'passive citizenship' as during the début of reforms designed to unambiguously differentiate the farm's formal economic function from its other civic and political roles. It is because of the harsh logic of differentiation that *demokratiia* is seen as the antithesis of civic entitlement and of civilisation itself.

Cohen and Arato are not ignorant of the fact that societies are meant to be lived in, rather than engineered by social theorists. Aside from their classic examples of modern institutions, they puzzle over how best to interpret 'plural forms of property' (1992: 441, 624n., 625n., 712n., 714n.), 'corporatist institutions' (1992: 5–8, 432, 461, 703n., 740n.) and types of social welfare rights such as dual-rights and client rights (1992: 441, 450, 461–2, 612n., 645n., 696n., 711n.). These institutions are usually categorised under the rubric of 'mediations' between spheres.[19] As if to emphasise their secondary status, the mediating institutions tend to be discussed in the 130 pages of small-print endnotes at the back of the book. While Cohen and Arato's analytic theory broaches the question of how to go beyond the dualism implicit in the debate on civil society, when it comes to imagining actual social institutions which transcend this dualism in everyday life it would be much more useful to turn the model inside out. 'Mediating institutions' should be boldly at the forefront of the analysis. It is to this end that anthropological writing can play an important role in enriching the institutional vocabulary of theorists, and in correcting the Euro-American biases in analytic models.[20] This sentiment leaves open the main question which should trouble reindeer herders, World Bank economists, and social theorists: upon what institutional foundation can a post-Soviet society be constructed?

In marked contrast to the differentiated models of western political parties and shareholder societies, there are numerous examples of institutions which truly mediate civil, political and economic interests. This chapter has examined the example of the citizenship regime in a complex region at the frontiers of Soviet industrialisation. Within the history of the differentiated 'west' there are also models which accomplish similar goals. Siberian native activists are particularly interested in the example of land reservations for the First Nations of North America. This example has been elegantly called an example of 'treaty federalism' in the United States (Barsh and Henderson 1980). In Canada, a Northern European model of 'consociational democracy' has been adapted to describe the societal models of the Dene in the Northwest Territories (Asch 1984). Australian aborigines have been equally articulate in advocating complex models of property, political representation and social infrastructure in order to consolidate their societies (Wilmsen 1988). Although Siberia has now become an even more distant frontier from the mainland of corporate business culture, this does not imply that its citizens have no experience of complex, mediated institutions. Rather, their experience and history has much to teach social theorists, anthropologists and development economists alike when it comes to drafting concepts which bridge the gulf between bourgeois and civic understandings of society.

NOTES

1 Many of my ideas on civil society were formed during fieldwork in 1989 in several Evenki and Buriat villages in the mountains to the east of Lake Baikal. The results of this work are published in Anderson (1992, 1993). Between 1992 and January 1994 fieldwork was conducted in a mixed Evenki and Dolgan hunting, herding and fishing state farm near the mouth of the Yenisei

River on the southern border of the Taimyr (Dolgano-Nenets) Autonomous District. The illustrations in this chapter are from the latter research.

2 The early stages of Soviet Siberian development policy assumed that the primal communalist traditions of indigenous people could be harnessed in the design of a socialist society. The first socialist organisations were 'clan soviets' (later renamed 'nomadic soviets'). These organisations persisted in Taimyr until 1953 when the Khantaiskii Nomadic Soviet was offically made a village soviet (*sel'sovet*). All village soviets in Taimyr since 1993 have been renamed 'village administrations'.

3 Derek Smith (1975) discusses a similar phenomenon in the raucous meeting place of nationalities of Canada's Mackenzie delta.

4 Following Cohen and Arato (1992: viii, 84, 97), it seems that the translation of 'citizen society' is closer to the Aristotelian original than is the usage of Hegel and Marx. Some recent work on social theory from Russia attempts to discover citizen society within Russian history (see the bibliography in Reznik 1994). Most such attempts locate citizen society in a pre-Soviet past (Chernykh 1994; Serbinkenko 1994) although Romanenko (1994) re-discovers citizen society persisting in 'quality but not in quantity' within artists' circles, *samizdat* and wall-newspapers. Other works which document the various *neformaly* ('non-formal') movements and discussion clubs since 1965 are Igrunov 1989 and Berezovskii and Krotov 1991. Reznik (1994: 21) takes the firm stand that citizen society is to be equated with market relationships. This is perhaps a sign that scholars using the formal Russian term are already duplicating the debates of their western counterparts.

5 Serbinenko (1994) and Kamenskaia (1994) confirm my impression that the meaning of the word *demokratiia* has changed through its popularisation in the Russian press. Both of their articles are enthusiastic attempts to uncover (or recover) the term's history in both pre-revolutionary Russia and in ancient Greece.

6 Vadim Volkov (forthcoming) notes in its original usage during the 1880s *kul'tura* was opposed to *tsivilizatsiia*. The former stood for a holistic growth of enlightenment and spirituality while the latter referred to an 'age of secondary simplification and decline of a national culture'. Raymond Williams (1983: 57–60, 87–93) notes a similar engaging ambiguity in the English usages of these two words. For an ethnography of the building of *kul'tura* in another Siberian village see Grant 1995.

7 This was resolution number 300 of the Central Committee of the Communist Party of the Soviet Union (16 March 1957). I occasionally find it useful to translate the word *narodnost'* as 'proto-people'. As the following section will explain, civic practice was thought to vary with the development of communities from clans, to proto-peoples, to peoples, and finally to nations (Stalin 1936). This parallel hierarchy of identity, which Soviet ethnography greatly refined, also puts symbolic meaning behind distinctions between citizens.

8 A much more influential association was formed in the district capital of Dudinka: The Association of Northern Peoples of Taimyr. While it is significant that native peoples had united under the rubric of their 'aborigin-ality', the characteristic activities of this association were to block attempts by Russians to take parcels of land out of state farms for private use. This

also confirms the link between such political associations and the strategies of private economic activity.

9 The history of stratified types of citizenship within Russia dates back to well before the Soviet period. In the nineteenth century, Russian society was broken into 'estates' (*soslovye*) each of which had differential obligations to the crown (Freeze 1986). Likewise, Siberian native people were divided into 'wandering', 'nomadic' and 'settled' categories each with their own special rates of tribute, obligations to the Tsar and bodies of common law (Bakrushin 1955; Raeff 1956). Just as Gregory Freeze argues that the estate paradigm can be read into the fabric of Soviet society, so can the hierarchy of peoples established in 1822 be seen in the differential positions of various aboriginal nationalities.

10 Although positions can be distinguished by their salary scale, a far more important indicator of status is the capacity to access goods and services (Humphrey 1983). Within the state farm Khantaiskii, ranking individuals by the size of their salary does not show any significant degree of stratification. However, when people are ranked by their access to transport, machinery, or to redistributive posts the list stratifies strongly along national lines.

By civic leaders I am referring both to party members (who most often occupy positions in the top of the state farm *apparat*) and to the leaders of the settlement administration.

11 A central characteristic of the *state* farm (as opposed to the *collective* farm) is a closer integration with the structures and recruitment regulations of the state bureaucracy (Humphrey 1983: 13–14, 137). In Taimyr there is a requirement that all members of the *apparat* have formal education and that the fishermen and hunters perform multiple roles as mechanics and account-keepers as well as producers. This centrally dictated formal requirement, which is an essential one if the farm is to continue receiving its subsidies, is directly responsible for the flood of newcomers into influential and lucrative positions and the 'crowding out' (*vytesnit'*) of native peoples from their local farm.

12 The word *kollektiv* translates awkwardly because of the relative poverty of English for collective terms for alliance. *Kollektiv* tends to be more localized than 'colleague', 'profession', or 'trade'; and at the same time more collegial than 'staff'. Most importantly, its similarity to the English word 'collective' tends to imply to the reader that it means 'members' of some multi-tiered institution like a 'collective farm' (the correct term for this idea is *kadry*). Instead, one institution, like the state farm 'Khantaiskii' can have many different 'communities of producers' (*trudovie kollektivy*).

13 The central place of occupational positions and *kollektivy* in the state-led economy was brought home to me by a group of sociologists from Novosibirsk who were conducting a questionnaire on attitudes toward employment amongst native peoples in the Canadian Arctic. Their forms had only one space for 'occupation' while many of their Canadian native informants had taken as many as five seasonal jobs within a single year. The leader of their expedition in bewilderment asked me how it was possible for one person to have multiple employment positions.

14 In 1992 the Norwegian anthropologist Ivar Bjørklund (University of Tromsø) accompanied an expedition of state officials on an official visit to an

unregistered group of Nenetses recently 'discovered' to be living an independent life on the northern reaches of the Yamal peninsula in western Siberia. Aside from bringing flour, metal goods and medicines, they also attempted to give these independent reindeer herders internal passports. Wary of the motives of the Russian state, these 'uncultured' herders took the trade goods but refused the passports.

15 The matter of national identity is a complicated affair in Taimyr. Informants and archival sources indicate that before the authorisation of nationalities there was a multitude of identities corresponding to territorial groups, clans and occupational gradations. A small sample of the almost untranslatable terms that one might find in this region are: *hakalar, betular, tongustar, khempol, yakol, tehol.* When discussing the genealogy of one senior woman – a woman who could recall only half as many generations as forbears with differing nationalities – exclaimed that being Evenki or Dolgan was 'just like tuning a radio' (from one channel to the other).

16 The bundle of rights allotted to women was one of the first spheres of the citizenship regime to be deflated by the reformers. Barbara Einhorn (1993) gives solid analysis of how 'democratic citizenship' in Eastern Europe has not only failed to make women 'active citizens' but has subordinated women into a citizenship status of a second order. Her link of 'active citizenship' to the demands for civil society in Eastern Europe is a valuable one. I understand active citizenship for women to be a good parallel example of the Evenki movement to restore the rights of their citizenship regime.

17 Evenki mothers had the bitter-sweet honour of the right to emergency health care for pregnancy due to the low rate of natural increase of this Soviet nationality. A pregnant mother could be expected to be evacuated by helicopter at the very least, or to be kept under a vigil approaching house arrest from the sixth month of pregnancy onwards. The fact that the demographic structure of Siberian peoples could be graphed as a stable distribution was due to the combination of the near elimination of the mortality rate of newborns combined with tragically high death rates for infants and adults alike (Pika and Prokhorova 1994).

    Among the other privileges granted to Evenki mothers (but not necessarily mothers of other nationalities) was the right to receive free milk, children's clothing, and mother's allowances multiplied by a special coefficient. Arguably Evenki women benefited from a more 'active' form of citizenship than Russian women due to their positions in villages closer to the sources of redistribution. Although legally they are not the heads of households, substantively many women act in this role.

18 There is some evidence that access to the market is seen by some reformers as a privilege consonant with the *kul'tura* of the entrepeneur. A recent working paper that I drafted for a consortium that wishes to privatise the sea lanes of the Northern Sea Route was criticised by a Russian reviewer for recommending the establishment of special retail and distribution organisations which would transport goods to native people as a matter of an aboriginal right. Such substantive principles were seen to be 'unreal' in the 'market relationship system'. As a concession, the reviewer suggested that native producers use the privatised sea lane to export their furs and reindeer.

19 Cohen and Arato often use mediation in a Hegelian sense (1992: xiv, 112–13,

477–80, 625n., 697n., 641n.). However when the discussion turns to their own interpretation of their 'three-part model', there seem to be gaps in the architecture. A common usage of 'mediation' is in conjunction with a concrete institution (like property, 1992: 624n.) which injects solidarity into the economy or helps satisfy the needs of people reproducing civil society (cf. 697n.). Here, civil society seems to dissipate into political and economic society and the state. In other contexts the institutions of political and economic society 'act as receptors' for civil society (1992: x, 416–18). In this context, civil society is present but the state is absent.
20 To be fair, Cohen and Arato admit that the mechanisms of Soviet-type societies are still poorly understood and that the 'interface of civil society and market economy' has not been adequately analysed in Latin America or Eastern Europe (1992: 70, 77). Despite this lack of understanding, the former Soviet Union is used as an example of the lack of a civil society (1992: 62–7, 442, 446).
      It is remarkable that a model that stresses the role of social movements devotes remarkably little space to the nationalist movements that are rocking the ex-socialist world. In one endnote (pp. 621–2), Cohen and Arato see these movements as a 'pathology' reflecting 'insufficient modernization' and 'growing insecurity'. The draw of the movements is dismissed as an 'illusory community'. In this study I have put forward the opposite argument, that nationalist movements can arise as a defensive strategy against the loss of a citizenship regime. It would follow that they could be alleviated by taking seriously the actually existing fabric of entitlements within a region.

REFERENCES

Anderson, D. G. (1992) 'Property rights and civil society in Siberia: an examination of the social movements of the Zabaikal'skie Evenki', *Praxis International* 12(1): 83–105.
—— (1993) 'Civil society in Siberia: the institutional legacy of the Soviet State', in H. G. De Soto and D. G. Anderson (eds), *The Curtain Rises: Rethinking Culture, Ideology, and the State in Eastern Europe*, New Jersey: Humanities Press, pp. 76–98.
Asch, M. (1984) *Home and Native Land: Aboriginal Rights and the Canadian Constitution*, New York: Methuen.
Bakhrushin, S. B. (1955) 'Yasak v Sibiri', in *S.B. Bakhrushin Nauchnye Trudy*, vol. 3, Part 2, Moscow: Izd-vo Akademii Nauk, pp. 49–85.
Barsh, R. L. and Henderson, J. Y. (1980) *The Road: Indian Tribes and Political Liberty*, London: University of California Press.
Bassin, M. (1993). 'Turner, Solovev and the frontier hypothesis: the nationalist significance of open spaces', *Journal of Modern History* 65(3): 473–511.
Berezovskii, V. and Krotov, N. (1991) *Rossiia: Partii, Assotsiatsii, Soiuzy, Kluby*, Moscow: RAU-Press.
Borneman, J. (1992) *Belonging in the Two Berlins: Kin, State, Nation*, Cambridge: Cambridge University Press.
Chernykh, A. I. (1994) 'Dolgii put' k grazhdanskuiu obshchestvu', *Sotsiologicheskie issledovaniia* 8–9: 173–81.

Cohen, J. and Arato, A. (1992) *Civil Society and Political Theory*, Cambridge, Mass.: MIT Press.

Einhorn, B. (1993) *Cinderella Goes to Market: Citizenship, Gender, and Women's Movements in East Central Europe*, London: Verso.

Freeze, G. L. (1986) 'The *Soslovie* (Estate) paradigm and Russian social history', *American Historical Review* 91: 11–36.

Grant, B. (1995) *In the Soviet House of Culture: A Century of Perestroikas*, Princeton: Princeton University Press.

Hann, C. M. (1995) 'Philosopher's models on the Carpathian lowlands', in J. Hall (ed.), *Civil Society: Theory, History, Comparison*, Cambridge: Polity, pp. 158–82.

Humphrey, C. (1983) *Karl Marx Collective: Economy, Society and Religion in a Siberian Collective Farm*, Cambridge: Cambridge University Press.

Igrunov, V. (1989) 'O neformal'nykh politicheskikh klubakh Moskvy', *Problemy vostochnoi Evropy* 27–8: 60–82.

Kamenskaia, G. B. (1994) 'Genezis ideia demokratii', *Sotsiologicheskie issledovaniia* 4: 29–40.

Keane, J. (1988) *Democracy and Civil Society*, New York: Verso.

Kornai, J. (1990) *The Road to a Free Economy: Shifting from a Socialist System: The Example of Hungary*, New York: Norton.

Kumar, K. (1993) 'Civil society: an inquiry into the usefulness of an historical term', *British Journal of Sociology* 44(3): 375–95.

Pika, A. I. and Prokhorova, B. B. (1994) *Neotraditsionalism na rossiiskom Severe*, Moscow: Institut narono khoziaistvenogo prognozirovaniia.

Raeff, M. (1956) *Siberia and the Reforms of 1822*, Seattle: University of Washington Press.

Reznik, Yu M. (1994) 'Formirovaii institutov grazhdanskogo obshchestvo', *Sotsiologicheskie issledovaniia* 10: 21–30.

Romanenko, L. M. (1994) 'Grazhdanskoe obshchestvo sushchestvet v Rossii, no . . .' *Sotsiologicheskie issledovaniia* 4: 12–16.

Serbinenko, V. V. (1994) 'O perspektivakh demokratii v Rossii', *Sotsiologicheskie issledovaniia* 4: 17–29.

Smith, D. (1975) *Natives and Outsiders: Pluralism in the Mackenzie River Delta, Northwest Territories*, Mackenzie Delta Research Project, 12, Ottawa: Department of Indian Affairs and Northern Development.

Stalin, J. (1936) [1913] 'Marxism and the national question' in J. Stalin, *Marxism and the National and Colonial Question*, London: Lawrence and Wishart, pp. 3–61.

Volkov, V. (forthcoming) 'The Stalinist concept of culturedness', in D. Shepherd and C. Kelly (eds), *Russian Cultural Studies*, Oxford: Oxford University Press.

Williams, R. (1983) *Keywords: A Vocabulary of Culture and Society*, London: Fontana.

Wilmsen, E. (ed.) (1988) *We are Here: Politics of Aboriginal Land Tenure*, Berkeley and Los Angeles: University of California Press.

Zaslavsky, V. (1982) 'The régime and the working class', in V. Zaslavsky (ed.), *The Neo-Stalinist State*, White Plains, NY: M.E. Sharpe Inc., pp. 45–65.

—— (1993) 'Success and collapse: traditional Soviet national policy', in I. Bremmer and R. Taras (eds), *Nations and Politics in the Soviet Successor States*, Cambridge: Cambridge University Press, pp. 29–42.

Chapter 6

The social life of projects
Importing civil society to Albania

Steven Sampson

The transition towards a market economy and a democratic polity in Eastern Europe and the former Soviet Union is not just something which is happening east of the Elbe. Transition is also a strategy being implemented by international development agencies, western financial institutions, foreign aid programmes and humanitarian or other non-governmental organisations (NGOs). The east–west divide formerly based on 'cold war' has now been replaced by the west's concerted effort to 'modernise' the east and to 'integrate' the former communist states into European economic, political and security frameworks. Spear-heading this effort is a gamut of western aid programmes aimed at helping the Central and East European States achieve 'privatisation', 'agricultural reform', 'higher-education restructuring', 'democratic institutions', 'legal reform', and 'a developed civil society'. These objectives may be articulated in a variety of ways: as 'strategies', 'indicative programmes', or 'plans'. At the basic level, however, they exist as concrete activities called 'projects'. The transition in Eastern Europe is a world of projects.

This chapter focuses on how one such project, to develop civil society, is being exported into Albania. It describes how a Danish-funded civil society foundation attempts to assist Albanian NGOs. In short, it is the story of how the term civil society takes on a social life. I am a member of this world. As an anthropologist who has done field research in Eastern Europe since the mid-1970s, mostly in Romania, I was soon drawn into the transition industry as a consultant to various Danish aid agencies and companies. As the only Romanian specialist in Denmark, I participated in several Danish projects in Romania in the areas of environment, social impact assessment and civil society/NGO issues. In 1994 I was asked to carry out an assessment of civil society and NGOs in Albania, and for the last year I have functioned as coordinator for a Danish 'civil society' project in Albania. The project itself is uncomplicated: on the basis of the 1994 assessment and feasibility study, the Danish government has established a foundation to help Albanian NGOs. I have participated in helping to set up the foundation in Albania, hire staff, recruit board members and provide technical assistance during the fund's first two years of operation. The foundation's main activity is to fund Albanian NGO activities, organise training and build up an NGO information centre for Albanian NGOs and foreign donors. I visit Albania about once every five to six weeks.

The purpose of this front-line report is twofold. First, I will show that civil society as a concept is good to think with. It functions as a window towards understanding the transition, and especially its global character. Second, I will emphasise that the transition is not simply the flow of resources, but also the export of models, that is, of representations. We can use 'civil society' development in Albania to show what happens when representations – accompanied by millions of dollars and the apparatus of projectisation – take on a social life in specific contexts. What happens when discourses like 'civil society' become projects? In the world of projects, concepts have to be defined institutionally, and one definition becomes dominant. The transition in Eastern Europe is not a fundamental, irrevocable social change along western lines, nor is it the controlled transfer of western experience to the east. Rather, the transition is a social space in which various resources – material, organisational, human, symbolic – are manipulated and reconstituted by a variety of actors in an organisational setting of global character. The transfer of civil society from Denmark to Albania will serve to show how this reconstitution takes place.

I begin by offering a more detailed view of the transition as project. I will describe the various resources involved in the transition, the main actors in the civil society field and how they attempt to appropriate these resources. The second half of the chapter focuses on how civil society is brought into Albania in its Danish-project variant and how Albanians deal with the resources, including the discursive forms. Finally, I draw some conclusions about the nature of concepts when they become projects, and ultimately, about an anthropology of the transition.

RESOURCES AND MAGIC IN THE WORLD OF PROJECTS

'The transition' is a flow of resources between east and west. It involves, for example, institutions of the European Union member states setting up offices in East European capitals, loans from the World Bank and grants from the Soros Foundation which supports education, particularly the social sciences. The transition produces conferences on small-business enterprise, human-rights education and NGO capacity building. It attempts to impart skills such as project management and fund raising. And it produces an army of specialists: the consultants, organisations, support staff and evaluators who ensure that the concepts of the transition are communicated precisely and projects implemented correctly. The traffic in specialists and the pervasiveness of training ensure that the world of projects has its own discourse. A contract is called 'terms of reference'. Having a foreign consultant is 'technical assistance'. The staff of an office become a 'project-management unit'. Teaching people to teach others is 'training of trainers'. Getting a free computer is called 'infrastructural development'. Lasting beyond a grant period is 'sustainability'. The goals of an organisation are a 'mission statement', and so on. The ubiquity of English and of what we might call 'project-speak' enable communication to take place among the transnational actors on the transition scene. For example, a Swedish diplomat may refuse to speak his native language with a Danish colleague, insisting that conversations about development can only take place in English. Any Albanian who wants to make a career in this world must acquire competence in English and in 'project-speak'.

It is tempting to regard the transition as simply the transfer of funds, technology, organisations and discursive forms from west to east. It would be easy to see East Europeans as passive recipients of western resources and discourse. Part of the western understanding of the transition is to emphasise this transfer: whenever a new highway opens, a new telephone or satellite cable is hooked up, a new border crossing is modernised or a new McDonalds opens, it is an occasion to celebrate this more rapid flow of people, the more efficient traffic in information, or the entry of western life-style and consumption habits into virgin territory.

This flow is not entirely positive, however, and nor is it unidirectional, as European concerns about uncontrolled migration, cross-border crime, agricultural dumping, or Russian Mafia all attest. While West Europeans travel east as consultants, East Europeans come west for study tours and training. Western specialists arrive as trainers and coordinators, while East Europeans participate as 'target groups', as programme officers, project managers, 'staff', as interpreters, or as participants in training-of-trainers courses. Some East Europeans now even travel to other East European countries as consultants paid by western organisations. East Europeans are pursuing western resources: jobs, trips, education; but the flow of resources, especially symbolic resources, is two-way. It involves manipulating and reworking resources in one's own context.

Behind the apparent rationality of projects and the discourse of 'institutional development' and 'capacity building', there also lies a considerable amount of magic or mystical thinking. Concepts such as 'human rights' or 'civil society' originate in a superlocal space (European Union (EU) in Brussels, European Parliament in Strasbourg, World Bank in Washington, the UNDP in New York, ILO in Geneva, etc.). These concepts then become programmes and projects, and the whole apparatus of fund-raising, the often unfathomable application forms, and even the currency used all have their own mystique. (Consider the fact that all funds for projects in Eastern Europe are expressed in United States dollars, European Currency Units (ECUS) or millions of ECU (MECUS), and almost never in any ordinary West or east European currency.)

The material and institutional flows which take place in the transition industry revolve around key concepts, such as privatisation, democracy, institutional development, and transition itself. The concept of civil society operates in its own discursive space. The symbolic struggle to utilise 'civil society' can be mapped out according to the *interests* of the various actors, the *contexts* in which they operate and the *resources* they have at their disposal. The interests and contexts certainly vary between east and west. There are quite large differences between what a western aid organisation, an EU diplomat, a private company, and an east European ministry can each bring to the transition. The interests and resources of individual east Europeans pursuing combinations of social goals and private strategies complicate the picture still further.

Resources are often unequal and incommensurable. After all, it is the east which requests aid and the west which sets conditions on awarding it, such that much of it eventually ends up back in western hands. Consider the two giant hotels constructed recently in Tirana, costing an individual well over $100 per night, whose construction, financed by World Bank tourist-development credits, has lined the pockets of an Italian and Austrian firm. Many skills are also unequally distributed, and so too is access to information and symbolic resources: information about money, and information about dominant concepts. It is here that the magic of the transition appears. The ability to master the symbolic resources of the transition, to gain access to knowledge and to manipulate it, determine whether an enterprising young individual in Eastern Europe becomes a party politician, an NGO leader, an employee of a western agency or firm, a local entrepreneur, or a mafioso. Each of these trajectories is part of the transition relation between east and west, each with its own separate flow.

TRANSITION AS TRANSFER OF MODELS

In the usual western view, the transition is a transition *to* something, implying that what exists in Eastern Europe must be converted or transformed into what we have in the west. Western agencies make assessments of the situation, formulate proposals, apply for money from their own governments or international organs (sometimes with an east European partner) and execute projects. The parallel with development work in the third world is obvious here and, as in the south, it is often assumed that it is the foreign experience or reality which is being transferred, rather than a model. Here is perhaps the most exotic aspect of what Danes call 'system-export': the assumption that western models reflect western realities, that things in the west somehow work according to the way they are depicted on project documents, tables, charts, plans and management diagrams.

Of course, most actors in the transition industry are well aware of the differences between ideal and reality. Like social scientists, they understand that what makes things 'work' are both the formal structures and the informal organisation and private incentives. However, this aspect is generally overlooked in the schemes for 'system export' to Eastern Europe. Failures are then explained in terms of 'legacies' from the past, 'socialist mentality' or 'resistance' by those being affected. In fact, many 'system-export' schemes fail because systems or units are exported without their western context. The advanced office technology which comes to some Albanian project offices is based on technical English manuals, nearby service and parts, reliable electric power and high quality telephone/fax lines, all a far cry from the daily life of any Albanian project office. The well-functioning NGOs and interest organisations of Danish civil society exist in an environment of effective public administration, an open press, and a political system which knows how to react to public pressure. In addition, Danish NGOs are in close contact with their funding sources; many are subsidised by state funds. Danish NGOs are thus well embedded in society, and they do what they do well. In Eastern Europe, where states are weak and finance nearly non-existent, where social problems are acute and confidence in social organisations is low, where kin, network and ethnic groups resolve problems which associations resolve in the west, the entire context of civil society differs. In this situation, the export of Scandinavian interest organisations is bound to be problematic. It is a case of what the Romanians call 'form without foundation'.

One might expect knowledgeable East Europeans, those working with the western specialists and agencies, to provide the necessary corrective 'input' to the imposition of western models. However, the fragmentary nature of system-export, and fragmentary knowledge about western institutions by most East Europeans make this difficult. Western systems have either been idolised or demonised. Expectations were very high in 1990, and disillusionment with what appear to be broken promises is rife. Many East Europeans have a material incentive not to criticise those who pay salaries much higher than local job markets, but even if they did not, they lack any intimate understanding of the western institutions which generate models for these ideal systems. When East Europeans visit western institutions they see a model system and they absorb the symbolic paraphernalia of western institutions: the well-equipped offices, ergonomic working conditions, relaxed style and high salaries of their western counterparts. The Danish Democracy Foundation, derisively criticised as a travel bureau for élite East Europeans, provides just such services.[1]

My point is that the transfer of western models to Eastern Europe is not simply an imposition by the west. It is facilitated by structures and interests within Eastern Europe, which accept the forms and attempt to shape them to their own interests. The transition has many agents both foreign and local, and we need to unravel their mutual complicity.

FOREIGN AND LOCAL ACTORS

The foreign agents of the transition formulate, finance and implement projects. The UNDP, IMF, the European Union, the World Bank, and the European Bank for Reconstruction and Development are the most important international organs on the East European scene. The most important is undoubtedly the EU PHARE/TACIS programme, located in Brussels, which provides billions of dollars for economic restructuring, infrastructure, humanitarian assistance, social safety-net programmes and NGO programmes to the Central and east European countries (PHARE) and to the countries of the former Soviet Union (TACIS). The international agencies frequently collaborate with national foreign-aid programmes like those of USAID, the British East European Partnership or the Danish International Development Agency. International or national aid programmes may also be executed by charitable or human-itarian agencies like Save the Children, Oxfam, Red Cross or in Albania,

Islamic organisations such as Red Crescent or Mercy International. Alongside church and charitable organisations a host of more specialised foreign NGOs administer aid programmes in health, social services, education, and job training. There are also foreign *foundations*, notably the Soros Foundation, which has branches in every East European country. Soros pays for conferences and facilitates the coveted travel to the west for many young East Europeans. As the largest private foundation in Eastern Europe, and with a clear western liberal agenda, Soros is a well-known object of admiration, rumour and denigration. Like other far-off, wealthy, inscrutable institutions such as the World Bank, Soros personnel can be accused of unethical behaviour, of being a 'Mafia' a 'clan' or even 'neo-communists'. This critique often comes from nationalist groups or others who have not been able to secure their own routes to the official west. This critique of the transition retains the magic: all change comes from mysterious outside forces, but the magic is now black. Finally among the foreign actors, there are the private consulting companies and individual consultants and contractors who are paid by western agencies to deliver goods, services and know-how to eastern beneficiaries.

The operations of all these western agencies and companies in Eastern Europe are a visible aspect of the east–west relationship. Western aid is part of the diplomatic agenda in Eastern Europe and the westerners are prominent, especially in smaller towns such as Tirana or relatively poor ones like Bucharest. They contribute significantly to the magic of the transition.

At the local level of the transition government ministries, east European NGOs, political parties and politicians can make requests or pose demands on westerners coming with programmes, local branches of foreign embassies or aid organisations, and the local business community. Some of these may be idealistic: civil society of the Vaclav Havel variety. Others may be using civil society development as a political instrument, as when nationalist organisations organise NGOs whose goals are an irredentist 'uncivil' society. Still other local actors use civil society as sustenance. This applies to East Europeans who circulate in the transition conference industry, those who interpret their societies to the west, and those whose income derives from making themselves irreplaceable to western agencies and firms: the interpreters, intermediaries, assistants, and so on. Some of these individuals have genuinely social projects which they pursue under the umbrella of western aid agencies. Others may have solely private agendas which exploit the current fads for civil society, NGOs, human rights and environmental improvement, in order to enjoy the good jobs, free trips, free equipment, or other privileges which their counterparts enjoyed under communism. They guard these privileges and are the objects of jealousy, derision and intrigue. Many pursue individual career skills (with languages, computers, or office administration) which they will use to pursue more rewarding careers, often emigrating abroad. In my experience East Europeans have proven themselves to be both more dedicated to their public projects, *and* more ruthless in exploiting their private agendas than westerners can readily appreciate.

I do not wish to imply that private agendas are found solely among the East Europeans. One need only spend a few hours in the lobby of Tirana's larger hotels, overhear the chatter in the luxury restaurants, or sit in the business-class compartment on the Friday Swissair flight out of Tirana to understand how western specialists, aid functionaries and private firms manipulate their knowledge to ensure that Eastern Europe's transition remains firmly within the framework of western rhetoric and bank accounts. The transition is also a business, and along with the waste, inefficiency and mystification there is a good deal of sheer profit.

CIVIL SOCIETY PROGRAMMES

The original emphasis of European and western development programmes in Eastern Europe was on economic reconstruction, infrastructure development, agriculture and social safety-net programmes. Gradually, however, and under pressure from the European Parliament in Strasbourg, Brussels realised that democratisation also required healthy civil society. The 'democracy programmes' focused on making the parliaments more effective; civic and political education; human rights; helping the free media; and aiding non-government organisations.

The main focus of civil society development has been to increase the number of NGOs. 'Democracy' was understood quantitatively. Few NGOs meant less democracy, more NGOs meant more democracy. The goal in Poland, for example, was to increase the number of NGOs from 3,000 in 1988 – far above any other East European country – to 20,000 by 1992. This goal was largely accomplished. (Denmark, with 5 million people, has 25,000 NGOS.) This quantitative fascination is not lost on east Europeans of the entrepreneurial variety, who see certain benefits in forming their own splinter groups and then convincing donors that they are a legitimate beneficiary. Many of these groups are derisively known as 'shadow NGOs', 'phantom NGOs' or 'quangos' (quasi-NGOs); when they are government-affiliated, they are called 'GOs'.

NGO development also entails qualitative changes, including 'institutional development', 'capacity building', and 'sustainability'. The aim is to make NGOs more effective, open, autonomous and 'transparent' (the transparency/opacity metaphor is pervasive in the NGO business). In PHARE and NGO jargon generally there is continual discussion of NGO 'eligibility'. In a more practical – funding-oriented – sense, civil society becomes equated with 'free associations', and especially those which seek to influence public policy or improve social services. Generally, a bona-fide NGO has to be autonomous, voluntary, legally registered and non-profit. NGOs are often distinguished from political parties which seek state power, and trade unions, whose members are often not voluntary or are tied to specific parties. Church-related organisations are also excluded because of their religious mission, and nationalist organisations because they may not respect human-rights provisions or may advocate violence, instead of the dialogue which is supposed to typify democracy. A distinction is sometimes drawn between 'narrow' associations whose interests extend only to their members, and 'public-service' NGOs which have social projects. The first group might include associations of hunters or lawyers; the second are the traditional 'grass-roots' organisations often known in the west as 'new social movements'.

The problem with such definitions is that they are often difficult to apply in Eastern Europe. Poland's *Solidarity* was rather more than simply a trade union, and on a more modest level many a trade union or fishermen's association may carry out a *socially* valuable activity, such as nature conservation. In Denmark, some NGOs are 100 per cent state-supported but nevertheless considered 'independent'. In Eastern Europe it is difficult to explain such distinctions, and the question of NGO authenticity pervades the funding allocations. It is particularly acute concerning cultural-nationalist organisations, many of which have irredentist objectives or are tied informally to political parties. The associational form is now preferred in a variety of projects, not all of them laudable. Most East European countries, for example, now have associations of former secret-police functionaries seeking pensioners' rights. Just as the original East European dissident parties began as informal groups of intellectuals, today's networks, cliques and factions are incorporating themselves as NGOs.

One of the main instruments for supporting East European civil society was to finance projects enabling NGOs to 'imitate western NGOs' as one EU document stated. Western organisations themselves could gain funding from this programme. The smaller, 'microprojects' programme makes funds available only to East European organisations. Finally, there were the Civil Society Foundations, established in several countries to award grants, conduct training and provide information to the NGO sector. Albania, the country with the most need for civil society, had never asked for, and hence, never obtained, a civil society programme, focusing instead on much needed humanitarian aid.

Enter Denmark, whose foreign-aid policy often seeks to fill gaps left by other agencies or organisations. The Danish minister of development decided in 1994 that Albania would receive a total of 9 million dollars in aid, of which 1.2 million would be earmarked for civil society development. In practice this meant the implementation of the PHARE civil society foundation model, this time with Danish aid money. Of no small importance was the fact that the PHARE-financed model had been instituted in other countries by a Danish team which had won the contract through competitive bidding. Having met the head of the team while in Romania (same conference, same restaurant, same plane) I was asked to undertake an assessment of Albanian civil society as the basis for the Danish aid programme. I was given four weeks to find out the government's attitude, public attitudes, and the needs, desires, skills and resources of Albanian NGOs themselves.

DANISH DEMOCRACY COMES TO ALBANIA

Albania, the poorest, most repressive and most isolated of the eastern bloc countries, made world headlines in 1991 with the pulling down of Enver Hoxha's statue, bread riots in provincial towns, and thousands of young Albanians fleeing in ships to Italy. Since the crisis the country has endured the pangs of transition: many factories have closed completely, land has been privatised, and new classes of rich and poor have arisen. Today Albania's economy and its people are dependent largely on foreign aid: this ranges from the credits given by the European Union and World Bank to the remittances sent back by approximately 400,000 Albanians working abroad (many illegally). Tirana, the smallest of European capitals, is full of cafés and kiosks, and now has its own squatter settlements of migrants from the poorer northern regions. While conflicts range in parliament and accusations of corruption affect all the parties, the transition industry makes its inroads.

Aside from foreign aid and remittances, Albanians' unofficial incomes are generated by illicit trade, much of which involves the smuggling of stolen cars or gasoline going eastward to embargoed Serbia. Salaries in the public sector are in the order of 100 to 200 dollars a month. Those in the private and foreign sectors are three to five times higher. Pensioners and other marginal groups are hard hit as the state is unable to provide welfare payments at reasonable levels, or meet social demands for housing and employment. The resulting social differentiation is marked. As one Albanian medical student expressed it 'there are two kinds of people in this country: the ones who drive Mercedes and the ones who sell bananas'.

It was into this world of transitional Albania that I arrived to assess the situation of civil society. My only initial contact was the Albanian NGO Forum, located in the former mausoleum of Enver Hoxha. The Forum, a coordinating organisation for several Albanian NGOs, turned out to be a single staff member with a small office and no telephone. The office and the coordinator's salary were being paid for by grants from a Dutch development agency (SNV), Catholic Relief Services, and by an Islamic foundation known as Mercy International.[2] I soon learned that Albanian NGO life was intimately tied to the western aid organisations in Tirana.

The Albanian NGO Forum had about fifty organisations as members, and the total was increasing rapidly. About half of them were foreign NGOs – the Forum had actually been established by foreign organisations to coordinate humanitarian aid. Most of the original Albanian NGOs were offshoots of the foreign NGOs or wholly financed by them, with foreign chairs. Albanian organisations included various environmental-protection groups, youth groups, organisations of pensioners, orphan-aid, women, disabled veterans, and other social associations. Every Tuesday the NGO Forum would hold a meeting in a small conference room at the UNDP complex. The meetings were led by the Forum's chair, a Palestinian doctor working on a Kuwaiti-financed hospital project. They were conducted in English with Albanian translation. About thirty or forty persons attended the meetings to discuss coordination and future plans. The Palestinian doctor was excellent at keeping the discussants from each others' throats. Passions often ran high when break-away groupings would return to present themselves as new NGOs, only to be challenged as illegitimate or unregistered. Among Albanian veterans' organisations, for example, the members of one group had fought in the Second World War with the partisans, while another had fought against them. The foreign NGO representatives attended these meetings out of loyalty or moral obligation. Their view was that the Forum's meetings were symptomatic of the sad state of Albanian civil society and of Albanian mentality: too much chaos, lack of creative thinking, dependence on foreign models and advice, and poor organisational and meeting discipline.

On being presented at the weekly meeting, I quickly became popular: I announced that the Danish government was considering a programme to aid Albanian NGOs and that I was here to assess the situation. I had the magic from abroad that was needed. I was both the connection and the source, and I was on the spot. (The participants often expressed their scepticism about foreigners who had 'come and made many promises', and were then never heard from again.) The next few weeks were spent interviewing various Albanian NGO activists, leaders, government officials, diplomats and foreign specialists. I also visited the towns of Durres and Shkodre to talk to local government officials and to search out NGOs in these towns. I then arranged a one-day seminar to explain the Danish view of NGOs and to hear representatives of sixty Albanian NGOs talk about their goals, visions and problems. I then drew up a long report, including a list of about 250 NGOs.

Spending day after day, night after night, with socially engaged people makes for a curious kind of fieldwork. You want to help out personally, with a name or phone number or money, but you cannot please everybody. Ordinary people who have never heard the expression 'civil society' and are unfamiliar with projects or NGOs reveal themselves to have a tremendous amount of ingenuity, able to organise meetings without money, telephones, fax machines or mail. These same people can also be vicious towards each other; support and comradeship go together with suspicions of betrayal and opportunism. The competition for the resources offered by the west exacerbates this tension.

ALBANIAN NGOs AS ORGANISATIONS

While Albanian villages certainly have a tradition of family and voluntary aid, Albania's autonomous social organisations, 'civil society' in the modern western sense, effectively began with the emergency aid given the country during the economic chaos of 1991. The brutal nature of the Hoxha regime prevented the emergence of any political organisations in the Charter 77 style. Official atheism made even religious organisation impossible. The emergency-aid effort was mainly conducted by the Italian government and European NGOs. These foreign groups established Albanian affiliates and worked with Albanian volunteers, often groups of women or students. These affiliates and volunteers came to form the nucleus of the first Albanian NGOs, so that foreign aid and civil society were inextricably linked.

Despite these origins, Albanian NGOs had many ostensible similarities with civil society in other East and West European countries: there were environmental, youth, women's, human-rights groups, virtually all of them affiliated or wholly financed by western donors or partners. More isolated and organisationally less developed were various social-service NGOs, for veterans, pensioners, the handicapped, and so on. NGOs in the rural sector, only recently decollectivised, were sorely lacking, as were economic or commercial organisations. Large grass-roots organisations such as farmers' cooperatives, chambers of commerce or trade unions were either non-existent or so stigmatised from the former regime as to be ineffective. Several were being reorganised and wholly financed by foreign-aid programmes. Minority-group organisations were poorly organised. The country's large Greek minority was under severe pressure: its *Omonia* organisation was increasingly politicised and had few links with the NGO community. Gypsy and Vlach/Arouman organisations were dormant. However there existed a host of Albanian cultural nationalist organisations with names like 'Albania – Fatherland of all Albanians', which sought to promote cultural contact or even political unity with the thousands of Albanians living abroad, especially in Kosovo. Virtually all of Albania's NGOs were in the capital, where their proximity to foreign donors gave them a clear advantage over NGOs and informal groups trying to establish themselves in the provincial towns.

Most Albanian NGOs consisted of a core group of activists who operated simultaneously as board, staff and effective membership. All NGOs pursued contacts abroad and needed money for basic operating costs, trips, publicity campaigns, computers and telephone lines. While one often heard complaints of inefficiency among the NGOs by foreign-aid workers or Albanian members, I was impressed by their ability to find solutions under arduous conditions. To be sure, some NGOs were either false or simply fronts for individual operators, and others were tied to political forces.[3]

In Albania, as in other East European countries, the inheritance of former 'front' organisations of women, youth, culture, minority, and academic groups posed problems. When the government allowed former members of these groups to continue them, they were accused of operating without a mandate, or of being mouthpieces for government policy. Some governments in Eastern Europe, in order to cash in on western aid, have established their own organisations, the so-called 'GOs' in environment and fields such as youth affairs. Since Albania also has a Youth and an Environment department in its government, conflicts arise as to who should have access to foreign donors, attendance rights at foreign conferences, and so on.

The most pervasive difference within the NGOs was the gap between those groups led by young, anglophone, well-travelled intellectuals and others whose members were less articulate and more isolated. The first group, including youth, environmental, women's and human-rights groups, often had wide-ranging public-service projects; they knew the language of projects and had often been to seminars abroad. The second group, older, Albanian-speaking and unfamiliar with the world of projects, tended to focus on increased social services, entitlements, or payments for their constituents. They included groups for aiding orphans, haemophiliacs, veterans, the handicapped, disabled workers, pensioners and the political-prisoners group. These 'entitlement' NGOs sought to have their members declared a specific status, such as 'handicapped', 'disabled veteran', 'parent of mentally retarded child', in order to benefit from special allocations from the state. Being declared a 'former political prisoner' or 'family member of formerly persecuted person' qualified you to jump the queue for housing and to obtain preferential loans from western-financed credit associations. The struggle for these entitlements was often the only goal of the organisation: as if to turn the socialist hierarchy upside down into a new hierarchy of entitlements. Relations between the two categories of NGOs were often oppositional: the young, activist-oriented NGO members would accuse the others being provincial, of failing to understand the NGO sector, of being out for their own material interests, using NGOs as a social club, and disguising their own culpability for their silence during the communist regime. Several older academics felt that they were being shunted aside when they offered their services to environmental groups, while young people would sometimes complain that the older ones would not listen to them.

With few resources and an uncertain institutional framework, only a small portion of the 300 or so NGOs with a formal existence are truly active. Virtually all of these are dependent on foreign funding.

ALBANIAN ASSUMPTIONS ABOUT NGOs

In the early days of 1991, the new Albanian government welcomed the European aid organisations and their Albanian assistants. NGOs meant free labour to distribute emergency aid. The government associated NGOs with charity, although some officials became sceptical when some Albanian NGO leaders were arrested in highly publicised cases of corruption of emergency relief. Officials were not prepared when Albanian NGOs began to expand into other sectors, including environmental protection, women's rights, autonomous youth organisations, human rights, minority rights, and the rehabilitation of torture victims. They found it difficult to deal with their many requests for support.

The Albanian government was not hostile to NGOs. Unlike Romania, for example, where the ruling neo-communist group around President Ion Iliescu has often viewed NGOs as a cover for the political opposition, Albanian officials were either sceptical or ignorant of NGO influence. They saw NGOs as voluntary organisations to help the government implement its plans. They were much less familiar with NGOs as lobby organisations, pressure groups, or as partners with the government in determining social needs and forming policy. Concepts such as civil society or NGO (used in Albanian as well) were simply slogans. Soon 'independent organisations' were seen as uncontrollable and unreliable, and groups such as *Omonia*, the organisation of ex-political prisoners, or the Helsinki Group, as embarrassing or even subversive. Many officials were clearly upset that western aid to Albania should go through NGOs instead of the government. The tensions generated from this situation stemmed from the fact that aid to Albanian NGOs had still to be approved by the Albanian prime minister's office. Suspicion and scepticism were mutual, even though many Albanian NGOs continued to suffer from a reflexive dependency on the state apparatus for carrying out tasks they could well have undertaken themselves.

There was also an exaggerated fear among Albanian NGO activists of government plans and conspiracies; that 'they' were still acting as if they ran things as in Enver Hoxha's time. An undelivered letter or disconnected phone was evidence enough of a government conspiracy. When I invited a government official to a meeting of NGO activists, it was assumed that the official would dictate the terms. When we agreed that a government representative should sit on the board of the NGO foundation which the Danish government set up in Albania, NGO activists feared that the board would become an instrument of the government. When I suggested that the other Albanians on the board might work to influence the official, as a kind of informal lobby, I was dismissed as naive.

In their daily operations Albanian NGOs were, according to many observers – Albanian and foreign – characterised by inefficiency, suspicion and tension. Many Albanians express the view, common in much of Eastern Europe, that private agendas lie behind all public or altruistic activities. There is an assumption of untoward motives by those whom one does not know personally. Since most NGOs are small, it is generally their leaders who are the most active. If the leader is invited abroad, for example, it is invariably interpreted as a personal project. The idea also exists that personal criteria are decisive in the distribution of resources. Virtually all competitive awards for jobs, money or travel are seen as going to friends or connections, regardless of better qualified recipients. Albanians talk of this system in terms of 'clan'. At the same time, there is a lack of confidence in any system of selection which does *not* depend on personal knowledge: 'I know him' outweighs any formal shortcoming.

Albanian NGOs have a view of western agencies and representatives as resources to be used. Westerners are assumed to have their own hidden agenda, are out for material gain, or are simply naive. While it is not my impression that Albanians are inherently manipulative, 'playing along with the western representative' is an assumption that many Albanians make about each other. They often insist on this aspect when they tell western NGO donors 'how things really work', or about 'the Albanian mentality'. The suspicion of collaboration that is associated with this mentality seems to be based upon a division of the world into friends and enemies, such that disagreement on a single point makes one an opponent on all points. There also exists in Albania, possibly as a consequence of communist rule, a tendency to equate centralisation with efficiency and decentralisation with anarchy, confusion and inefficiency. The very possibility of independent, autonomous groups collaborating via *ad hoc* networks is seen as problematic.

It goes without saying that Tirana-based foreign officials, donor representatives, experts and consultants all gravitate to those NGOs with the younger, anglophone activists. Foreigners feel good when surrounded by younger, energetic, intellectual, socially engaged, English speakers who are willing and able to utilise the available resources given them, be it a new computer or a trip to a human-rights seminar. A foreigner who deals with the second group of older, more provincial NGOs, has to proceed more slowly. Older Albanians may only speak Italian, thus necessitating an interpreter for the anglophone or francophone consultant. They may have moving stories of repression to relate or they may be obsequious to the foreign representative and embarrassed to admit ignorance about the terminology of foreign aid. Others may feel the need to give moral lessons to the foreigner, or to explain Albanian history. Not knowing the 'culture' of projects, many of these older NGO members place the emphasis on getting money, rather than on their ideas for projects or the goals or their organisation.

As an agent of western civil society, one of my tasks was to separate the legitimate from the shadow NGOs. Sometimes this task was un-complicated, as when an NGO with a nominally large membership (often without dues or budget) had not carried out any activities except seeking money. In other examples, I found that NGO leaders were more interested in telling of travelling and of future plans, and that their offices were curiously silent when compared to the chaos of more activist organisations.

It sometimes happened that competing foreign donors would arrive looking for partners, and the more capable Albanians could play off one against the other. All the western experts and aid delegations were in Albania to implement projects, and their expectations often came into conflict, both with each other and with local requests. The nature of western contacts with Albania often contributed to unreasonable expectations. New personnel would suddenly appear and then fly out. The unexplained appearance and disappearance of foreigners – and the costs involved – was another example of how western magic operated on the Albanian scene.[4]

Even more problematic were the one-day conferences or workshops in which western specialists would participate with a standard presentation which they had already delivered in other countries of the region. Such meetings were particularly frustrating for Albanians. The experts and the locals knew so little about each other that 'seminar' has now become a word of derision and even comic routine on Albanian television. As one Albanian NGO activist whispered to me during yet another NGO seminar, where we were hearing platitudes uttered by a Council of Europe NGO specialist, 'with the money for his airplane ticket I could have financed my entire organisation for a year'.

BUILDING CIVIL SOCIETY

Following Danish government approval of my preliminary study of Albanian NGOs, a team from Denmark returned to Albania to construct the organisational framework for civil society. The Danish scheme to help NGOs would take the form of a Civil Society Foundation. Forming such a foundation would require approval by the Albanian government, as this was part of the official Danish aid programme. Our concrete tasks included finding members for a board (preferably persons from the NGO community with untarnished reputations), establishing the legal and financial basis for the foundation, hiring an executive secretary and staff, renting offices and purchasing equipment. Once the foundation was operational there would be a press conference, solicitation of applications by NGOs for projects, the awarding of grants to Albanian NGOs, the opening of an NGO information centre and the arrangement of training courses. The primary goal of the foundation, in line with the EU PHARE foundation in other countries, would be to help Albanian NGOs to become more effective and more autonomous of foreign support, and by building NGO capacity to help Albanian civil society have a greater impact on government policy and on the public. The foundation structure was intended to enable the Albanian NGOs to obtain hands-on experience in administering funds, instead of just searching and begging for them.

Tirana being a small town and government officials being receptive to the Danish programme, the formalities were rapidly resolved. Our press conference received wide coverage, and our board members – all of whom had some connections with NGOs – set about assessing our first applications. Following the publicity given to the fund, in which I appeared on television and in the press together with several board members, I became a minor celebrity in Tirana. Many Albanians assumed that I was solely responsible for dispensing the funds, and that the remaining eight Albanian board members were simply window dressing. I was approached on the street, telephoned and visited at the office and at my apartment by well-meaning Albanians who needed money for various projects, many only remotely connected with NGOs. Ex-diplomats handed me résumés. A former sports hero offered me his apartment for use as an office. New graduates of the English faculty came looking for translation work. Everyone was intent on making a connection with me. Albanian society was still a network society, and with their privileged access to scarce resources, foreigners are still a key resource. My insistence that our fund could not finance such projects, and that I myself did not make the decision, seemed to have little impact. I later discovered that general statements I had made that the fund would certainly like to give money for good projects, and that these persons should apply, had been interpreted as a promise of funding.

Eventually, fifty-seven applications were received, and our board sat down to evaluate them. Each project was thoroughly discussed as to the NGO's eligibility, the project's feasibility, and the budget. Since our board members and secretariat were well connected, it was usual for one or more of us (including myself) to have some knowledge of the NGO or of the individual project leader applying. Even among board members, this personal knowledge led to an emphasis on the project leader's personality as opposed to the project proposal as it appeared on paper. 'I don't know him' was a sign that something was wrong. 'He is a serious person, I know him', was a sign that something was right.

The board ended up by awarding funds to forty NGO projects, and these reflected the variety and range of civil society initiatives in Albania.

They included a women's counselling centre, a training programme for a farmer's association, a workshop for village women to learn about their inheritance rights, and a variety of environmental-awareness and health-education campaigns on activities ranging from problems of solid waste in Tirana to anti-smoking, drugs, and AIDS. Greek and Rom (Gypsy) organisations received grants to register their respective populations by drawing ethnic maps. Conference and seminar grants were awarded to groups of pensioners, haemophiliacs and cultural groups. Virtually all the applications in this first round came from Tirana. None of them asked for any training, even though our budget had funds for training in various aspects of NGO activity. The NGOs apparently thought that they had all the skills and knowledge they needed. For some organisations the application form itself is the most difficult hurdle in becoming a legitimately recognised part of civil society. The NGO applying for funds has to designate its 'target group', a phrase almost untranslatable in Albanian. It has to provide a 'mission statement'. Making detailed budgets and providing indices for 'evaluation' and 'sustainability' has also proved problematic. The foundation's staff is doing what it can to help organisations in making their applications.

One of the more interesting applications was one from The Mission to Resolve Blood Feuds, which was seeking to buy a used car with which to visit families involved in clan disputes. The organisation, with branches in most Albanian cities, was led by a Catholic priest in Shkodre, and was concerned with alleviating all kinds of family conflicts. The Albanian press has reported that thousands of people are afraid to leave their homes because of various kinds of vendettas. The association had resolved 168 such feuds, often using an elaborate ceremony in which documents were signed, songs sung and oaths chanted. This organisation expressed an interest in links with similar western groups, and it was tempting to direct them toward the world of 'conflict-resolution' consultants and training seminars.

The board rejected various ethnic cross-border projects of questionable value to Albanian civil society, together with several projects with vague content or unrealistic budgets. In the world of projects there is theoretically no room for running costs. In reality, projects are proposed in order to cover these costs. This means that the project application process stimulates a degree of misrepresentation. Aid agencies are aware of this, attempt to sharpen their control, and thereby add to the vicious circle of distrust between western donors and Albanian NGOs.

As money is allocated and grant contracts signed for this first round of projects, and as a new round of supplicants enters, I am already being advised by other Albanians that I should just wait and see: 'By the end of the project, the leader will have his own Mercedes.' The assumption by Albanians is that every NGO organisation (except that of which the accusing individual is a member) is the instrument of a kind of clan. Regrettably, the scandals and tensions which circulate as rumour are not counterbalanced by any genuine and visible socially beneficial activity in Albanian society. This society remains largely impenetrable to all the foreign observers. However, it also demonstrates the sort of voluntarism which one rarely finds in the sophisticated, fund-raising, market-oriented, state-supported world of western NGOs. Much of the real social work which in the west is channelled into NGOs or charitable organisations is in Albania carried out on an interpersonal, face-to-face basis in urban neighbourhoods and villages. True, mass grass-roots organisations of agrarian cooperators, Green activists, and lobby organisations of various kinds are missing. Yet if we examine Albanian society in terms of its civilising everyday life, instead of looking at its civil society solely in terms of the number and strength of its NGOs, a completely different picture emerges. Interpersonal relations in local settings are difficult to integrate into that world of projects which has become the focal point of Eastern Europe's transition.

CONCLUSIONS: CIVIL SOCIETY AND THE GLOBAL TRANSITION

Social scientists and NGO funding agencies can employ various definitions of 'civil society': in terms of group characteristics or concrete activity, as narrow interest groups, or broad civic movements, and so on. Social analysts and evaluation reports can pinpoint whether civil society is 'underdeveloped' or 'nascent' or 'progressing' in a given country. It is up to anthropologists, however, to reveal how people themselves define, redefine and utilise concepts in their social practice. An anthropology of the current transition in Eastern Europe needs to investigate how representations like 'civil society' take on a social life, and what happens to concepts that move about in very different social contexts – from the plush Brussels consulting firm to the Albanian NGO trying to stop blood feuds.

In the west, civil society is said to have grown up with the rise of capitalism. More specifically, it grew up around the free association of individuals in secularised, democratising, pluralist capitalist states. These factors were missing, or cut short, in Eastern Europe and have had to be reconstituted or totally recreated. Albania's civil society has thus remained dependent on concepts, organisation and funds from western agencies. This dependency has meant that Albanians must manipulate imported concepts in order to procure western resources. Some Albanians have proven better at this manipulation than others, and one sign of the transition is that some individuals who were very good at the 'wooden language' of socialism have now mastered the jargon of democracy programmes, project management, capacity building and other catch-phrases such as 'transparency', and 'empowerment'. Such individuals serve as brokers in the unequal relationship between the west and the east. Like brokers everywhere, they manipulate resources and thrive off the maintenance of barriers. The forum for such activity is the world of projects, and civil society development is part of this world.

Manipulation and exploitation of the representations used by others is hardly new in the aid context: East Europeans could profit by visiting East African communities where local officials and headmen, skilfully manipulating the discourse of 'community development' and 'decentralisation', prodding the guilty conscience and massaging the socialist leanings of Scandinavian aid workers, were able to channel millions of dollars of foreign aid for their own private agendas. There are similarities between western aid to the third world and transition aid to Eastern Europe. Does this mean that 'the transition' in Eastern Europe is only a facade for new kinds of private entrepreneurship? Certainly not. There is a great deal of genuine, public-spirited social energy at work. As individuals, as informal groups and as NGOs, people are making extraordinary contributions with little resources in difficult conditions. Whether all this is 'civil society' ought to be irrelevant for us. However, it *is* relevant for various actors, eastern and western, in the world of projects, inasmuch as procuring scarce resources depends on conforming to a certain kind of organisation. Put bluntly: social networks can't get grants, but autonomous associations can.

The players in this world of projects range from major donor agencies to the consultants, project managers and other operators (legal and illegal) who appear on the scene whenever new resources are distributed in unclear situations. This uncertainty creates the 'magic' of the transition, in which inexplicable wealth comes down from a place called Europe, or from other foreign donor countries or agencies. The magic of transition requires strange jargon, and a host of rituals and ceremonies in which inequality between west and east masquerades as 'partnership' or 'coordination'. A key aspect of this magic is the transmission from west to east of 'models' for development by which the east is supposed to replicate (if not imitate) a western experience which is only a representation taken out of context. The more out of context this representation is, the more magical aura and organisational paraphernalia are needed to surround it. As part of this transition magic, Civil Society as autonomous social activity coexists with 'civil society' as a discursive field and as a structure of resources. Brokers manipulate and control the representational forms which have become so essential to the transition.

In this chapter I have explored the interaction of these two types of civil society in the world of projects. I have tried to emphasise that the transition in Eastern Europe has a global component: the formal transfer of resources interacts with the informal circulation of money, objects, people and representations back and forth across the east–west divide. New borders are being erected between east and west just as old ones disappear. The borders are more subtle, but they are there. After all, it is *we* who are developing *them*, and *our* concepts are becoming *their* projects. *We* social scientists are studying *their* transition and underneath the magical world of projects lie mystification and power.[5]

NOTES

1 For example, a visit by an official from the Albanian social-service sector to Danish hospitals resulted in a positive impression of the Danish health-care delivery system. He was never told, however, that during the week he was there all the nurses had been on strike, that three hospitals were being closed, and that private health-care facilities were doing a booming business because of long waiting times for operations.

2 Islamic organisations are also at work building hospitals and mosques, and providing cash payments to (Muslim) families. They are a significant part of the NGO scene in Albania, although their notion of civil society has little in common with the cosmopolitan, secular and grass-roots thinking of Albanian youth, women's and environmental organisations.

3 Some Albanian irredentist organisations were clearly of this type. The Association of Ex-Politically Persecuted (composed of former political prisoners and family members) has sought to run candidates for office, and the (Greek) *Omonia* organisation is affiliated to the Party of Human Rights. The tendency for NGOs and parties to overlap has occurred elsewhere: Poland's *Solidarity* and the Romanian *Civic Alliance* are prominent examples.

4 Within the space of a few days, I myself was asked for information by groups dealing with eco-tourism, AIDS awareness, orphan information, a geologists' group, a fish-farming group and finally, by the Society for Gay Albania to try and make connections with parallel agencies abroad.

5 The ideas for this chapter arose out of the EASA session on civil society in June 1994. It reached its current form in August 1995, when it was presented at a session on the politics of aid to Eastern Europe at the Fifth World Congress of Central and East European Studies in Warsaw.

Chapter 7

Civic culture and Islam in urban Turkey

Jenny B. White

SELECTIVE OCCLUSIONS OF ASSOCIATIONAL LIFE

In urban Turkey, voluntary associations, grass-roots protest actions and other forms of civic activities often are organised on the basis of mutual trust and interpersonal obligation, rather than on an individual, contractual membership basis. Trust and reciprocity characterise communal life in general and are the means by which individuals, and particularly women, express and reinforce their family and community identities. These voluntary associations are not based on clan, tribe, family or other primordial ties; rather they represent a free choosing of individuals with whom to associate within the web of one's acquaintances and community. This creates a political space for women to act publicly without leaving the privacy and security of their communal and gendered roles. Furthermore, this web of already existing community ties is the foundation of a civic culture upon which both Islamic and secular groups build organisational infrastructures among the working class. In this chapter I shall argue that such a civic culture exists and has preceded recent Islamist political successes in Turkey. This leads me to question the usefulness of speculation about the compatibility of Islam and civil society. Informal civic association teaches citizenship skills that may, in time, lead to further politicisation and institutionalisation and thus pave the way for a more participatory system and encourage more accountable governance.

Much of the civil society literature, particularly that dealing with the Middle East, is dominated by discussions of organisations of free individuals bound by a more or less specifically articulated social contract, symbolised by such artefacts as the membership list. These organisations generally have a middle-class constituency. The type of informally organised civil society found among the Turkish working class and described below forms a conceptual bridge between such free associations of unbound individuals and other, primordial forms of association, the inclusion of which under the rubric of civil society is the subject of some debate.

The term civil society has a long history specific to political and philosophical developments in Europe and the United States. Its conceptual role for most of this century has been as a buffer between human aspirations and totalitarian regimes. The failure of these regimes has given new impetus to seekers of democratic potential and also to those who seek new foes. The term civil society has become entangled in these political currents, emerging as a kind of litmus test for the democratic potential of non-western regimes. Recently, there has emerged a small but burgeoning optimistic literature on the presence of civil society in the Middle East.[1] Arguing against an essentialising of Islam, some scholars have pointed out that groups with an Islam-oriented political agenda are a diverse lot, and include groups that are willing to participate in the democratic process, as indeed they have done in Turkey, Jordan and Lebanon (Norton 1993a: 10–11, 1993b). They argue, in other words, that civil society is possible under Islam. However, an accompanying chorus of sceptics points to what it perceives to be an inherent incompatibility between civil society and Islam, for some the new enemy on the world stage.[2] Civil society as an individualistic, market- and contract-based form of associational life is counterposed to an Islamic discourse that seeks to subjugate society and the state to its own interests. Because of its singular history as a secular republic, Turkey is considered by many to be a test case for the incorporation of Islam in a democratic system.[3]

Whether the discussion incorporates a tractable or an intractable Islam, the civil society debate in the Middle East generally remains focused on the relative presence of feminist groups, trade unions, and other groups that fit the western model of free association of individuals and a contractual if not adversarial relationship with the state. Many of these are middle-class or élite associations. Excluded from the category of civil society by many, though not all scholars, are associations based primarily on kinship or primordial ties, such as those of family, clan and tribe, since these are exclusionary rather than inclusionary forms of association.[4] Preliminary research into urban working-class associational activity in Turkey, however, has turned up a variety of hybrid groups that operate on the fringes of these categories.[5] These associations are not forged of contractually bound individuals, nor are they kinship-based. Religion may organise their activities but is not their *raison d'être*; their organisational framework may be *either* religious *or* secular. Indeed, these associations are sometimes short-lived, emerging to address one particular problem. They are concerned, at least initially, not with obtaining or sharing state power, but with addressing local conditions: the lack of water and electricity, the need for a health centre, or the need for job training for girls. Some, over time, become more inclusive, politicised and institutionalised. These groups fall between the conceptual cracks: they do not have Islam as a political agenda, but they are very different from the secular bourgeois associations such as professional groups, human-rights organisations and women's groups, which dominate in the literature on associational life.

The literature on civil society and democracy in Africa is replete with examples of 'informal' associations.[6] These are often deprecated as primordial, parochial, or taken as evidence of a weak civil society.[7] Carapico (1994) goes so far as to differentiate between an 'African model' and a 'classical' western model of civil society, analogous to the difference in organisation between the informal and formal economic sectors. On a cautionary note, Waylen (1994) points out that studies of popular movements in Latin America and elsewhere often do not take account of gender, nor are such movements incorporated in theoretical examinations of the relation between civil society and democratisation. With regard to the Middle East, despite the recent blossoming of a variety of social movements and civic activities, scholarly attention has remained firmly focused on recognisably 'classic' forms of civil society. The complete occlusion of the Arab world in some discussions of democracy is even more disturbing.[8] It derives in part from characteristics of various states in the region, including discrimination against women and minorities, human-rights abuses, intimidation by secret police, and other vices of totalitarian or authoritarian regimes. Yet these alone cannot account for the singular treatment accorded the Middle East in discussions of democracy and civil society. Africa and Latin America share many of these faults, yet civic life is registered at many levels of social action, even if popular and gendered aspects are incompletely acknowledged at a more theoretical level.

The reason for such differential treatment is to be found in the aspiration of Islam to determine the criteria underlying not only personal behaviour, but also social and political life. Whether such an Islam can cohabit with the modern state is the question around which both sceptics and optimists have taken their stance. Scholars wishing to demonstrate that Islam is indeed compatible with a pluralistic society and polity have underlined the variety of individualistic, universalistic 'classical' civic organisations to be found in Muslim nations, and shy away from associational life that appears more particularistic. The latter, based on community, family and regional ties, smacks of the tribalism with which the region has for centuries been tarred (or romanticised). What is at stake in the dispute over the compatibility of Islam and civil society is nothing less than the political legitimacy of different types of social bonds.

CIVIL SOCIETY AND WOMEN'S 'INFORMAL' ASSOCIATIONAL LIFE

Civil society is a concept that tries to explain what binds people together in modern state societies in a civic life beyond their individual interests. The meanings attributed to the term have followed the trajectory of western philosophical thought, beginning in the seventeenth century when the term took on attributes of reason and rationality in opposition to revelation and the state of nature (Cohen and Arato 1994; Seligman 1992; Shils 1991). The concept gained popularity in the eighteenth century because it provided a 'rational' basis for social order and law in European societies increasingly divorced from the traditional bonds of God, king and family. Increasingly, new capitalist market relations required new forms of social action based on self-interest, and no longer kept in check by a shared vision of the cosmic order. What could be the moral basis of a community of competing individuals acting out of egoism and self-interest?

Adam Smith was among the first to suggest that social order and morality originated within people, not from God. People are motivated by egoism, it is true, but also by altruism, a 'natural' sympathy with fellow men, and a desire for recognition, respect and approval from them. Mutual validation took place through the act of exchange. The impetus for social order was located directly in human interaction, particularly in its manifestation in the public arena of the market-place. As Adam Seligman has recently summarised the position taken by David Hume, 'The universal good was nothing beyond the calculus of individual or particular goods, and the public good was supported solely by the workings of private interests' (1992: 38). 'Man's autonomy' was validated and guaranteed through his participation in the public arena in the civil structures of political activity (Seligman 1992: 43).

The entwining of market and social order has two important implications for the term civil society as it continues to be used today. One is that economic and commercial interests came to be seen as distinct from primordial ties. The other, related, distinction is one between a public sphere that is an arena of mutual and rational consent, involving values, rights and duties, and a private sphere that is the locus of ethics and morality, which had been pushed out of the public sphere along with the belief in a cosmic order. It is from this point on that the concept of civil society became associated with property ownership (in many cases also a criterion for citizenship) and separable from religion and its moral imperatives.

During this period, partly as a result of the decline of home manu- facturing and the spread of factories, women and children came to be associated ideally with a private home sphere separate from production and the market, and therefore out of range of the sphere of rational and civil society and the political order. In the eighteenth century, civil society also came to distinguish civilisation from barbarism, and to characterise a market sphere distinct from that of the 'folk' (Shils 1991). The long-term exclusion of women, children and the working class from the rights of citizenship is still mirrored today in the elision of many of their activities from discussions of civil society. Furthermore, the recent use of the concept to differentiate states according to their potential for democracy and civilisation (Huntington 1993) carries on the tradition of using rationality and individualism as the yardstick to measure the distance between the civilised individual and the collectivist barbarian. Civil society, in its 'classic' form, has little conceptual tolerance for associational bonds based on religious ethics, on 'private' relations of kin and clan, or on regional 'folk' loyalties.

In the twentieth century, the sense of a political community and of citizenship came to be added to the definition of civil society. However, the rights that secure modern civil society continue to be political rights and property rights (Cohen and Arato 1994: ix; Shils 1991) characterising a society of atomised individuals competing in the market.[9] Civil society, defined in this way, finds little resonance in societies in which social and economic order is maintained through bonds of religion, tribe, ethnicity or community. In other words, the 'classical' sense of civil society is of little or no use in describing most of the non-western world below the level of government and the activities of a segment of educated westernised élites. It also excludes women, who are seen to be embedded within the family rather than freely associating as citizens in the public sphere.[10] As Waylen (1994) points out, orthodox political-science demo- cratisation literature is characterised by 'narrow definitions of demo- cracy, politics, and citizenship, the concentration on the public sphere and the use of simplistic notions of civil society' (1994: 335). The élite bias of much of this literature means that women's political participation finds little place, since women more often participate in popular move-ments and do so on the basis of their gendered social roles, for instance as mothers and household providers.

This is certainly the case in Turkey, where a wide array of popular movements can be found in working-class communities. Some, like regional self-help and community charity groups, are officially registered and of long standing; others seem more ephemeral and oriented toward specific goals: for instance, motivating the local municipal government to carry out infrastructural improvements. Women participate in many of these, but are particularly active in voluntary activities and associ-ations which are based on networks of already existing community relationships, rather than on any formal type of membership. Here are some examples from my field research to give an idea of the variety of activities involved:

• In one community, sewage pipes broke and mixed with the tap water. A retired worker organised men at the local coffee-house to phone others in the community. Joined by their families, these men marched on municipal headquarters and presented officials with open jars of reeking tap water. The pipes were repaired.
• Four children were run over and killed on a particularly dangerous stretch of road. Neighbourhood women visited and telephoned each others' homes, then sat on the street and blocked traffic for several days. The municipality permanently closed the street.
• With municipal funding and volunteer labour, local women opened several informal schools to teach young women marketable skills such as typing, book-keeping and sewing, as well as literacy, child-care, art and music. The association, like those in the examples above, was forged of personal ties based on familiarity and trust. The women organised as 'cells' on the basis of already existing community ties. This form of organisation brought in women who would not otherwise have been able to participate because of cultural and religious proscriptions enforced by husbands, other family members, and the community itself. The schools were enormously successful and 'gradu-ated' hundreds of women over their years of operation. They were closed down when an Islamic-based party won the municipal election and withdrew municipal resources. More recently, using their own limited resources, these women opened a formally registered women's centre, with more explicitly political and feminist goals.

The success of such initiatives in poor neighbourhoods (which tend to be socially more conservative than middle- or upper-class areas) is due in large part to their very 'informal' organisation, based on pre-existing webs of mutual support and trust. It allows women to participate in civic and overtly political activities that improve their lives without fear of social disapproval. It creates a political space within which women can act as citizens in a public manner without leaving the privacy and security of their gendered roles.

Islamic political parties in Turkey and throughout the Middle East owe much of their recent popularity and electoral successes to the very same strategy of organisation by social 'cell' (Newman 1994). They are building, however, on an already existing form of association that is available to secular projects as well. A major difference is that Islamic groups, including those in Turkey, have the financial resources to provide and support organisational frameworks based on religion. How much of the recent success of Islamic groups and pro-Islamic political parties is due to financial liquidity and consequent enhancement of organisational opportunities is an open empirical question. It would also be interesting to know to what extent and in what manner non-élite women participate in Islamist political activities. Unfortunately, most of the existing literature on Islamist women in Turkey pays attention only to élites (Göle 1991 1996; Ilyasoğlu 1994; Toprak 1996).

ÜMRANIYE'S FOLK SCHOOLS

For a deeper understanding of the associational base and long-term potential of 'informal' reciprocal associations in Turkey, I will elaborate on the example given above of volunteer schools which teach women vocational skills. Ümraniye is a neighbourhood in Istanbul, a city of 10 million people. Thirty years ago, Ümraniye was designated as an industrial area and since then has attracted migrants from all over Turkey. It is a working-class district with a large squatter segment living in illegally constructed housing. Many of these migrant women want to become integrated into city life, but face formidable problems, mainly due to the poverty of the area. In addition, it is not considered proper for women to work outside the home and their movement in public space is restricted to visits to nearby relatives and neighbours. Their identities as women are derived from their social roles as daughter, mother, wife, and so on. These roles and the women's socially important identities as good neighbours are expressed and maintained through participation in a web of exchanges of labour, information, food, money, and other goods and services. In other words, women's identity is expressed through parti-cipation in a system of generalised exchange. This ideology of exchange requires that you do things for others with no expectation of return from that individual (although it *is* expected that when you need help yourself, the family or community will provide). The important thing is to keep relations open-ended, rather than closing them through direct reciprocation. This creates a broad communal web of mutual indebtedness, which provides long-term security. The desire to pursue individual goals and individual profit, although it exists and is acted upon, generally is not openly acknowledged.

These women, when they engage in political action, are far more likely to organise situationally to improve local conditions for their family and community (to get water services, health care, education and job training) than they are to support universal principles of, say, women's rights or human rights. Many of these community women might well disagree with the idea that individual women have rights that supersede their duties to family and community. Informal or more formal frameworks for their activities may be provided by Islamic or by feminist organisations, but often the impetus comes from within the community itself, especially from the relatively more educated segment: pharmacists, nurses, schoolteachers. These women may, in turn, draw support from university-educated women from outside the community or even from a sympathetic local municipal official, creating new urban networks that supplement or even displace traditional patron–client ties.

In Ümraniye in 1989 a group of local women, nurses, teachers, housewives and other volunteers, approached the municipality for permission and funding to open a *Halkokulu* (People's School) for local women. The school was founded and staffed by amateur volunteers from inside the community. Soon after it began functioning, the state tried to close it down on the grounds that it was breeding militants. The women surrounded the building and continued holding classes in the yard. With the support of the municipality, they fought the closure in court and were eventually allowed to continue as a 'local experiment'. In the years that followed, hundreds of women attended classes and the group of organisers grew to over 200. Eighty per cent were under the age of 40; half came from families with income near the poverty level. In 1993, these women organised a two-day conference in a cinema in Ümraniye, to which they invited representatives of national feminist groups and women's centres, and university women. These women gave talks alongside local women on issues affecting Ümraniye, ranging from economic independence and the politicisation of women to the problem of domestic violence. A representative of the municipality gave the opening address. One speaker even suggested that women should vote

only for political parties that have a woman on their slate. Over 400
women participated. Women in Islamic dress sat side by side with women
in modern western dress. The conference was reported in the major
newspapers. The organisers presented the event as an attempt by migrant
women to forge an identity of their own in contradistinction to the
identity of the city woman, whom they saw as corrupt and commer-
cialised, and to the identity of élite educated women, whom they believed
looked down on their life-style, their clothing, their food and their beliefs.

The People's Schools were a means of representing the community's
needs to the state, as well as a means of obtaining resources from the
state. In this sense, the association clearly was based on an understanding
of citizenship. It was characterised by civility in the representation of
diverse views, life-styles and religious beliefs. In the later stages of the
conference the association became widely inclusionary, crossing neighbourhood as well as class lines. Eventually, the citizenship skills learned
through informal associational activities were put to use in organising
more formal representation of community needs to the state as an
officially recognised women's centre.

The schools were not organised by reference to an Islamic framework,
though other neighbourhood schools were. Both secular and religious
frameworks were prevalent in the squatter and working-class areas. The
Ümraniye association, though not explicitly Islamic, was not based on
the bourgeois secular individualist ethos that moblises élite feminist and
human-rights groups. Strategies of inclusion were based on the same
webs of reciprocity and group membership that characterise the community as a whole. In other words, this association was not based on
religion or kinship, nor did it fall into the category of 'classic' civil
society. Rather, it was a form of 'informal' reciprocal association for the
purpose of exerting pressure on the state to improve community conditions.

One aspect of many reciprocal associations that sets them apart from
what generally is conceived of as civil society is a lack of reference to
universally relevant abstract principles of individual rights and justice.
It is perhaps for this reason that such associations, if they are noticed at
all by civil society scholars in Turkey and abroad, are relegated to either
the kinship or the Islamic camp, and are thought of as weakening civil
society. Yet, it is in the particular that individual–state relations are made
manifest, whether the locus of connection is the political or the communal
arena. For Turkey, and perhaps for other Middle Eastern societies,
broadening the definition of associational life that makes up civil
society to include reciprocal associations would open up a wide range of

activities previously overlooked in the debates. Despite their short life span and limited goals, such associations have a strong foundation in the community ties from which they blossom and, as I have shown, they may form a basis for further, more formally organised, political action.

CONCLUSION

Free association within civil society should not necessarily be restricted to the basis of a contract between individuals. It can occur on the basis of shared experience, trust and the bonds of reciprocity. These are not the exclusive domain of kinship and religion, but can and do mobilise political action among friends and neighbours, in the squatter areas of Turkey as in the slums of Africa (cf. Hart 1988).

James Turner Johnson (1992) pointed out that, even if one accepts that democracy is tied to European culture and history, it *can* travel to non-western societies. What is necessary, first of all, is a democratic culture that supports a variety of social units formed by voluntary or natural relationships.

Membership in democratic societies in fact *consists* in the web of relationships formed by membership in neighborhoods, clubs, families, and as many sorts of communities as may come together, and identity as a member of a democratic society is shaped by participation in these local associations ... Moreover, in democratic societies these communities are always coming into existence and dissolving, changing and being changed in various ways, and shifting their relationships with one another.

(1992: 46–7)

This civic culture is undeniably present in Turkey and perhaps in other areas of the Middle East. Both Islam and secularism, in all of their varied manifestations, stand on the ready stool of local associations and webs of communal relationships. However, while a civic culture that supports democracy from the bottom up is necessary, it is an insufficient condition. Johnson adds that the state must be responsible for providing a top-down legal and political framework that allows and protects plurality and diversity. Middle Eastern states have had different levels of success in meeting these goals. The problem, as Johnson points out, is one with which western democracies also struggle. The question, then, for scholars of the Middle East, should not be whether civil society and democracy are compatible with Islam, but rather to what extent particular state ideologies (of which Islam is but one of many) nourish civic culture.

NOTES

1 See, for example, Goldberg, Kasaba and Migdal 1993, Norton 1995, and various special issues of the *Middle East Report* (1992) which deal with the Middle East, Islam, and democracy.
2 For example, Huntington 1993 and rejoinders.
3 For recent discussions of the problematics of combining Islam and pluralism in Turkey, see Ahmad 1991; Kazancigil 1991; and Lewis 1994.
4 The exact attributes of civil society are the subject of much recent debate. For detailed discussions of the historical development of the concept and representations of competing views, see Cohen and Arato 1994; Seligman 1992 and Shils 1991.
5 Preliminary research was carried out in Istanbul in the summer of 1994, and was funded by the University of Nebraska at Omaha and the Institute of Turkish Studies.
6 See Harbeson, Rothchild and Chazan 1994, and Bratton 1989.
7 See, for example, Chazan 1992 and Diamond 1993.
8 Hudson (1991) points out that the Arab world is entirely absent from Diamond, Linz and Lipset 1989, a recent four-volume international survey of democracy.
9 Cohen and Arato critically discuss this and other current approaches to civil society; they argue for the inclusion of a cultural rationalisation of normative action (1994: xvii).
10 This ideology of women's place is prevalent even in western countries and affects the evaluation and effectiveness of women's political actions, despite their widespread participation in civic activities beyond the home.

REFERENCES

Ahmad, F. (1991) 'Politics and Islam in modern Turkey', *Middle Eastern Studies* 27: 3–21.
Bratton, M. (1989) 'Beyond the state: civil society and associational life in Africa' *World Politics* 41(3): 407–30.
Carapico, S. (1994) 'Proto-civil society in Yemen', paper presented at the American Political Science Association annual meeting, New York, September.
Chazan, N. (1992) 'Africa's democratic challenge: strengthening civil society and the state', *World Policy Journal* 9(2): 279–307.
Cohen, J. L. and Arato, A. (1994) *Civil Society and Political Theory*, Cambridge, Mass.: MIT Press.
Diamond, L. (1993) 'Civil society and the development of democracy: some international perspectives and lessons', paper presented at the workshop 'Civil Society and Democracy: International and African Perspectives', Goree Institute, Dakar, Senegal, March.
Diamond, L., Linz, J. J. and Lipset, S. M. (eds) (1989) *Democracy in Developing Countries*, Boulder, Colo.: Lynne Rienner.
Goldberg, E., Kasaba, R. and Migdal, J. (eds) (1993) *Rules and Rights in the*

Middle East: Democracy, Law and Society, Seattle: University of Washington Press.

Göle, N. (1991) *Modern Mahrem*, Istanbul: Metis.

—— (1996) 'Authoritarian secularism and Islamist politics: the case of Turkey', in A.R. Norton (ed.), *Civil Society in the Middle East*, vol. 2. Leiden: E. J. Brill, pp. 17–43.

Harbeson, J. W., Rothchild, D. and Chazan, N. (eds) (1994) *Civil Society and the State in Africa*, Boulder, Colo.: Lynne Rienner.

Hart, K. (1988) 'Kinship, contract and trust: the economic organisation of migrants in an African city slum', in D. Gambetta (ed.), *Trust: Making and Breaking Cooperative Relations*, New York: Basil Blackwell, pp. 176–93.

Hudson, M. (1991) 'After the Gulf War: prospects for democratisation in the Arab world', *Middle East Journal* 45: 407–26.

Huntington, S. (1993) 'Clash of civilizations', *Foreign Affairs* 72(3): 22–49.

Ilyasoğlu, A. (1994) *Örtülü Kimlik*, Istanbul: Metis.

Johnson, J. T. (1992) 'Does democracy "travel"? Some thoughts on democracy and its cultural context', *Ethics and International Affairs* 6: 41–55.

Kazancigil, A. (1991) 'Democracy in Muslim lands: Turkey in comparative perspective', *International Social Science Journal* 128: 343–60.

Lewis, B. (1994) 'Why Turkey is the only Muslim democracy', *Middle East Quarterly* 1(1): 41–9.

Newman, B. (1994) 'Turning eastwards: Islamic party's gains in Istanbul stir fears of a radical Turkey', *Wall Street Journal*, 12 September.

Norton, A. R. (1993a) 'Inclusion can deflate Islamic populism', *New Perspectives Quarterly* 20: 10–11.

—— (1993b), 'The future of civil society in the Middle East', *Middle East Journal* 47(2): 205–16.

—— (ed.) (1995) *Civil Society in the Middle East*, vol. 1, Leiden: E. J. Brill.

Seligman, A. (1992) *The Idea of Civil Society*, New York: The Free Press.

Shils, E. (1991) 'The virtue of civil society', *Government and Opposition* 26(1): 3–20.

Toprak, B. (1996) 'Civil society in Turkey', in A. R. Norton, (ed.), *Civil Society in the Middle East*, vol. 2, Leiden: E. J. Brill, pp. 87–118.

Waylen, G. (1994) 'Women and democratization: conceptualizing gender relations in transition politics', *World Politics* 46: 327–54.

Chapter 8

Gender, state and civil society in Jordan and Syria

Annika Rabo

STATE, GENDER AND CIVIL SOCIETY

In the Middle East, as elsewhere, state power is to some extent dependent on the definition of gender roles. In this chapter, I will draw on examples from Syria and Jordan to show how this partial dependency creates a space in which both men and women can use symbolic manifestations of (mainly) female gender identity to contest the state's definition of 'private' and 'public' spheres.[1] This allows them to contest state power. Ideas of civil society are, therefore, not gender-neutral but gendered.

The impact of the state on the lives of citizens in the Middle East is widely recognised both inside and outside the region. This impact is usually the starting point for discussions about the relation between state and non-state structures. However, recent analyses tend to be macro-oriented and show little concern for how citizens perceive and react to the ideology and practices of representatives of the state. There is still too little analysis of the interface between citizens as living people and state apparatuses.[2] Furthermore, there is still very little interest in how gender relations are affected by state policies and state influence, or in how gender relations and gender ideologies in society-at-large affect the state apparatus. It is, of course, no coincidence that studies of gender relations are still very much the domain of female researchers, who study other women (often from a grass-roots perspective), while macro-level studies of state and civil society are still mainly the domain of male researchers, who are, in reality, studying other men. Both researchers studying and analysing the state and power-holders in state apparatuses tend to assume that the state is gender-neutral, even though, when we mentally imagine a citizen anywhere in the world, we see a man.[3] Citizens 'at home', however, can be imagined as either men or women. The 'private life' of citizens is seldom considered in a gender perspective, but rather as a domain in which men and women do their 'private' things. There is still little analytical interest in how profoundly these 'private' things are connected to – both influencing and influenced by – the state. The apparent ubiquity and 'naturalness' of the state (and, concomitantly, of something outside the state) prevents us from seeing how such naturalness influences gendered identities. There is also little interest in how the development and penetration of state agencies into the daily lives of gendered citizens affects ways of culturally constructing categories such as state and civil society, public and private, and male and female. The very concept of civil society hovers uncomfortably between diverse cultural ideas about 'public' and 'private'. By focusing on the gendered state and gendered civil society, we can gain insights of *general* theoretical value. An analysis of the relation between the state apparatus and civil society in Syria and Jordan, for example, necessitates a focus on gender, since ideas about 'good' men and women are important symbols in political struggles.

In much of the earlier anthropological and sociological literature, 'women' in general, and Middle Eastern women in particular, were thought to 'belong to' the private sphere.[4] Such analyses stressed that, especially in sex-segregated societies, the physical control of women is crucial to ensure the control of their sexuality and reproduction. The debate about 'private' women and 'public' men in the Middle East (or universally) proceeds with reference to women's role in childbirth and child-rearing (cf. Rosaldo and Lamphere 1974). These simple male/ female, public/private, domination/subjugation dichotomies have been often criticised.[5] Here, I shall draw on four basic arguments from these critiques. First, it is important to distinguish between emic and etic understandings. Second, one must recognise that emic definitions are highly variable. Third, it is crucial to differentiate between 'real' flesh-and-blood women, and women-as-symbols (e.g. of family honour). Fourth, it is important to realise that ideas about the public and the private spheres are historically rooted. In the west (and now elsewhere), there is a 'private sphere' *because* there is a 'public' one.

In recent debates about civil society, certain other aspects are closely related to this neglect of gender. First, civil society is often perceived as including only 'nice' voluntary associations outside state repression. Second, 'public' and 'private' are treated as concepts that lack historical moorings. These assumptions are both androcentric and ethnocentric. We should be very careful not to create a dichotomy between state and society in which the state is simply a locus of repression. Instead we should look at the interdependencies between state and civil society, and recently a number of scholars analysing the second and third worlds have stressed that 'more' civil society does not automatically lead to democracy and development.[6]

Are we better off not even trying to pinpoint a 'civil society'? Perhaps instead we should make greater efforts to analyse the state? Giddens (1985: 21–2) claims that the concept of civil society is too fraught with ambiguity to be useful. At the same time he follows Hegel in arguing that 'civil society' is an integral part of the development of the modern state. In a fully developed modern state, 'civil society' in a sense disappears (*ibid.*). Institutions outside the reach of state administration are nevertheless in a sense absorbed by the state. Following Giddens, I argue that such institutions should not be characterised as 'remnants' or as the 'authentic' social life of a society. Any notion of civil society is coloured by notions and understandings of the state, and issues concerning the public and private spheres, and how notions of 'family' act as links between them, are a central case in point.

In the Middle East, there is growing interest among scholars and political activists in delineating 'civil society'. Western scholars analysing Middle Eastern history or politics are also using the concept. Sadowski (1993: 14) links this new interest to general concerns about the state and democracy in the region. These current western trends, he argues, lean heavily on traditional Orientalism. In this tradition, the Orient, the Middle East, and the Islamic world are always shown to be *lacking* some basic ingredient for a happy marriage between the rulers and the ruled. Sometimes the state is too weak, sometimes it is too strong. Sometimes 'social groups' are too strong or too autonomous, sometimes it is the other way around. Historical 'facts' are applied haphazardly to 'prove' the long continuity of unjust rule and the deeply rooted tradition of Oriental despotism.[7] Traditional Orientalism has come under strong academic attack in the past few decades (see Asad 1975; Said 1978; Turner 1978); but now it seems that a strong group of neo-Orientalists is surging forward (Sadowski 1993: 18). Conceptual tools change depending on the current reading of political forces, but the underlying premises remain the same. For many western scholars, it seems to be vital to locate a specific 'otherness' in which a constructed west can be mirrored in all its glory. Today, more than ever, this 'other' is the Islamic world.[8]

Within the Middle East, the context of debates about civil society directed at indigenous audiences is obviously different. According to Zubaida (1992: 4–5), the Egyptian debate about civil society can be characterised in terms of two diverging understandings. The first is represented by secular-liberal intellectuals, who see civil society as necessary to strengthen democracy in the region. In their view, civil society is confined to voluntary associations, while both state agencies and primordial associations (family, tribes, etc.) are regarded as authoritarian and coercive. The other position is represented by thinkers who see civil society as 'an informal network of relationships' (*ibid.*); these thinkers often represent Islamic-communal ideologies. Representatives of both groups of intellectuals are very critical of the state, which they see not only as stifling and corrupt but also as detrimental to economic development. Both camps, therefore, see the promotion of 'more' civil society as a means to further specific political and economic interests.

Most contemporary Middle Eastern states have a short history. It must be remembered, however, that large parts of the region have been incorporated into state structures for millennia. Urban traditions are long, particularly when compared to Northern Europe, and urban dwellers have clearly been religiously and politically central to the Middle Eastern state. Both inside and outside the region there is a tendency to overemphasise the rural, 'tribal' character of the historical Middle East, and to forget that there was a constant flow between urban society, rural settled society, and nomadic society.[9] Historically, however, one can characterise these early states as peripheral to the lives of the majority of the population living within their borders. People were left more or less alone, as long as they paid taxes or tribute (see Zubaida 1989). Religious orders, urban guilds, and informal residential organisations were very common in the Middle Ages (Ibn Battuta 1929; Lapidus 1967). Urban classes in the Middle East, however, did not develop in the same direction as their counterparts in Europe.[10] With the direct or indirect impact of colonialism, the rather loose relationship between rulers and ruled changed. With the emergence of new independent nation-states, it changed even more. Today, men and women all over the Middle East live lives that differ enormously from those of their grandparents, parents, or even older siblings. The scope and scale of state interventions have profoundly affected people as citizens. Today, they are also being affected by drastic cut-backs in state expenditures in many countries.

Contemporary Middle Eastern states vary greatly, as do the economic and political resources of their citizens. The place where you were born and the passport you carry (or cannot carry) is of the utmost importance. Within each nation-state, class differences and ethnic or religious differences have also taken on new dimensions. Citizenship, as it was conceived in the west, is based on a male individual. However, in the third world (including the Middle East), personhood is deeply embedded in 'communities, families, in ethnic, racial, or other social groupings' (Joseph 1992: 23). This has a profound impact on gender relations, since the very idea of a civil society in the west is based on 'a fraternity, not a sorority, and not a family' (*ibid.*). In spite of all the regional political and economic variation, women (and/or the family) have been and are still used to represent symbolically both the progress and cultural tradition of societies throughout the Middle East. The struggle for power in new states continues to be expressed through a discourse in which women are important symbols.

Laws on personal status are extremely interesting from a gender perspective. They can be regarded as a symbolic intersection or link between ideas about gendered personhood and moralities. Personal status laws in the Middle East regulate marriage, divorce, custody of children, and inheritance. Such laws are obviously a very important public statement about how power-holders in each state order relations between men and women, and how they believe the ideal family should be constituted. These laws are, in effect, public manifestations of 'private' issues. It is important to stress that contemporary laws are not remnants of early Islamic periods. In many countries the laws have only recently been codified, after great political struggle. In most countries, the codification and systematisation of personal laws started during the colonial period. This legal work was part of building a centralised state. At the same time, it was a symbolically important way for men involved in power struggles to underline their commitment to 'authentic' Islamic values. Personal status laws were perhaps the most important locus of a (constructed) cultural tradition.[11] The legal status of Middle Eastern women differs significantly from that of men in personal status laws.[12] Hence, women are regarded by officials in legal institutions as 'different' from men with respect to rights and obligations in the 'private' sphere.

In some Middle Eastern states, like Kuwait, Morocco or Saudi Arabia, educational policies and employment opportunities firmly underline the belief that men and women have *different* roles to play, and that the natural order of society is one in which fathers, brothers and husbands are responsible for the conduct of their daughters, sisters and wives. This is a *patriarchy* fostered and enhanced by the state. Here, ideas about a 'private sphere' (*hayaat el khaas* 'private life') which is separated and radically different from those about a 'public sphere' (*qata'a/hayaat el 'am* 'public sector/life') are cultivated directly or indirectly by power-holders.

In other states, such as Iraq, Syria or Tunisia, suffrage, educational policies or employment opportunities are used to stress the inherent *similarity* between men and women. Here, the dichotomy between public and private receives less official emphasis, and there is a great discrepancy between the content of personal status laws and political rhetoric. In official discourse there is often talk about the need to 'modernise' society, and women are said to have an important role in this process. Citizens are told that men and women, side by side, should build a new and developed nation for the good of all. However this does not imply equality: for radical nationalists in the Middle East who favoured *state feminism*, the seclusion of women had to be abolished because secluded women were a 'wasted national resource', not because they had equal rights (Kandiyoti 1991: 10).

GENDER AND THE MODERN STATE IN SYRIA AND JORDAN

At the beginning of the First World War, the eastern Mediterranean was still more or less part of the Ottoman Empire. During the war, the British enlisted Arab support against 'Turkish' (i.e. Ottoman) domination. In return, Arab leaders were promised national independence in a large Arab territory after the war.[13] These leaders wanted to build a specifically Arab nation, as opposed to a multi-ethnic Islamic empire. After the war, however, the region was divided and controlled by Great Britain and France. During the interwar years, the policies of the two great powers succeeded in forming both massive pan-Arab sentiments and more limited 'national' feelings. On the one hand, the opposition to artificial boundaries set by the great powers formed the basis for a feeling of shared Arab political destiny. On the other hand, Syria, Jordan, Lebanon, Palestine and Iraq were in a sense created by the European powers. With the political boundaries complemented by slowly emerging differences in administrative, economic and educational policies in each of the so-called 'mandates', the artificiality of these political units was transformed over the years into an apparent naturalness.

Syria was administered by France during the interwar years, and became independent after the Second World War.[14] French administration had, to some extent, created a national bureaucratic structure, but the population was far from integrated into a nation-state. The French manipulated cleavages between different ethnic and religious groups, who still had very little contact with one another. The rich and better educated took political control after independence. However, political life was lively, not to say chaotic, with *coups* and counter-*coups*.[15] Effective nation-state building did not start until 1963, with the *coup* that brought the Ba'th Party to power. At the time of the take-over, the party was small and had a very limited political base, but it soon came to dominate political life in Syria. It is a pan-Arab socialist party which sees itself both as a vanguard force leading the people, and as a party with historical responsibility to control the state for the benefit of the people. According to Ba'th ideology, social and economic differences will wither away and disappear under party rule. Through educational, distributional and political measures, the party has aimed at abolishing traditional institutions which it defines as 'feudal, tribal and patriarchal'.

The economic ideology of the Ba'th Party asserts that the natural resources of a country belong to its people and should be administered by the state. Thus, large-scale nationalisation campaigns, as well as land reform and the redistribution of land to poor peasants, were implemented. Syria was basically an agricultural country, and the state controlled (and still controls) prices on major crops. The state has encouraged agricultural cooperatives and made large-scale investments in agriculture and industry. The centre controls most important economic and political decisions, and Syria is often characterised as a 'planning state' much like the states of the former eastern bloc. However, in the last few years, new 'open-door policies' and economic liberalisation have been implemented.

During recent decades, the Ba'th Party has built a very strong state apparatus, dominated by the party. The party is commonly equated with the state. Ba'th membership has increased dramatically, and now is mandatory for employment in most of the state sector. The public sector is the motor of the economy, and an enormous number of people are employed as civil servants of various sorts. Ba'th educational policies have made Syrians not only literate, but also relatively well educated, and for decades the state guaranteed employment after a certain level of education. This policy has been changed, but formal education is still a right and duty for all citizens. Ba'th ideology is an integral part of the curriculum in all Syrian schools and universities. The party also dominates so-called popular organisations (e.g. the Women's Union, the Students' Organisation, and the Peasants' Union) and all trade unions. From this point of view, it is clear that 'civil society', in terms of voluntary non-governmental organisations, hardly exists in Syria.

During the last decades, state (i.e. Ba'th) policies have affected Syrian women in a number of ways. Women and men, *as citizens*, are constitutionally equal and have the same (few) basic rights and (many) obligations. Six years of elementary education is mandatory for both boys and girls. Jobs in the state sector have been distributed to both men and women. Women in the state sector have the right to three months' paid maternity leave. There are also state-supported day-care centres. Girls participate in basic military training while in school, but are not enlisted in the regular army. Since independence, both men and women have the right and duty to vote.

In party rhetoric, both men and women are 'cadres' in the struggle to build a new and better society. This rhetoric is morally charged, and juxtaposes the 'good' future against the 'evil' past. 'Traditional' gender ideologies are decried as the remnants of a patriarchal order which the party strives to eliminate. In this rhetoric, kinship links are seen to foster a kind of solidarity which threatens the progress of society. The organisation of people into clans, tribes or large families is regarded as 'feudal', and a threat to the nation.[16] Kin-based ideologies in the Middle East stress the different but complementary roles of men and women, and underline the need to control the reproductive capacity of women for the sake of the kin group. The locus of authority is the *pater inter pares*: a family patriarch or a *sheikh*. Women are not singled out in party literature as victims of 'feudalistic social relations'. The official rhetoric is directed more generally at oppression through tradition. But study groups for adult women, which are organised by the Ba'th-controlled Women's Union, are seen by the party as an important instrument to train women to 'rid themselves of traditional attitudes'. The rhetoric employed by the party cadres is vague and ambiguous. Women are portrayed as both victims of traditional attitudes and, when they cling to family bonds instead of embracing the progressive ideas of the party, as among those who reproduce such attitudes.

Syrian women are very important to the economy and are prominent as public employees. In most regions, rural women form the backbone of the labour force. Young and middle-aged urban woman are employed and can expect to continue their employment after marriage and child-birth. Today, it is possible for educated employees to quit public employment, but a decade ago, this was extremely difficult. The public sector employed both men and women and tied them closely to the state. Formal employment bonds became legally very tight and in a sense they superseded the legal bonds of the family unit. This, of course, has enormous consequences for all Syrians, but especially for women, who work whilst still expected to put their families first. As in so many other countries, women in Syria are thus squeezed between the ideal of the good woman and that of the good employee or worker.

Women today are represented in most professions. Syrian women have been encouraged to take up medicine, pharmacy and engineering. They have an employment profile closer to that of women in the former eastern bloc than to that of women in Western Europe. Women hold about one quarter of the seats in parliament, and there is one female minister (the minister of culture).[17] Most of these women were hand-picked by the party and would probably not have won their seats without heavy backing.[18] Syria can in this way be said to practise 'state feminism'.

Reactions to state feminism have been mixed. Many young educated women consider their lives to be better than that of their mothers. They can read and write, they 'know' more, and they have more 'rights'. They stress that 'progress' has been made. Yet these woman also often complain about the compounded economic pressures under which they live. The new post-Ba'th generation has new expectations. Young women want to choose their own spouse, and to live alone with him and their children. The cost of living, however, puts great pressures on young couples. Two salaries are hardly enough to make ends meet for many urban couples employed in the public sector. Furthermore, women are still unevenly burdened with housework and child-rearing. They often claim that relationships within the family are full of stress. In some rural areas, women in agricultural production work much harder today than they did a generation ago. Men often leave the countryside to seek employment as casual workers in towns or in foreign countries, leaving women with extensive economic responsibilities.

Syrian women are visible in most areas of life, yet their contribution to production and reproduction is not reflected in state political representation, authority or influence. 'State feminism' has, in fact, increased Syrian women's economic burdens. These women complain that the promises of 'modernity' have not been fulfilled, and that a woman's work increases every day. They react to the new 'open-door' economic policy in different ways. In the last few years, agricultural prices have increased and women in some rural areas say that the family economy has improved. The situation is different for many employed urban women. They have been raised to have urban middle-class tastes and aspirations, and now they are increasingly faced with economic difficulties. Economic segregation is increasing in Syria, and urban men are less and less inclined to seek work in the public sector.

The modern history of Jordan differs radically from that of Syria.[19] Syria became a republic under the French mandate and later became a one-party state. Jordan (originally Transjordan) became a hereditary kingdom under British rule. King Abdallah was imported to the sparsely populated mandate. His claim to Jordan was based on his descent from the prophet Muhammad and his father's involvement in the struggle against the Ottoman Empire. The king was totally dependent on British economic support, which he used to build a political structure in which he emulated 'traditional' Arab leadership qualities. He was personally accessible and he bolstered the rule of tribal *sheikh*s. Compared to Syria, Jordan was much more rural. The king therefore encouraged migrants (mainly from Syria and Palestine) to come to Jordan and expand urban activities. King Abdallah's position was precarious. He had pan-Arab ambitions of his own (particularly with regard to Palestine), yet he was constrained by and dependent on the British. Moreover, he was not particularly popular either inside or outside the mandate. His popularity was further damaged after the occupation of the West Bank of Palestine and its incorporation into Jordan during the war against Israel in 1948. Abdallah was murdered in 1951, and was succeeded in 1952 by his grandson Hussein, the present king. In spite of many difficulties, Hussein has continued to build Jordan as a nation-state. He is a heroic figure in many ways – he actively portrays himself as such – and has survived a number of attempts on his life.[20] In 1970, Jordan was racked by civil war when Palestinian guerrillas tried to oust the king. The army crushed the attempt, and Palestinian organisations were later banned in Jordan. During the 1970s and 1980s, only Islamic associations were allowed to organise openly.

Compared to Syria, Jordan is a small country poor in natural resources. Jordan's economic survival has been difficult. When Palestinian refugees poured into the West Bank in 1948, and into Jordan proper after the Israeli occupation of the West Bank in 1967, Jordan survived only thanks to the economic assistance of Britain, the United States, and (later) oil-rich Arab countries. After the war against Iraq in 1991, roughly 300,000 Palestinians and Jordanians returned to Jordan from Kuwait. This has put severe strain on the Jordanian economy. Not only have demands on infrastructure and social services increased, but national earnings from expatriate workers have decreased dramatically. These earnings from migrant workers were Jordan's major source of foreign-currency earnings, and large sections of Jordanian society had become accustomed to this 'oil economy'.

In the west, Syria is still portrayed as a sinister socialist state with strong anti-western political sentiments. Jordan, on the other hand, has long been considered an ally of the west and a propagator of 'market values'. Jordanians in official positions stress that free enterprise is necessary to stimulate economic growth. Yet, in fact, the strength and growth of private enterprise has always depended on state policies and the patronage of the royal house. It is the state which has promoted and nurtured a 'private' economic sector. The king and the royal family have controlled the Jordanian state apparatus in, much the same way as the Ba'th Party controls the Syrian state apparatus. Since the 1980s, however, a process of democratisation has taken place. Emergency laws have been lifted. Parties have been registered. Women are finally allowed to vote. Democratisation, like everything else in Jordan, has been instigated by the royal house. In the first free election in 1988, Islamic candidates won over a quarter of the seats and were able to form a fairly tight coalition. In the election of 1992, when political parties were allowed, the Islam-oriented parties were not quite as successful, but still formed a block to be reckoned with in parliament. The king selects the Upper House himself, and in the Lower House, a majority of members (whether or not they have an Islamic orientation) are still loyal to the king and regard the presence and stability of the royal house as a safeguard against chaos and anarchy. Most Jordanians today seem to believe that King Hussein is the best available political leader.

The Jordanian state has used its revenues to invest heavily in the public service sector. Education, for example, is seen as very important. Jordan has been very successful in getting the younger generation into a basic education that now lasts ten years. More young girls from rural areas attend school than their Syrian counterparts. Moreover, many Jordanian women continue their education at university. Female students constitute a slight majority at state universities, and a large majority at the mushrooming private colleges and universities. Jordanian families invest in foreign education for their sons, but not their daughters.[21] However Syrian women have a higher rate of employment than their Jordanian sisters. Jordanian women have not been absorbed by the state sector to the same degree that Syrian women have, nor are they subject to the same pressures to work that Syrian women have been.

In Syrian official rhetoric, women, like men, have an obligation to society through their ties to the state. This view (at least so far) has been successfully inculcated into the young. These ideas clearly originated in the notion of 'civil society' that was promulgated by ideologues from various progressive political movements during the fight for independence. In the Jordanian official view, on the other hand, women have a societal obligation through their families. Jordan, in a way, oscillates between 'state patriarchy' and 'state feminism'. In the 1970s, Jordan had to import labour due to the export of its own (mainly male) labor force. At that time, the Ministry of Labour actively tried to encourage Jordanian women into employment. These efforts were successful to a certain extent (Hijab 1988: 112), but also created ideological debates. Foreign, often non-Muslim, maids were employed in the homes of the newly employed married women. Islamic discourse presented these maids as a danger to society. Children would be brought up by alien women who were ignorant of the country's cultural and religious traditions.[22] Married women with jobs were told that they were not good mothers and that they threatened the cultural authenticity of the country. When the economic recession hit Jordan in the late 1980s, many Jordanian married women lost their jobs (as did many maids).

Islamic movements have capitalised on 'popular' sentiments and claim that women compete with 'breadwinners' if they ask for the same jobs as men. According to these movements, women should only compete among themselves in (for example) the education sector. The great majority of Jordanian first- and intermediate-level teachers are women, and the educational sector employs more women and men than any other sector. Many women also work in government bureaucracies. Up until a few years ago, it was possible for families in Jordan to survive on one salary. A married woman who worked was a sign of family poverty, unless the woman was highly educated and employed in a prestigious position. Today, it is said that almost one quarter of Jordan's population lives below minimum income levels. This, of course, has dramatic consequences for gender relations and perceptions of gender roles in daily life.

In Jordan, as in Syria, men and women officially have 'equal' value as citizens. In Jordan, the official position of women is based on the Islamic concept of 'equal but different'. Men and women are said to have different roles to perform in society. The royal house has been active not only in 'preserving' but in creating 'tribal' sentiment. The male Arab Bedouin is evoked as a cultural ideal. Hospitality, honour, independence and fierce loyalty to the group are stressed as virtues, both by the royal house and by many Jordanians. Women have honour through men, and their virtue is important to the honour of men.[23] Women are ideologically linked to the state (i.e. the royal house) as women have always been linked to their kin groups. (This is the opposite of Syrian ideology. Syrian women have not been politically mobilised by the state *as women*.) Women's organisations have not been encouraged if they are seen as 'political'. However, charitable organisations which cater to 'women's needs', (e.g. sewing, knitting and gardening for 'poor and needy women') have been instigated by middle- and upper-class women, often with royal patronage. Islamic organisations have begun to 'target' women politically in the last decade. Activities in these organisations are generally 'female' and religious training is mainly confined to 'women's matters' and family ideals (Roald 1994). For many women, however, these activities are the stepping stones to political commitment outside the kin group.

POLITICAL RHETORIC AND THE STRUGGLE OVER THE PRIVATE

It is clear from the discussion above that there are great differences in political ideology between the royal house in Jordan and the leaders of the Ba'th Party in Syria. At the same time, however, there are many similarities in how relations between rulers and ruled are formed and maintained. In both countries, the state apparatus has been of the utmost importance in carving out national identities in recent decades. Syria is a much more heterogeneous country than Jordan in terms of regional differences, urban-rural life-styles, and the number of religious and ethnic differences. Yet, Syria has become a nation. A number of people in Syria are opposed to the Ba'th Party (many of whom are in exile or in prison), and most people are sick and tired of economic mismanagement and corruption. At the same time, though, people born and bred in Syria are firmly Syrian (with some exceptions) and feel that they share a national heritage apart from and above links to the present state. Jordan is much less heterogeneous, yet its population grapples more acutely with problems of national identity. More than half of Jordan's inhabitants are of Palestinian origin and relations between the Palestinians and the royal house have been and continue to be (to put it mildly) ambivalent. King Hussein and the royal house *are* Jordan. This links the past and the future with the fate of the king. In Jordan, the metaphor of *the family* is salient in symbolically representing political power. The family is officially expressed as the basic building block of society and the state. The king is portrayed as the family father – the father of all Jordanian families, just, fair, and above reproach.[24]

In both countries – despite pan-Arab rhetoric – the goal of the political leaders controlling state resources has been to create *national citizens*. In both countries, the state apparatus has been crucial in this effort. Schools, military service, mass media, and health services link people to the state. In both countries, the political leaders have a welfare programme, and their control over political and economic resources has been crucial in the reproduction of the relation between ruler and ruled. The very ideas of 'private' and 'public' are conditioned by state involvement. In both Jordan and Syria, the public sector is the main employer of women. The public sector is, in the eyes of citizens-at-large, generally seen as 'safe' and 'protected' for women. Salaries in Syria are often lower in the public sector, but a private employer is likely to demand much more from his employees in terms of loyalty and on-duty behaviour. Many public offices and bureaucracies are used by the employees as a 'home away from home'. Visitors pass by, and employees conduct private or family business, use the facilities for private errands, and so on. The private sector is usually only thought of as 'safe' for women in cases when small family enterprises employ their own kinswomen. Thus, ideas about private and public 'spaces' do not coincide with the public and private economic sectors.

Embedded in the official Syrian rhetoric, we find the idea that the ('private') individual needs the public sector to be economically, politically and socially liberated from the family or kin group. In Jordanian political rhetoric, we find ideas about the interconnectedness of family life and the public sector's political life. Only the royal house, it is implied, can guarantee a fair balance between private and public economic and political interests. Leaders try to control political life in both countries, and to turn inhabitants into malleable and loyal citizens. From one point of view, they have been quite successful. Control over political symbols has been much harder to achieve, however. Political rhetoric is always morally charged. It deals with hopes and aspirations for a good life and a good society. It plays on emotions and on ideas about self and history. In Jordan and Syria, as in many other countries with repressive state apparatuses, political rhetoric is directed by the state. Opposition forces have few opportunities and few spaces in which to formulate alternative visions. Hence, critique of the state is usually formulated using well-known symbols, as with the multiple meanings of the female Islamic veil.

Modern Islamic female veiling has become one of the most potent moral symbols in the Middle East because it is a *public* manifestation of a 'private choice'. In many contexts, veiling signifies that women are taking on new and different political roles. It can symbolise both the locking of women into 'primordial ties' and their defiance of state political authority. It is important to differentiate between gender and gendered activities and symbols of gender, though these are often fused by men contesting for power. In 1983, women were attacked in the Damascus bazaar. They were *unveiled* by teenagers from the Ba'th-controlled youth organisation. People I talked to were all very shocked by this incident. Even young women who scorned the 'ridiculous' dress of heavily veiled women felt that this was a terrible violation. Some people predicted that there would be fights and demonstrations at the university. Christians who usually underline their more 'modern' attitude to women were angered by the fact that 'innocent (female) shoppers' had been the target of political violence. Most people I talked to linked this incident to the struggle between Ba'th and the Syrian Muslim Brotherhood.

The relationship between the secular Ba'th Party and the Syrian Muslim Brotherhood has been tense for decades. The Brotherhood organisation came to Syria from Egypt at the end of the 1940s, at the same time as the foundation of the Ba'th Party. Their constituencies have largely coincided, and their political philosophies have much in common. Before the Ba'th Party came to power – through a *coup* – the two movements did at times cooperate. At the end of the 1960s, the Brotherhood and other religious parties were banned. During the 1970s, the conflict between the Ba'th Party and the Brotherhood developed into one between *the state* and the Brotherhood. Cadres from the Brotherhood killed officers and party functionaries, and organised strikes in bazaars in various parts of Syria. The conflict escalated in 1979, and in 1982 the Syrian army attacked and killed about 30,000 people in the city of Hama. This massacre has come to have great symbolic significance for a great number of Syrians, regardless of their political views or religious/ethnic background.

Long before the emergence of modern Syria, Hama had been the seat of strong Muslim organisations. Opposition to state control and allegiance to Muslim values were fused. For decades, female veiling in Hama had been on a scale and intensity not found in other Syrian towns. Even Christian families in Hama veiled their women, as did families with allegiance to the Syrian Communist Party! In Syria, opposition to the Ba'th Party's economic policies has often emanated from traders. The bazaar quarters are usually closed and dark, and they attract many female shoppers. It is a public space under 'private' economic control.[25] Relations among large traders and small retail traders and between traders and customers are multistranded and hard for public authorities to control. Hama, with its bazaar and its veiled women, was therefore popularly seen as a no-go area for the state. Hama was firmly within the state's territory, yet it was regarded by many people inside and outside the town as 'uncontrolled'. As a social and economic space, Hama was difficult for outsiders to penetrate. When large parts of Hama – notably its city centre – were destroyed, this was a warning to all in Syria that the state was not going to tolerate opposition. During this period, many male Muslim activists were imprisoned or killed. In consequence, young women all over Syria increased their public politico-religious commitment. Young women in the streets, in offices and at the university wore modern Islamic dress with a special *hijaab* (head covering) and long coat more frequently. When women were attacked in Damascus, it was an interpreted as an attack on this increase of female public Islamic politics.

The situation was temporarily defused by President Assad, who in a rare public announcement that I heard live on national television said that elements in the youth organisation had been overexcited and had overstepped their proper role. In Syria, he stressed, dress was a matter of *'private choice'*, adding that 'customs and traditions could not be overcome by violence'. The president chose to talk about veiling as a 'private' issue. Yet, in many Syrian public spaces, veiling is forbidden.[26] Girls and boys both have to wear uniforms, and scarves covering the hair are not allowed. Female Syrian teachers can lose their jobs if they cover their hair. In many public government offices, there have been campaigns to 'convince' women not to wear a *hijaab* to work. In Syria, as in other Muslim countries, 'traditional veiling' (whether in deep black with double face veils or with a colourful headscarf) indicates class and place of origin. This is not seen either by Ba'th Party cadres or by Syrians at large as 'political' dress, but as an expression of 'customs and traditions'. These are styles that the ruling party thinks will disappear with 'progress and modernity', and which they contrast with the mandatory school uniforms. Yet, many Muslim women all over the Islamic world today discard regional and class indications in their dress, and wear the fashionable modern Islamic dress that is spreading throughout the Islamic world. This is the style of dress which is politically threatening to most regimes, because it indicates that women take a political stand in public. Hence, to Syrians, female veiling or the wearing of a headscarf today can be much more than 'custom and tradition', and is seldom seen as simply a 'private choice'. Veiling may be regarded as a clear political demonstration against the state and the Ba'th Party. By wearing modern *hijaab*, women are protesting against the current political situation. In Syria, the language of the veil is a language of silent protest. In a sense, the *hijaab* represents the *visible* site of Syrian civil society.

To some Syrians I talked to, Assad's speech and his stress on 'private choice' signalled political concessions.[27] They predicted – they were later proven right – that there would be no renewed efforts to reform the personal status law. The Ba'th Party leadership intermittently tried to put forward a secular personal status law, to make it possible, for example, for Christian women to marry Muslim men. Such a law would also make polygamy illegal and give equal inheritance to men and women. However, opposition to such reforms has been strong, even within the Ba'th Party. Assad's speech can hence be interpreted as a 'peace offering' to all those *men* who refuse to relinquish their control over women 'in private' – that is, *within the family*. Women who have been the victims of public violence could continue to be victimised by male 'private' inequalities or violence.

Islamic veiling has a different history in Jordan, where political parties were banned for decades and where 'traditional' female dress was very much associated with Palestinian national pride. All political activity in the 1980s was expressed in terms of Islam. Islamic revivalism was initially more or less supported by the state and the royal house. Today, the situation is more complex because Islamic parties attract large groups of followers, not all of whom are loyal to the king. In her study of the Muslim Brotherhood in Jordan, Roald (1994) underlines the fact that the organisation is gender-segregated both in ideology and in praxis. The leadership is strictly male, and women and men are thought to have different political needs. Women should be trained religiously and politically, but for gender-specific roles – to be good wives and mothers. Jordanian women from poor or middle-income backgrounds have, however, found new means of expressing themselves within this religiously sanctioned gender segregation. For many, the Islamic movements have given women a new kind of public freedom outside the web of family patriarchy.[28] It is within the confines of 'Islamic' dress that young women become physically mobile, verbally articulate and able to choose their own (Muslim) husbands, jobs and friends outside family control. By wearing modern Islamic dress, Jordanian women embody a 'private' sphere in public. Women who want and need to work in Jordan signal their 'good intentions' by wearing modern Islamic dress. They show that they are concerned about an Islamic life-style and that they can combine work and religion.

After the 1989 government reshuffle, the new minister of education was a staunch Islamist. He immediately tried to impose gender-segregated offices in the Ministry. Male visitors could henceforth only visit male employees, and female visitors only female employees. Many Jordanians who initially seemed happy about this new gender order later became rather upset. The minister made it impossible for 'natural and innocent' relations to be pursued at work or in schools. Fathers could not visit girls' gymnastics tournaments, for example. More and more people started to resent this imposition, in which all relations and contacts between men and women were interpreted as potentially sexual. The minister was removed after about a year.[29]

Situating women outside the 'private' has always been more ambiguous on the part of the state in Jordan than in Syria. On the one hand, the royal house needs to demonstrate a 'liberal' face to its western allies and donors and to underline for its external audiences that the state caters to all its citizens. On the other hand, the king has to rely heavily on his Islamic/Arab legitimacy and has to try to build a modern state that can be perceived as 'authentic'. One of the paradoxes of Jordan is that this symbolically very 'male' state depends heavily on the presence of women in the public sector. Female students at Jordanian universities, many of whom will become part of the state apparatus, are increasingly veiled. In Jordan, the veil has so far been a symbol of liberation from family oppression and at the same time, a symbol of (constructed) cultural authenticity.

WOMEN AND MEN IN A WORLD OF STATES

Ideas of private and public are interconnected in the Middle East just as they are in the west. They contribute to the symbolic representation of gender, as seen in the case of veiling in Jordan and Syria. In both the west and the Middle East there is a strong feeling that institutionalised politically organised violence against women (and children) is more repellent than institutionalised violence against men. Soldiers and police-men killing and beating up civilian men in situations of political conflict or war is, if not accepted, at least seen as part of the game. But, women and their offspring should not be touched. On the other hand, the beating of women inside the home is often considered a 'private' or 'family issue', both in the west and in the Middle East. The sanctity of women in 'public' has been successfully utilised in political conflicts. During the Algerian war of independence, women were used in the underground movement because they could smuggle arms and messages more easily than men could. The *intifada* caught the imagination of the world when 'defenceless' women and children fought a superior army practically bare-handed. In Jordan, it was women who demonstrated in sympathy with the Palestinian *intifada* in 1987. They were harassed less than men would have been.

Behind these conscious political manipulations of gender symbols we seldom question what real women represent in a world ordered by states. In order to be good *citizens* and good *wives and mothers*, Syrian women had to be 'prised out of backwardness'. There has been a systematic devaluation of female traditional culture in countries like Algeria, Iraq and Syria. Instead, the 'modern' woman is almost totally dependent on powerful men in the public sector for access to economic and political resources. *State feminism* in such countries is hence quite partial. Women might be encouraged to regard the state as a benefactor, and in fact it may be so for individual women. Yet women have had to take the consequences of this emancipation all alone.[30] When state feminism is regarded by many citizens as sponsored by an unpopular regime, women's organisations will be viewed with suspicion. But state feminism is, in reality, a part of a larger state patriarchy. From a gender perspective, women in a state patriarchy like Jordan inevitably become locked into the private/domestic when opposing male groups contest political power. Individual women may break out of this symbolic ordering of the world and take on roles that are generally defined as 'male', but the pattern remains the same.

In Syria, this kind of 'breaking-out' by women is officially sanctioned because it tells Syrians and the world what kind of society the state plans to build: one in which all citizens are 'productive and equal'. Many Syrian women, like women under similar conditions elsewhere, not only have a political right to what is defined (from above) as productive work, but are economically obliged to exhaust themselves. They not only create an economic surplus which is appropriated by the state, but it is they who reproduce society. The Jordanian state also tries to prise women out of 'backwardness', but with a softer and yet more patriarchal touch.

Women have had to pay, and continue to pay, a very high price for the contradictions between state patriarchy and state feminism and between what might be conceived of as state and civil society. Everywhere, the influence of the state has redefined the make-up and meaning of the family. In the Middle East, families or kin-based groups are prised open. National identities and national loyalties are actively fostered by political leaders, often at the expense of other identities and other loyalties. Both women and men are treated as children, and most citizens lack basic democratic rights. Thus, it is tempting for women to feel that overt state patriarchy will offer them more security and dignity. The attraction of state patriarchy today is that it claims to provide emotional satisfaction and cultural identity where other 'un-Islamic', 'untraditional' or 'western' models have failed. This is also the lure of most Islamic movements. These movements try to create a 'larger' civil society – a space for 'free' political and economic associations opposed to current state apparatuses. However, the overt patriarchy of contemporary states and of political movements reaching for state power shares little of the redeeming qualities of the patriarchal kin-group upon which it models itself. The patriarchal family provided economic security and emotional satisfaction within mutually interdependent gender roles. The patriarchal family order existed in societies where ideas of public and private were not symbolic spaces for political power. 'More' civil society in the contemporary Middle East could well mean increased symbolic and practical burdens for women.

NOTES

1   I have carried out fieldwork on various topics in Syria in 1978–80 and 1988; and in Jordan in 1987–88 and 1991.
2   See, for example, Luciani's otherwise excellent four-volume work (1987).
3   One notable exception is Kandiyoti 1991.
4   See Al-Qazzaz 1977 for bibliographical summaries.
5   See Moore 1988: 13–40 for a summary of these arguments.
6   Tostenson (1993: 116), for example, argues that 'profoundly undemocratic social movements' are also part of civil society in Africa. Fatton (1992: 6) stresses that civil society is constantly 'colonised' by the ruling class.
7   For an excellent example of a recent Orientalist perspective, see Vatikiotis (1987), who argues that Islam can never become democratic in the 'right' western sense.
8   Samuel Huntington is such a scholar today. He predicts (1993) that the new locus of global conflict, after the fall of the Soviet Union, will be between the west and the Islamic world.
9   Ibn Khaldoun, the famous fourteenth-century scholar, claims that only cohesive tribal groups could overturn bad governments. Yet, once in power, these tribal groups would lose their solidarity after a few generations (1978: ch. 2). Ibn Khaldoun has inspired many later theorists inside and outside the region, such as Gellner (1981: ch. 1).
10 For an interesting analysis of this difference highly relevant to current debates about civil society see Turner 1974.
11 For very interesting discussions about political struggles, personal status law and women as symbols of national identities, see Charrad 1990, Hakiki-Talahite 1991, Mayer 1991 and Kandiyoti 1991.
12 This difference varies: for example, it is small in Tunisia but much greater in Morocco.
13 For a short historical summary, see Yapp 1987: chs. 4–6.
14 Good introductions to Syria's modern political history include Seale (1956) and Petran (1972).
15 The majority of the Syrian population was born after the take-over by the Ba'th Party and the living 'collective memory' of the pre-Ba'th years is probably fading. However, older people stress the importance of transmitting the memory of the 1950s, which was a decade of political conflict, but also a decade of great hopes for democracy. Compared with today's Middle East, this decade now appears as a period in which 'civil society' had more political influence.
16 'Feudal' relations (in the Ba'th sense) are none the less prevalent in Syria, and the political leadership is itself a prime example of a tightly knit kin-based group. We should not see this as a 'remnant' of 'traditionalism', as

Syrian political opponents are prone to do, but as a highly modern and contemporary use of ethnic and kin ties.

17 The minister of culture has held this position for more than fifteen years. This ministry is not regarded either officially or popularly as particularly 'female', and the minister is not a 'token woman'. I have heard her described as a 'very tough lady' who could get any ministry she chose, but who has particular interests in cultural affairs. However, some ministries are more 'female' than others – notably the Ministry of Education and Ministry of Planning.

18 All candidates are, in a sense, hand-picked by the party leadership, but women are in a much more ambiguous position than men. Opponents speak of these women in a very denigrating way. Men imply that they have made a political career at the expense of their virtue. See the discussion below.

19 Day 1986 provides an introduction to Jordan's political history.

20 See Lunt 1990 for a biography of King Hussein.

21 In Syria the expansion of state universities made them much more accessible to both male and female students. In Jordan, it is very difficult and costly to gain admission to a state university. Families are reluctant to send their daughters to study abroad alone, either to other Arab countries or to the west. However, girls are very ambitious and, in general, have better grades than boys (see Rabo 1992; Roald 1994).

22 There were 12,000 maids from Sri Lanka alone in Jordan in 1985 (Hijab 1988: 113). Maids also come from the Philippines. They were concentrated in the well-off quarters of the capital. Hence, criticising these maids could be interpreted as a political critique of the 'foreign' life-style of the wealthier strata.

23 Jordan is not a tribal Bedouin society. Most Jordanians now live in urban centres, and the pastoral sector is not economically significant. The royal house is 'urban' with roots in Mecca. The tribal idiom is, however, very important in Jordan (cf. Layne 1989). Tribal relations and virtues are regarded by many as 'Jordanian', rather than Palestinian, characteristics.

24 King Hussein is now married to his fourth wife. Queen Noor is American and is *never* portrayed as a mother figure. The king was not a father figure when he succeeded to the throne because he was only 18 years old. It is with age that he can use the patina of maturity. His wife is perhaps twenty years his junior. King Hussein is the father of twelve children. He is affectionately called *Abu Abdallah* ('father of Abdallah') in laudatory poems, songs and 'spontaneous' popular outbursts. The custom of naming adults after their oldest son (*Abu X* or *Umm X*) is prevalent throughout the Middle East. Political leaders, especially Palestinian ones, often have an *Abu- nom de guerre*. Yassir Arafat is called *Abu Ammar* although he is not the father of Ammar.

Along similar lines, there have been efforts in Syria to 'humanise' the distant President Assad by utilising the image of a father. President Assad is sometimes called *Abu Sleiman*, which is not the name of his eldest son. Assad is, however, called by his *Abu-* name much less frequently than is King Hussein. In laudatory poems, Hafez Assad is more often simply called *Ya Hafez* ('Oh Hafez'). Both *Abu-* name and 'real' first-name usages indicate a lack of distance between the speaker and the leader. An *Abu-* name usage also indicates patriarchal ideas. Since there are so few female political leaders, we have no comparable data on women. It may be noted that the most famous singer in the Middle East, the late *Umm Kalthoum*, was childless – that is, she was not the mother of Kalthoum.

25 In the language of both men and women, darkness and lack of control are symbols of femininity, while order and penetration are symbols of masculinity.

26 According to my female urban Syrian informants, the wearing of *hijaab* in schools has increased in the 1990s. The issue of the veil is one of the most debated inside and outside the region. For an excellent summary of the issues, see Hijab 1988: 50–62.

27 Syrians with interests in politics are very skilful in making elaborate interpretations of public statements. Syrians of all political convictions agree that political information should never be simply interpreted at face value; it must always be analysed carefully for more complex meanings.

28 This is not to deny the patriarchal order of Islamic movements in Jordan. Roald (1994) discusses the key word *usra* ('family') in the context of the Muslim Brotherhood. The *usra* is the basic unit of the organisation, patterned on the family, in which mutural trust and responsibility are encouraged. The Brotherhood *usra* is usually exclusively male.

29 Newspapers, which at that time were becoming less censored, were full of debates about this issue. It is, of course, very difficult to assess 'true' public opinion, but I think that debates such as this enabled many Jordanians to realise the stakes of political democracy.

30 See Hakiki-Talahite 1991 for further discussion of the Algerian case, which is similar to the Syrian in many ways.

REFERENCES

Al-Quazzaz, A. (1977) *Women in the Middle East and North Africa: An Annotated bibliography*, Austin, Tex.: University of Texas Press.
Asad, T. (1975) 'Two European images of non-European rule', in T. Asad (ed.), *Anthropology and the Colonial Encounter*, London: Ithaca Press, pp. 103–18.
Charrad, M. (1990) 'State and gender in the Maghrib,' *Middle East Report* 163: 19–23.
Day, A. R. (1986) *East Bank – West Bank*, New York: Council on Foreign Relations, Inc.
Fatton, R. (1992) *Predatory Rule: State and Civil Society in Africa*, Boulder, Colo.: Lynne Rienner Publishers.
Gellner, E. (1981) *Muslim Society*, Cambridge: Cambridge University Press.
Giddens, A. (1985) *The Nation-State and Violence*, Cambridge: Polity Press.
Hakiki-Talahite, F. (1991) 'Sous le voile ... les femmes,' *Les Cahiers de l'orient* 23: 123–42.
Hijab, N. (1988) *Womenpower: The Arab Debate on Women at Work*, Cambridge: Cambridge University Press.
Huntington, S. (1993) 'Clash of civilizations', *Foreign Affairs* 72(3): 22–49.
Ibn Battuta (1929) *Travels in Asia and Africa 1325–1354*, London: Routledge and Kegan Paul.

Ibn Khaldoun (1978) *The Muqaddimah*, London: Routledge.

Joseph, S. (1993) 'Gender and civil society', *Middle East Report* 183: 22–6.

Kandiyoti, D. (ed.) (1991) *Women, Islam, and the State*, London: Macmillan.

Lapidus, I. (1967) *Muslim Cities in the Later Middle Ages*, Cambridge, Mass.: Harvard University Press.

Layne, L. (1989) 'The dialogics of tribal self-representation in Jordan', *American Ethnologist* 16(1): 24–39.

Luciani, G. (ed.) (1987) *Nation, State, and Integration in the Arab World*, Rome: Instituto Affari Internazionale.

Lunt, J. (1990) *Hussein of Jordan*, London: Fontana.

Mayer, A. (1991) 'Personal status laws in North Africa: a comparative assessment', paper given at the Department of Legal Studies, Wharton School of Business, University of Pennsylvania.

Moore, H. (1988) *Feminism and Anthropology*, Cambridge: Polity Press.

Petran, T. (1972) *Syria*, London: Ernest Benn Ltd.

Rabo, A. (1992) 'The value of education in Jordan and Syria', in *Kam-ap or Take-off: Local Notions of Development*, Stockholm: Stockholm Studies in Social Anthropology and Almqvist and Wiksell International, pp. 98–122.

Roald, A.-S. (1994) *Tarbiya: Education and Politics in Islamic Movements in Jordan and Malaysia*, Stockholm: Almqvist and Wiksell International.

Rosaldo, M. and Lamphere, L. (eds) (1974) *Woman, Culture, and Society*, Stanford, Calif.: Stanford University Press.

Sadowski, Y. (1993) 'The new orientalism and the democracy debate', *Middle East Report* 183: 14–21.

Said, E. (1978) *Orientalism*, London: Routledge and Kegan Paul.

Seale, P. (1956) *The Struggle for Syria*, London: I. B. Taurus.

Tostensen, A. (1993) 'The ambiguity of civil society in the democratisation process', in A. Ofstad and A Wiig (eds), *Development Theory: Recent Trends*, Bergen: Chr. Michelsen Institute, pp. 106–18.

Turner, B. (1974) *Weber and Islam*, London: Routledge and Kegan Paul.

—— (1978) *Marx and the End of Orientalism*, London: George Allen and Unwin.

Vatikiotis, P. (1987) *Islam and the State*, London: Croom Helm.

Yapp, M. (1987) *The Making of the Modern Near East 1792–1923*, London: Longman.

Zubaida, S. (1989) *Islam, the People and the State*, London: Routledge.

—— (1992) 'Islam, the state, and democracy,' *Middle East Report* 17: 4–10.

Chapter 9

The deployment of civil energy in Indonesia

Assessment of an authentic solution

Leo Schmit

In Indonesia, the capacity to formulate and carry out development policies resulting in technological progress and economic growth tends to be seen as more important than the capacity to create open polities endowed with the benefits and virtues of Euro-American civil society. The Indonesian mode of governance is characterised by centralised authoritarian institutions, technocratic polities, diffuse class distinctions, and the high value attached to personal leadership, political consensus, religious morality and collective welfare. Thus, although there is a developing civil society in Indonesia, it does not take the forms familiar to European and American citizens. The right of political opposition and the liberal-individualist notion of civil participation are seen as incompatible with Indonesian political culture. Instead, over the last twenty-five years a regime of depoliticisation of civil life based upon the political leadership of President Soeharto, the active involvement of the military in societal affairs, and a state ideology known as *Pancasila*, has been a viable solution in this country. Other contributing factors have been Indonesia's position as a bridgehead against communism; a pragmatic approach to foreign and Sino-Indonesian corporate business investments; a massive flow of oil and gas export revenues; and a strong sense of commitment to development objectives, with a concomitant allocation of funds and some exposure to external influence.

When the sixth cabinet of President Soeharto was installed in 1993, Indonesia had to choose between three broad options (Bastin, Schmit and Schulte Nordholt 1993). The first was to keep on working towards Indonesian solutions appropriate to global circumstances in the 1990s. This would imply a strategy of containing civil energy by developing and deploying human resources for the sake of economic progress, industrialisation and international prestige. The second option was to adopt foreign standards of governance based on the premises of individual freedom and human rights. This would imply releasing flows of civil energy along unknown lines and exposing the nation to international interference. The third option was to intensify the military apparatus's security approach.

The military option was not a real option, but it would be the probable consequence of the failure of either of the two other options. It could not be the preferred option, because it implied going against the tide of globalisation and frustrating Indonesia's ambition to engage in the world market as an emergent industrial nation. Paradoxically, the security approach would also entail a high risk of internal strife and regional fragmentation, damaging the country's international reputation.

The second option, 'democracy' along European or American lines, was associated with Indonesia's traumatic experience of political strife in the 1950s and 1960s. The regime was also aware of the futility of trying to repeat a foreign historical experience, no matter how valuable, and instead it applied a reverse Orientalism. It appealed to Indonesian values in order to justify a security approach to civil matters, asserting that the complexities of democracy in the modern world were not compatible with traditional Indonesian forms. In 1994, this assertion implied the repression of independent trade unions, the closure of periodicals, and the supervision of private organisations.

An emphasis on the first option is expected to enable those in power to stay there and to pursue a vision of the nation as an emergent technological and industrial force. The prospect of becoming an industrial nation capable of competing on the world market appeals to a sense of national pride that can be reconciled with Islamic religious values. By means of this mode of governance, Indonesia also expects to become an example to other developing nations. Finally, such an attempt is not discordant with thinking in international development agencies, which stresses the role of authentic institutions and values in improving the governance capacities of developing countries.

Consequently, the Indonesian New Order regime is putting forward a dual model of civil society in which economic activity is decentralised and diffuse, while political power is concentrated in the hands of a technocratic élite. The first element of this strategy is the substitution of economic participation for political participation, in accordance with the principle of economic democracy. Tens of millions of job-seekers are encouraged to become economically active as self-employed individuals and as small entrepreneurs. To facilitate their efforts the New Order regime has made a concerted effort to restructure the economy at the expense of conglomerate business interests. The second element of the

Indonesian governance strategy is the substitution of a nationalist-technocratic 'politics of expertise' for politics based on party interests or political opposition. Within Indonesia's 'national-conference' model of policy-making, which is based on the principle of consensus, experts and intellectuals have ample opportunity to make recommendations. Competition among these experts is based on problem-solving capacities and budget allocations, not on the acquisition of popular support. These principles of political consensus and economic democracy are grounded in the national *Pancasila* ideology, a set of basic tenets to which all Indonesian citizens are required to adhere.[1]

Basically, two core assumptions underlie the Indonesian mode of governance: consensus and cooperation. Consensus means the containment of pluralist forces among the educated élite, while cooperation stands for the containment of market forces. My assessment of these notions follows two parallel avenues of inquiry. The first investigates how the New Order regime expects to maintain consensus. The second seeks to discover whether the institutional and human capacity necessary for this purpose is in place. The Indonesian mode of governance provides a case study of the usefulness of supposedly 'authentic' institutions and values in solving problems of governance and civil participation, which may require adjustments to the classical liberal understanding of civil society. The analysis may also be instructive for other developing nations, and for international development agencies.

GOVERNANCE AND CIVIL SOCIETY IN INDONESIA

The New Order regime has had a long relationship with the international donor community, and development funds from this source have reached over 5 billion dollars annually – about 40 per cent of all development expenditure in Indonesia. Through this consortium, Indonesia has been exposed to the most recent ideas on how to sustain development momentum (World Bank 1993). In World Bank circles, a fascination with the 'East Asian miracle' (World Bank 1994) and a feeling of dismay over the 'African crisis' (Jaycox 1993) have sparked a resurgence of interest in building governance capacity. A broad internal evaluation of projects by the World Bank (1992) has revealed major problems in the implementation of adjustment policies in many developing countries: lack of attention to feelings of 'ownership', and hence political commitment to implementing adjustment policies; failure to assess adjustment policies' beneficial and harmful effects on particular categories of the population; failure adequately to assess institutional capacities, especially as they concern knowledge gaps, operational deficiencies, and aspects of sustainability; and failure to provide opportunities for popular participation in the formulation, implementation and evaluation of policies. These findings have been supported by evidence from academic studies in the fields of new political economy (Nelson 1992), which is concerned with questions of policy commitment and pluralist interest articulation, and New Institutional Economics (North 1990), which is concerned with questions of agency, transaction costs, and contractual arrangements. For example, Wade's (1990) case study of Taiwan demonstrated the importance of improving the quality of human resources, and of deploying this capacity through a policy advisory structure consisting of strategic councils, advisory boards, research foundation, private-sector laboratories and consultancy agencies. This mode of governance can be defined as technocratic, in that there is governance by a single party, backed by a military apparatus, which gives priority to economic development objectives. This polity is dominated by experts and professional bureaucrats who see the expansion of entrepreneurial opportunities and the proliferation of institutional arrangements in support of these activities as viable alternatives to political development.

Basically, the idea of economic participation through entrepreneurship rests on the assumption that without increased access to economic opportunities, political participation is at best meaningless, and at worst disruptive. According to this line of thinking, economic activity depends on transparency, accountability, and responsiveness in governance, and sustainability in institutional and environmental resources (Sarageldin 1993). Hence, capacity building and participatory development have become international agencies' key strategies in the 1990s. States' new roles are defined in terms of formulating strategic industrial policies, investing in infrastructure, promoting technology, improving the quality of human resources, fostering private institutional arrangements, providing legal security, and widening the scope for private entrepreneurship and popular participation in societal affairs. The concept of participatory development has been defined by a confusing mix of policy objectives. These include fostering the functions of market institutions, building local capabilities, reforming public services, decentralising, safeguarding environmental sustainability, developing small and micro enterprises, promoting political pluralism and elections, forming trade unions, calling for gender autonomy, protecting human rights, and upholding the rule of law. Yet, all approaches share a common commitment to the notion of entrepreneurship as a primary strategy to increase popular participation (Healey and Robinson 1992).

Experiences in East Asia have shown that a critical mass of outward-looking entrepreneurial people can play an important role as a partner in institutional arrangements and as a proponent of interests and ideas in policy-making. Other potential advantages of promoting widespread entrepreneurship for Indonesia are the possibility of industrial and economic restructuring and a way out of the low-wage labour trap. The New Order regime wishes to follow the example of other Asian nations and to discard Indonesia's image as a low-wage nation. Individual entrepreneurship is seen as alternative to the authoritarian management of wage–labour relations, which has become less feasible following the relaxation of east–west international relationships (Bürklin 1993). The management of labour relations is further complicated by the large share of foreign or Sino-Indonesian ownership in labour-intensive sectors of the Indonesian economy. An ideology of class operates here, but is blurred by ethnic sentiments rooted in centuries of history.

In the New Order regime's mode of governance, the notion of consensus is represented as a core Indonesian value which has its roots in Javanese culture and in the nationalist movement which turned Indonesia into an independent nation. The notion of consensus was reinforced by the failure of the democratic Indonesian Constituency in the 1950s and by the bloody political chaos which occurred at the end of President Soekarno's rule in 1966 (Nasution 1993; Vatikiotis 1994). Since 1966, party politics have been confined to the periods immediately preceding national elections and party conventions. Parliamentary legislation and control of the executive are possible in theory, but do not take place in reality. Voting procedures are seen as disruptive of consensus and harmony. Personal vetting and a commitment to the national ideology are requirements for political activity. This subjugation of civil liberties has been justified in terms of political stability and economic progress. However, since President Soeharto will leave office after his sixth term, doubts about the continuation of these practices are rising. The underlying assumption is that the prevailing mode of governance and ideological discourse has become sufficiently institutionalised and accepted by the populace to be carried on regardless of changes of leadership (Liddle 1992; Syamsuddin 1993).

The New Order regime appears less sure of this, and continues to be concerned with matters of internal security. In the Indonesian context, the security approach refers to the prevention of expressions of extreme political or religious viewpoints which might disrupt national stability.

Security is also at stake when the ideological foundations of the nation or the authority of the president are challenged. Public protest by citizens who are increasingly appalled by economic mismanagement, collusion of interests and abuse of power, is also considered a threat to national security, in part because of the damaging effects such protest can have on foreign investment and hence on the economic stability of the country.

Since 1991, when President Soeharto declared an era of openness, public debate in Indonesia has become increasingly focused on issues with direct bearing on civil society. Instead of focusing on developmental issues and problems with policy implementation, the public media became concerned with a list of sensitive issues, none of which could have been discussed previously. Among the most debated topics were bank scandals, cases of corruption and collusion, lack of transparency in budget allocations, the prohibition of alternative trade unions, and expressions of political zeal at conferences of the two non-ruling parties (the *Partai Demokratis Indonesia* (PDI: Democratic Party of Indonesia) and the *Partai Persatuan Politik* (PPP: United Political Party)) or at meetings of the Islamic mass organisation *Nahdatul Ulama*. People were also concerned with land-eviction procedures and compensation schemes, the state's exploitation of welfare institutions and lottery schemes, the ownership of crop-purchasing agencies and strategic business corporations by members of the president's family, and the disadvantages that small-scale enterprises have in the face of the economic dominance of Sino-Indonesian entrepreneurs. The New Order regime has deliberately triggered some of these discussions on public occasions, thus violating its own prohibition on debating sensitive issues related to class, religion, ethnicity and the distribution of power.

In 1994, this process was abruptly stopped when President Soeharto decided to close three periodicals and to introduce new regulations on organised civil activities. He did so on the grounds that 'without rules and their observance, what will emerge is anarchy, not democracy'. The president has hinted several times that he sees a link between expressions of public discontent and the activities of the forbidden Communist Party of Indonesia (*Partai Kommunis Indonesia*, or PKI). Expressions of extremist religious zeal are dealt with similarly. Reference is made to fatal incidents in Tanjung Priok in 1984, in Lampung in 1988, in Kuningan in 1993, and in Madura in 1994, or to the military repression of separatist movements in Aceh, Irian Jaya and East Timor, all of which have been justified in the name of internal security. Civil activities in such areas as sports, culture, recreation and communication have all been strictly regulated and supervised. Apart from the issue of state-run lotteries, which were abolished at the request of Islamic student protesters, no concessions have been made. When the reputation of the president was involved, judicial verdicts were very severe. Minor tokens of societal discord have been dealt with under criminal law. Security considerations lay behind a spate of quasi-military operations against traffic violators (*Operasi Zebra*) and Draconian measures against brawling students and petty criminals (*Operasi Bersih*). The military leadership has denied there is any link with a previous spate of extra-judiciary killings in 1983 (known as *Petrus*) or with 'mysterious shootings'. Nevertheless, these actions have frightened many people away from politics.

There is a good deal of public support for this security approach. Indonesians admit quite frankly that, in explosive public situations, discipline is often lacking. As long as economic growth continues, it seems that a large proportion of the emergent Indonesian middle class places more value on its material well-being than on exercising political influence. Close relationships between the affluent middle classes, the bureaucracy and the military may thwart expectations that the bourgeoisie will act as a lever in the democratisation process. Most members of the civilian élite (politicians, scientific experts, intellectuals, and so on) have become accustomed to their roles as participants in a technocratic polity, and have no experience in creating bases of popular support. Most intellectuals and experts aspire only to secure institutional safeguards against authoritarian whims, and the regime has mobilised their expertise as it begins the second long-term development period (1994–2019).

Indonesia's developmental strategy for the next twenty-five years consists of a combination of 'narrow-based' and 'broad-based' policies. The former refer to state investment in high technology, infrastructure, and human-resource development, policies aimed at turning Indonesia into an industrial exporting nation such as Japan, South Korea and Taiwan. The assumption underlying this strategy is that basic conditions in terms of capital, manpower, knowledge, and skills are already met, and just need to be triggered into action by the 'spin-off' effects of strategic investments. Thus, policy-makers have emphasised transport, communications and education. The term 'broad-based policies' refers to the notion of economic democracy, as the Indonesian leadership envisages it. Participation is seen primarily as a socio-economic activity, with lack of participation caused by structural imbalances in the economy. The basic assumption underlying this part of the strategy is that household-based entrepreneurship can replace corporate business activities. This form of business is supposedly more in line with the principle of family cooperation, as laid down in the 1945 constitution. The two elements of this strategy are mutually reinforcing. By leading the way in core areas, the state is supposed to create broad opportunities for household businesses and micro-enterprises. At the same time, as the masses seize these opportunities they are expected to refrain from political participation and leave the technocratic élite to make optimal policy decisions. The potential benefits of this strategy are high, but so are the risks. Failure to maintain consensus at the level of policy-making will negatively affect the chances of creating a cooperative market system, and vice versa.

THE POLITICS OF EXPERTISE AND THE SIXTH CABINET OF SOEHARTO

Recent analyses of the politics of expertise in Indonesia (Bastin, Schmit and Schulte Nordholt 1993; Vatikiotis 1994; Schmit 1994a) suggest that it is becoming increasingly difficult to maintain consensus between three clusters of expertise which have emerged within the national élite. The first is a group of financial and economic experts who are disciples of the professors – who were the managers of the economic stabilisation and structural adjustment processes during the 1980s. The second is a group of technological experts who have clustered around the minister of science and technology, Ir B. J. Habibie, to whom President Soeharto gave a special mandate to create a technological infrastructure. The third group is a cluster of socio-cultural expertise which is made up of an amalgam of nationalist, religious, and socio-cultural experts gathered in the Indonesian Association of Islamic Intellectuals (ICMI) and other intellectual organisations.

After 1993, the internal balance within the sixth cabinet of President Soeharto shifted in favour of a technological-intellectual coalition under the leadership of Minister Habibie. Within the cluster of financial and economic expertise, a new generation of economists with a nationalist orientation replaced the financial experts who masterminded the de-regulation policies of the 1980s. Minister Habibie, who has enjoyed the personal support of President Soeharto since his return to Indonesia in 1978, after a sixteen-year stay in Germany, is the architect and manager of virtually the entire technological infrastructure in Indonesia. He acts as director of national scientific and technological institutions, and he manages a cluster of ten strategic industries, which include armaments, aircraft and shipbuilding. In this last capacity, he has considerable influence over military expenditure patterns. He formulated the basic outline of the second long-term development programme. He can also exert his influence in several line ministries, such as Education and Transport and Communication, where numerous former associates are installed.

Minister Habibie's priorities have been described as reckless and ill-advised by some observers, and as bold and visionary by others (Schmit 1995). The large-scale budget expenditures required to implement his grand vision have become a threat to consensus. For instance, the new minister of finance has not been able to restrain Minister Habibie from investing massively in the shipping industry and in inter-island communications, or from purchasing used warships from Germany. A short public exchange of viewpoints regarding this issue ended with the closure of three periodicals in 1994. Without the financial skills and the international connections of their predecessors, the new economic team is no match for Minister Habibie, who is convinced that the key to growth lies in engineering, rather than economics. Disagreements over budget allocations have been complicated by the economists' commitment to the idea of economic democracy. They are more concerned with tax reductions for entrepreneurs and poverty-alleviation schemes for the poor than with promoting fiscal austerity or assessing the economic feasibility of Minister Habibie's projects.

Discord over priorities and budget allocations implies the use of political arguments which could easily spill over into public domains such as the national configuration of professional associations, the national assembly and political parties, the Islamic mass organisations, the public media and society at large. For instance, professional associations of intellectuals have been formed according to the religious background of the members. First, the Christian Association of Intellectuals was reconstituted in 1990. Subsequently, in 1991, the Islamic Association of Intellectuals, a Hindu association and a Roman Catholic association were formed. The ruling party, *Golkar*, and the military security board have both watched this outburst of civil energy among the educated élite with considerable apprehension, fearing that these initiatives would stir up religious strife and therefore harm the national interest. The fact that some members of these associations left the ruling party was a cause of great concern, and led to the formation of a nationalist intellectual umbrella association in 1993.

Within the domain of party politics, the PDI and the (Islamic) PPP are now geared for a more active role in policy making. For instance, at a tumultuous party conference in 1993, a new PDI leader was elected despite interference from the Ministry of Internal Affairs and the security forces.[2] In 1994, she openly criticised the regime for scaring people away from politics and for causing political disorientation among citizens. In the national assembly individual members of the three political groups and the military faction have become increasingly vocal during debates and committee sessions. On several occasions, cabinet ministers have been summoned before parliamentary committees to account for controversial policies. Even within the ruling party, members have suggested that this 'functional grouping' be turned into a genuine political party and that its membership be decoupled from the bureaucracy.

The principle of consensus is also maintained in the world of private associations and voluntary organisations. Religious foundations, business associations, cooperative unions, youth and sport organisations, environmental associations and about 10,000 other registered non-governmental organisations (NGOs) are bound by the Law on Mass Organisations to follow the national ideology and to fit into a national organisational structure. New accreditation rules pertaining to NGOs were formulated in 1994, which included individual screening and vetting procedures for executives similar to those used in political accreditation. Enforced participation in national umbrella organisations further contains the civil energy of tens of thousands of highly educated persons from all backgrounds. Despite these obstacles, NGOs have combined to defend their common interests against the regime.

Outside parliament, several democratic fora and the famous dissident group *Petition Fifty* are seeking to join forces with the non-ruling parties. The leadership of the Islamic mass organisation *Nahdatul Ulama*, which has over 20 million members, has also become involved in political discussions, out of frustration and lack of confidence in the leadership and programme of the Islamic PPP party. Overall, the New Order regime is very anxious about 'embryonic' party formation and the potential constituencies of the PDI and PPP among the emergent middle class and the rural élite.

In the domain of labour relations, the government is trying to maintain consensus by setting a minimum wage level and by creating a tripartite model known as *hubungan industri pancasila*. Representatives of government, industry and the official all-Indonesian Labour Association are expected to work out their differences and create harmonious relationships. Yet, minimum wage levels (which are between US $1.15 and $3.75 per day) are often ignored by industry and this has become a cause of social instability (Tjiptoherijanto 1993). Although the official association is not doing much about the matter, attempts to set up an alternative labour union were blocked in 1992 and 1993. When this blockage failed to have the desired effect, the new union was simply forced to merge with local branches of the official association. Unauthorised strikes have been suppressed by the security forces, leading on occasion to the death of militants. In 1994, a bout of labour unrest throughout Indonesia ended in public rioting and a violent clash with security forces in Medan, Sumatra. Following these incidents, leaders of the new union were arrested for inciting public disorder.

Consensus is of the utmost importance for President Soeharto's reputation as a unifying medium amidst potentially divergent forces. Apart from the provision of material welfare, this capacity is a major source of the president's legitimacy and has acquired almost magical significance. Moreover, consensus within the élites has an exemplary function for the whole of society in the overarching context of *Pancasila* ideology. Yet as we have seen, the technocratic polity contains many sources of discord, actual and potential.

As for Minister Habibie's claim that a critical mass of scientific expertise and institutional capacity now exists in Indonesia, one may doubt whether the new team of engineers and intellectuals can match the effectiveness of the financial technocrats during the era of structural adjustment and deregulation (Pangestu 1991; Schmit 1991, 1995). Case studies from elsewhere in Asia have demonstrated that technological independence can be achieved through an institutional infrastructure that is capable of providing high quality educational services and research facilities to industry and corporate business (Chamarik and Goonatilate 1994). Such institutions are not yet available in Indonesia, where the main sources of policy input are located in the National Planning Agency, the state ministries, and the state universities (particularly the National University of Indonesia and the technological universities in Bandung and Surabaya). During the 1980s, Indonesia made extensive use of advisory services and policy inputs provided by external agencies such as the World Bank and the Harvard Institute for International Development. After 1993, influence from these quarters diminished considerably. However, due to Minister Habibie's dominant position in the technological infrastructure, there is not yet sufficient scope for Indonesian non-governmental think-tanks and so-called 'arm's-length institutions' to play a significant role. With one man having the final say in all technological research programmes and applications, there is a risk that the assessment of alternative solutions will be neglected.[3] The number of private consultants has been growing, but no transparent institutional arrangements allow the expertise available to be transmitted to policy-makers. The education system has been unable to produce sufficient numbers of engineers and managers capable of technological innovation, even though the number of foreign-trained graduates is now increasing rapidly (BPPT 1993; Djojonegoro 1988). Indonesia, like other Asian nations with fast-growing economies, is facing a general shortage of educated and skilled people. It is becoming dependent on importing thousands of Asian expatriate executives. By insisting on a limited number of technological priorities in the high-tech sector, Minister Habibie is denying the private sector a regular supply of other types of technological knowledge and skills. This policy could turn out to have negative consequences: high mobility and high wages in the private sector may drain Habibie's own apparatus and dependency on highly paid expatriate staff may reinforce latent feelings of hostility against large conglomerate businesses, particularly those owned by Sino-Indonesians. The end result of efforts to link the state-owned high-tech sector and the mass of small entrepreneurs and self-employed individuals could well be a further concentration of economic power in the hands of those who presently hold it. This could reinforce existing sentiments regarding the concentration of economic power and growing income disparities, and hence make it more difficult to achieve economic democracy.

DEPLOYMENT OF CIVIL ENERGY FOR ECONOMIC DEMOCRACY

The notion of economic democracy refers to a strategy of containing economic forces by deploying untapped civil energy through household business endeavours. The core elements of this strategy are economic cooperation among firms of different sizes and capacities and the development of individual entrepreneurial capacity. The idea is that cooperation between economic entities of different sizes and individual entrepreneurs will lead to peaceful economic restructuring, analogous to the way in which consensus among different clusters of expertise is supposed to smooth the process of policy-making for industrial re-structuring. These ideas must be situated in the context both of new trends in international development thinking, and of the Indonesian notion of economic participation. This is rooted in the national *Pancasila* ideology and a long history of nationalism combined with deep antagonism towards the business activities of the Sino-Indonesian community.

The notion of economic cooperation has historical precedents in Indonesia. It was derived from European notions of cooperative endeavour during the late colonial era. In the European context Black (1994) makes a distinction between 'communal' and 'individual' liberties. These correspond to two notions of civil society, represented by guilds and entrepreneurs respectively, which have oscillated in importance through time. In Western Europe of the late nineteenth century the spirit of cooperative endeavour reflected the ascendency of the communal notion, particularly as a means of protection against capitalist forces. This notion was implanted in Indonesia by the Dutch through the colonial popular credit system. This cooperative ideology has continued to offer an Indonesian alternative to extreme capitalist or socialist orientations (Schmit 1991, 1994).

The influence of contemporary international development agencies is reflected in the notion of sustainability as expressed in World Bank (1993) and Serageldin (1993). The main point made in both these works is that economic participation and some degree of private affluence are vital for implementing and maintaining regulations and institutional arrangements for sustainability. Other influences come from theories of industrial restructuring and institutionalist economics. These theories are concerned with new forms of industrial organisation and international competition associated with the process of globalisation. East Asian experiences with industrial restructuring and human resource development are seen as successful examples of this trend (Best 1990; Wade 1990; World Bank 1994).

The Indonesian idea of economic coordination is consistent with some of the tenets of the new institutional economics (see, for example North 1990). Economic activities are seen as strategies aimed at reducing transaction costs, raising mutual trust and improving the enforcement of contracts by means of non-market institutional arrangements which evolve in specific cultural and socio-political environments. Even conventional economists are becoming aware that there is more to progress in developing countries than economies of scale, and that they have to get a grip on notions such as creative destruction, flexible specialisation, and collective entrepreneurship (Best 1990). Meanwhile, sociologists and anthropologists have pointed out the resilience and creativity of household-business endeavours. They have drawn attention to notions such as social enforcement, cultural embeddedness, and 'knowing the work' (see Granovetter 1984; Gudeman 1990).

In the Indonesian context, the idea of millions of citizens working together and catering to larger economic entities on the basis of contractual relations cannot be disentangled from the objective of displacing Sino-Indonesians from their positions of economic power.

The idea of dismantling the large conglomerate businesses appeals strongly to most Indonesian people, since the majority of labour-intensive export industries are owned by members of the Sino-Indonesian business community. Roughly 200 conglomerates, which control over 4,000 companies, contribute 35 per cent of Indonesia's gross national product (World Bank 1993). In addition, members of the Sino-Indonesian community, which numbers about 6 million, have a disproportionate share of the 75,000 small and medium-sized enterprises in Indonesia. In contrast, the number of micro-enterprises has reached more than 30 million. Out of about 200 million Indonesians, about 30 million people live in abject poverty. In these circumstances, the notion of economic democracy implies the creation of a critical mass of entrepreneurs, which is then expected to be stimulated by the government's technological investments and to generate income and job opportunities for tens of millions of citizens. The economy will be restructured through the dismantling of the conglomerates and potential labour unrest is to be contained by the substitution of subcontracting relationships for employer–employee relations.

In 1991, a group of about forty Sino-Indonesian owners of conglomerate businesses was called to an assembly at President Soeharto's Tapos ranch. There, they were given the message that it was time to assume more social responsibility for the Indonesian people. Since this meeting, the issue of indigenous (*pribumi*) versus non-indigenous (*non pribumi*) ownership of economic assets has been hotly and publicly debated. Following exposures of bank scandals, and the misuse of export certificates and re-discount facilities, this debate reached peaks of emotion in 1994. The president's view on this issue is clear: the utility of large business conglomerates was exhausted during the first long-term planning period, 1968–94. During the current long-term planning period, these companies are expected to retreat and dissolve. The New Order regime is going to hasten this dissolution through measures such as breaking up the closed family boards of these companies and installing new managers, splitting the conglomerates up into smaller entities which will work on the basis of subcontracting arrangements which are beneficial to all participants, and providing legal protection and technological and infrastructural facilities for economic participation by the mass of the citizens, who will be in household businesses.

The objectives of economic democracy are being pursued through a series of policy measures. In 1994, the issue of entrepreneurship was given the status of a national movement in which all segments of Indonesian society are expected to participate. State-owned enterprises, national and provincial universities, provincial and local governments, and private associations have all been mobilised to encourage aspiring entrepreneurs The president has ordered local governments to reserve a fixed proportion of their expenditures to support small and micro entrepreneurs. Other measures include the restructuring of the ministries of Cooperation and Manpower and the distribution of poverty-alleviation grants to neglected villages. Funding for entrepreneurial development will come from profits made by state-owned enterprises and conglomerate businesses, private contributions, and allocations from the state development budget. In addition, the government will try to redirect financial flows from the banking system by means of enforced loan quota schemes in the banking system. Finally, according to the new Law for the Protection of Small Enterprises, large enterprises are prohibited from operating in specific economic sectors.

The deployment of civil energy on this large scale makes the outcome unpredictable and implies the risk of unintended political consequences. Blaming Sino-Indonesian businessmen for working in collusion with high-ranking bureaucrats and not allowing the Indonesian population to participate in the economy could easily lead to public outbursts of ethnic strife. This strategy could also distract public attention from the concentration of wealth and power in circles close to the president and the New Order leadership. Moreover, protective legislation and preferential policies may be highly effective in terms of political legitimacy, but they are likely to prove less effective in terms of entrepreneurial development. In this respect, the notion of economic democracy seems to refer to a class ideology in which entrepreneurship is reserved for a privileged minority of the Indonesian population.

In their review of the various stages of policy-making and implementation in Indonesia over the last forty years, Isono Sadoko, Maspiyati and Haryadi (1994, 1995) point to two major institutional deficiencies which bear on the question of whether adequate institutional and human capacity for entrepreneurship exists in Indonesia. The first is a conceptual confusion with regard to the meaning of economic cooperation, the interpretation of which varies from the very political (in the sense of forging a completely new national economy) to the pragmatic (in the sense of establishing intra- and interindustrial partnerships based on mutual interest). The second institutional deficiency is the proliferation of semi-official organisations and institutions, many of which do not have the necessary professional and operational capabilities to implement official policies. Many cater to exclusionary constituencies and depend on subsidised resources. Since 1945, many financial institutions have been involved in developing small enterprises and household business with varying degrees of success. Given their traumatic experiences during earlier episodes of policy-making, they view new appeals for financial support for small and micro enterprises with extreme caution. Nevertheless, intellectuals and popular leaders have adopted the notion of economic democracy with great vigour.

Indonesian policies and programmes comprise a mixture of social and economic objectives and are influenced by a complex institutional history. Ministries are mandated to achieve social-policy objectives such as promoting village specialisation and increasing employment (Bappenas 1993; Mubyarto, *et al.* 1994). One may even suspect that some of their new programmes have been designed specifically to inject new energy into tens of thousands of semi-official cooperatives, village-development institutions, and ministerial support institutions. Unfortunately, due to the political overtones of this policy, there is a persistent tendency to concentrate support on the supply side instead of the demand side of small-scale enterprises. Ignorant of the real market prospects and the cultural, social and economic characteristics of household businesses and self-employed persons, the government often neglects their real needs. Moreover, the provincial- and district-level government agencies involved in these support schemes are weakened by a lack of fiscal autonomy. The real potential of local governments, acting in partnership with local business leaders, to create business and employment opportunities, remains to be tapped. Without more autonomy, the involvement of local governments in national programmes will cause high opportunity costs: the money would be better spent in supplying routine services fairly and efficiently.

The question of how and by whom the national support funds for small entrepreneurs and household businesses should be managed is also problematic. The number of claimants is huge. If the fund were handled by a private-sector institution, it could be used to link large and small business entities within vertically organised production chains by means of subcontracting arrangements and intra-industrial partnerships. Such a private institution could coordinate educational and training services, help transfer technology, and create new marketing facilities for small and micro entrepreneurs, in a manner similar to that found in Europe, the United States, and some East Asian countries. However, it seems more likely that the Ministry of Cooperation will retain the power to manage and allocate these support funds. Allocations will then tend to be determined by political and ideological considerations, and the result could be that these schemes will once again acquire the reputation of being compensation schemes designed to redress disadvantages. This is detrimental to the promotion of real entrepreneurship. The same risk would present itself if professional and business associations with close links to the regime were to become involved: for instance, the Indonesian Chamber of Commerce has a long tradition of stirring up emotions by means of nationalist rhetoric and expressions of ethnic hostility.

The empirical evidence does not support assumptions that there is plenty of scope for individual entrepreneurship in Indonesia, nor that this sector has the capacity to replace conglomerate businesses. There is scope for expansion in certain areas, but in general, the share of cottage industries and household-businesses in the national economy, has been declining. Falling demand for simple household-business products and services is matched by a rising demand for more sophisticated products and a concomitant growth of wage labour in small-, medium-, and large-scale businesses (Evers 1993; Haryadi, Isono and Maspiyati 1994). Moreover, it is clear that household businesses' capacity to innovate and invest is insufficient to replace that of conglomerate businesses.

Finally, the institutional and cultural conditions for entrepreneurship in Indonesia differ both from those of successful East Asian nations and those of crisis-ridden Latin American economies. For instance, in the context of Latin America, Gudeman (1990) has identified the capacity for creating local value and turning it into exchange value by means of economic thrift, innovative recasting and 'knowing the work' as a potentially strong characteristic of household businesses. These characteristics have not been noted in studies of household businesses in Indonesia, which are full of terms like 'exclusionary practices', 'survival strategies' and 'deskilling of labor' (Haryadi, Isono and Maspiyati 1994). In comparison to some East Asian countries, the Indonesian situation is characterised by a mismatch between educational facilities, individual career expectations, and demand for knowledge and skills in the market-place. The problem is that in the present stage of transition, the educational system fails to prepare people for either wage-labour relations or individual entrepreneurship (Cobbe and Boediono 1993; Haryadi, Isono and Maspiyati 1994).

The costs and benefits of the policies described above still have to be assessed in detail. Among the expected benefits are social stability and legitimacy for the New Order regime, technological progress, international prestige, domestic employment and income generation for the broad mass of economically active people. In this respect, the idea seems to follow the example of the East Asian developmental states. However, developing countries in general and Southeast Asian nations in particular lack many of the characteristics of the East Asian developmental states and are operating in a different historical context (Siriprachai 1993). The social opportunity costs of starting a national movement for the development of small and micro enterprises must not be underestimated. The massive deployment of civil energy from the level of ministries and societal institutions down to the collective or individual levels of micro-entrepreneurship could be diverting attention away from urgently needed institutional reform and civil participation. Even if one supposes that a critical mass of capacity is available and that the objectives are feasible, there is still the risk of 'inciting' feelings of discontent towards the Sino-Indonesian community. It is difficult to see how the idea of replacing the owners of conglomerate businesses squares with the ambition to narrow the gap between Indonesia and other Southeast and East Asian nations, where overseas Chinese business networks are working very successfully.[4]

CONCLUSION

The Indonesian idea of substituting economic democracy for civil participation is consistent with some themes in international development thinking. Indonesia is being given the benefit of the doubt because of the risks of political unrest and environmental degradation caused by unemployment and poverty. International agencies are aware that making aid conditional on political changes modelled on European and American democratic traditions has not been effective. All hopes are now placed on expanding the scope of civil participation through the market and through tapping the potential of authentic forms of governance. In the long run, the purpose of assisting the technocratic élite and of promoting economic participation is to instigate a further spontaneous process of embourgeoisement, which will in turn generate new civic initiatives from within.

This emphasis on authenticity is congenial to the World Bank residential office in Jakarta, which is testing a new model for sustainable development. Both Indonesia and the World Bank hope that the Indonesian solution will be a positive example to many other developing countries, which have not coped well with foreign models of governance and civil participation. The international employment crisis was identified as a problem with global implications at the Social Summit of the United Nations in 1995, because of the associated risks of political unrest, environmental degradation, and international migration. As chair of the Non-Aligned Movement, Indonesia is particularly keen to set an example in dealing with this problem and to demonstrate the success of its solution to problems of civil participation.

Paradoxically, however, the above analysis suggests that international support for the Indonesian solution implies assisting the efforts of the New Order regime to reduce the opportunities for persons outside the technocratic élite to participate in politics. Perhaps the most chilling implication is that national political formations are seen as 'obsolete' in the face of technocratic and allegedly transnational solutions to problems, and as a threat to the internal stability of developing nations.

If, on the other hand, the risks which I have outlined in my assessment of the politics of expertise and economic democracy can be avoided or neutralised, then the Indonesian solution will be exemplary. Summarised, the model would look like this: economic and technological experts and intellectuals would be given opportunities to participate in policy-making within the boundaries of a 'national conference' which would consist of the president's advisory council, professional associations, political parties and voluntary associations. Popular participation would be channelled through the economy according to contractual arrangements based on mutual benefit. The legal system would serve this strategy in two ways: by punishing deviant expressions of civil energy under criminal law, and by arbitrating contractual relationships between economic actors.

This pursuit of an authentic national solution has implications for our analytical concepts of civil society. At present, it is not so much a model as a learning experience. Only time will tell whether mass-support programmes and notions of collective entrepreneurship are an appropriate way to forge highly complex institutional arrangements between economic actors and to create the basic range of civic endowments that we associate with the liberal-individualist version of civil society.

NOTES

1 These tenets are national sovereignty, human dignity, popular democracy, social welfare and monotheism. For further discussion see Darmaputera 1988.

2 Miss Megawati Soekarnoputri is the daughter of Indonesia's first president, Soekarno, who was in office from 1945 to 1966.

3 In 1994, Habibie held sixteen positions including director of strategic industries, manager of research institutes in the technopolis (Puspiptek) in Serpong, member of scientific boards and advisory councils, and head of the free investment zone at Batam Island, off the coast of Singapore.

4 Two further problems could be listed here. The idea of getting out of the low-

wage trap by promoting the expansion of household businesses seems to go against the trend of a growing demand for wage labourers. In the field of labour relations, institutional development is seen as a threat, while the function of free bargaining in overcoming the low-wage trap is not recognised. Household-business associations and artisan groups would seem to be favoured by power-holders primarily because they are easier to control.

REFERENCES

Bappenas (1993) *Manual on the Presidential Instruction on the Development of Poor Villages*, Jakarta: Bappenas.

Bastin, J., Schmit, L. and Schulte Nordholt, N. (1993) 'Het zesde Kabinet van Soeharto: Mogelijkheden voor "Take off"?', *International Spectator* 47(7–8): 440–6.

Best, M. (1990) *The New Competition: Institutions of Industrial Restructuring*, Cambridge, Mass.: Harvard University Press.

Black, A. (1984) *Guilds and Civil Society in European Political Thought from the Twelfth Century to the Present*, London: Methuen and Co.

BPPT (1993) *15 Tahun Badan Pengkajian dan Penerapan Teknologi (BPP Teknologi) 1978–1993*, Jakarta: BPPT.

Bürklin, W. (1993) 'Strong states, cooperative unions, and the structure of the international system', *Internationales Asienforum* 24(1–2): 91–103.

Chamarik, S. and Goonatilake, S. (eds) (1994) *Technological Independence: The Asian Experience*, Tokyo: United Nations University Press.

Cobbe, J. and Boediono, (1993) 'Education, demographics, the labor market and development: Indonesia in the process of development', *Journal of Asian and African Studies* 28(1–2): 1–27.

Darmaputera, E. (1988) *Pancasila and the Search for Indentity and Modernity in Indonesian Society: A Cultural and Ethical Analysis*, Leiden: E. J. Brill.

Djojonegoro, W. (1988) 'Overseas training: human resource development for science and technology', paper presented at the NAFSA Conference, Washington, DC.

Evers, H.-D. (1993) 'The transformation of the informal sector in Indonesia: social and political consequences', Bielefeld: Institute for Development Sociology, Bielefeld University, South Asia Working Paper 192.

Granovetter, M. (1984) 'Economic action and social structure: the problem of embeddedness', *American Journal of Sociology* 91(3): 511–21.

Gudeman, S. (1990) 'Remodelling the house of economics: culture and innovation', *American Ethnologist* 18(2): 141–54.

Healey, J. and Robinson, M. (1992) *Democracy, Governance and Economic Policy: SubSaharan Africa in Comparative Perspective*, Brighton: Overseas Development Institute, University of Sussex.

Isono Sakoko, Maspiyati and Haryadi, D. (1994) *Expansion in Small Business and Self-Employment in Indonesia: A Review of Policies*, Bandung: Akatiga Foundation Centre for Social Analysis.

—— (1995) *Pengembangan Usaha Kecil. Pennihakan sefengah hati*, BandungL Yayasan Akatiga.

Jaycox, E. (1993) 'Capacity building: the missing link in African development', paper given at the conference 'African Capacity Building: Effective and Enduring Partnerships', African-American Institute, Reston, Virginia, May.

Liddle, R. (1992) 'The politics of development policy' *World Development* 20(6): 793–807.

Mubyarto *et. al.* (1994) *Keswadayan Masyarakat Desa Tertinggal*, Yogyakarta: Aditnya Media and P3PK UGM.

Nasution, A. (1993) *The Aspiration for Constitutional Government in Indonesia: A socio-Legal Study of the Indonesian Konstituante 1956–1959*, Utrecht: Proefschrift.

Nelson, J. (1990) 'Introduction: the politics of economic adjustment in developing nations', in J. Nelson (ed.), *Economic Crisis and Policy Choice: The Politics of Adjustment in the Third World*, New Jersey: Princeton University Press.

North, D. (1990) *Institutions, Institutional Change and Economic Development*, Cambridge: Cambridge University Press.

Pangestu, M. (1991) 'Managing economic policy reforms in Indonesia', in S. Ostry (ed.), *Authority and Academic Scribblers: The Role of Research in East Asian Policy Reform*, San Francisco: ISC Press, pp. 93–120.

Schmit, L. (1991) *Rural Credit Between Subsidy and Market: The Adjustment of the Village Units of Bank Rakyat Indonesia, 1984–1988*, Leiden: Institute of Cultural and Social Studies, Leiden Development Studies 11.

—— (1994) 'A history of the *Volkscredietwezen* (Popular Credit System) in Indonesia 1895–1935', in K. Kuiper (ed.), *A Provisional Manual of the Algemeene Volkscredietbank (AVB) by Mr A. Th. Fruin*, The Hague: Ministry of Foreign Affairs, pp. 1–36.

—— (1995) 'Rules, positions and programmes: the politics of expertise in Indonesia', in P. Silva and B. F. Galjart (eds), *Designers of Development: Technocrats and Intellectuals in the Third World*, Leiden: Research School CNWS, pp. 166–89.

Serageldin, I. (1993) *The Vice-Presidency for Environmentally Sustainable Development: Statement of Mission*, Washington, DC: World Bank.

Siriprachai, S. (1993) 'Can Southeast Asian nations emulate East Asian developmental states? A note', *Newsletter of the Nordic Association of Southeast Asian Studies* 8: 9–15.

Syamsuddin, M. (1993) 'Political stability and leadership succession in Indonesia', *Contemporary Southeast Asia* 15(1): 12–23.

Tjiptoherijanto, P. (1993) 'Perkembangan Upah Minimum dan Pasar Kerja', *Ekonomi dan Keuangan Indonesia* 41(4): 409–23.

Vatikiotis, M. (1994) *Politics under Suharto: Order, Development, and Pressure for Change*, London: Routledge.

Wade, R. (1990) *Governing the Market: Economic Theory and the Role of Government in East Asian Industrialization*, Princeton: Princeton University Press.

World Bank (1992) *World Bank Structural and Sectoral Adjustment Operations: The Second OED Review*, Washington, DC: World Bank.

—— (1993) *Indonesia: Sustaining Development*, Washington, DC: World Bank.

—— (1994) *The East Asian Miracle*, Washington, DC: World Bank.

Chapter 10

Community values and state cooptation

Civil society in the Sichuan countryside

John Flower and Pamela Leonard

While we were in China, from 1991 to 1993, the living standards of most of the farmers in the area where we did fieldwork declined. The gains made during the early 1980s in the immediate aftermath of decollectivisation were eroded by flat wage rates, inflation, and the increase of fees and taxes levied by the state. Farmers in this mountainous area of Southwest Sichuan province felt left out of the reform-era prosperity enjoyed by other regions in China, and increasingly disillusioned with their relation to the state. They complained of new burdens placed on them by local government authorities, and simultaneously expressed concern about the decaying social fabric in the countryside in the wake of receding state involvement. With many young people leaving the area in search of work as the income potential of agriculture becomes increasingly marginal, the care of old people was a particularly contentious issue in the village where we lived. Faced with new problems and unsure of how they would be resolved, farmers wondered who would assume responsibility for feeding and caring for the old. Who would ensure that education and medical care for all ages was affordable? Who would coordinate grass-roots efforts at economic development in the countryside? Would this be the responsibility of families, the work of the government, or would new rural non-government institutions also become involved? The answer is clearly some combination of these, but how they will fit together – the relative importance of state, public, non-state and private – is not clear.

Western observers of China have debated the extent to which a social realm between state and family existed in the Chinese past, and the possibilities of its renewed development in contemporary China. Most of these analyses, born of the celebrated 'public-sphere' theory of Habermas (1989), look to the rise of a market economy for signs of an emerging 'civil society' in which contractual ties and horizontal integration between economic actors challenge primordial ties to the family and to the ruler. This market-spawned civil society in turn serves as the precondition for free, rational, informed discourse on the political ends of society – the public good debated in the 'public sphere'. Implicit in this discourse of civil society, born of the western historical experience, is the notion of a clear boundary between state and society. We argue that this notion of boundedness is problematic in the Chinese context, where the vectors of social interaction involve both horizontal and vertical linkages of exchange and expectation. If the idea of 'civil society' is to have salience in the Chinese countryside, it must be reworked to embrace the blurry interpenetration of state and society, and understood in terms of the cooptation, negotiation and historicity at the heart of this interaction.

Leaving aside, for the moment, the problematic use of these terms in the Chinese context, the search for 'civil society' and a 'public sphere' in China's past has yielded results that speak to the Chinese countryside today. Rowe (1989), in his seminal work on Hankow, has described how a 'public sphere' emerged in China in the second half of the nineteenth century as a specific historical response to the trends of urbanisation and dislocation. As the old networks of family and locality were no longer able to ensure an equitable basic subsistence, new institutions (for example, the 'winter defence' which provided food to the masses in times of shortfall) emerged during this period to fill the gap.[1] Rowe points to three trends in popular welfare activities in nineteenth-century Hankow: first, the extension of relief to a broader sector of society than had been considered deserving in the past; second, the supplanting of state-sponsored welfare facilities by projects founded on local societal init-iative; third, a shift from a tradition of private philanthropy based on the individual gift to a practice of corporate and relatively impersonal sponsorship of public causes (1989: 130–2). He attributes these trends to the rapid urbanisation of the post-Taiping era, and to the 'none too orderly reconstruction' which led to a popular sense of anomie and decline in moral values. Significantly, Rowe identifies both a long-term secular trend from official to private responsibility for public services, and a cyclical trend where the state assumed these duties by coopting what had been initially private initiatives, only to wane as societal forces again resurged in the nineteenth century. A similar story of the cyclical power of the state can be told for communist China. After Liberation in 1949, the functions that these 'public' institutions fulfilled were superseded by a powerful centralised state. The communist system, in principle, provided the safety net that ensured food for the masses, developed and maintained infrastructure, and set standards for working conditions. Since the Deng era of reform, however, the nominal power of the state as guarantor of the social safety net has receded, and its former obligations are increasingly met by private concerns. Rowe provides a useful distinction in analysing these trends. It is not the participation in social-welfare activities of state or society that distinguishes these periods but rather, since 'such activities were always, in some sense, joint projects', we need to examine shifts in initiative and control of these undertakings.[2]

Unlike Rowe, we are less interested in documenting the fact of a resurgence of civil society at a particular historical moment – although the stories we will tell lend credence to such an interpretation of post-reform China. Rather, the aim of this chapter is to help define the nature of interactions with government and to point up some of the ways in which basic social functions are effectively fulfilled or hampered by the form of these relations. Rowe's point that all projects are to some extent joint projects suggests that the analysis of Chinese civil society should proceed not from a classical standard of competing state/society interests but from the investigation of the particular form of the interactions between the state and nominally non-state organisations, to see how power is negotiated and initiative channelled.

In contrast to Rowe's analysis of historical institutions, Yang (1994) approaches the question of civil society in contemporary China from the intriguing perspective of *guanxixue* – the art of social relations. Yang argues that *guanxi*, understood as dyadic relationships of exchange entailing both instrumental benefit and personalistic obligation, form the 'rhizomatic' warp and woof of Chinese social life through which people surmount bureaucratic obstacles and thereby 'subvert' the normative hegemony of the socialist state. Rather than positing a boundary between state and society, it is the very dispersed and fluid nature of *guanxi*, spreading across and through state organs, that is subversive of state power and its 'universalist ethics'. Yang describes the coalescence of *guanxi* networks in China as a kind of nascent civil society – the *minjian* 'realm of people-to-people relationships which is non-governmental or separate from formal bureaucratic channels' (1994: 288), long realised in social practice and now just beginning to emerge in institutional form.

While Yang consciously focuses on urban *guanxi* networks, she introduces the rural experience to highlight both the centrality of *renqing* ('human feelings, human sentiments, personal tie of affect and obligation') in the rural gift economy, and its importance for the possibility of a Chinese civil society in the *minjian* realm. This is most purely manifest in kinship-based ritual exchange in the countryside. The concept of *renqing* is also the linchpin of Yang's heuristic dichotomisation of Chinese social interaction along gender lines: the rigid 'masculine' vertical integration of universalist ethics, instrumentalism, and power, as opposed to the 'supple', 'feminine' horizontal integration of particularist *renqing* ethics, affective bonding, and 'the weak'. Despite the broad strokes used here to contrast the *minjian* and 'state redistributive' modes of social relation (which, along with the idea of 'subversion', seem to reinforce the idea of state versus society rather than their interpenetration), Yang's conceptualisation of a Chinese civil society based on networks of affective ties is a useful corrective to theories that emphasise economic interests alone. Indeed, Yang's treatment of the gift economy (like our own findings presented below) suggest that, while market relations are entwined with personalistic ties, the instrumental component of commoditisation actually weakens the networks of affective bonding that comprise Chinese civil society, rather than strengthening civil society as in the contractual model.

In both urban *guanxi* networks and rural rituals of exchange, the gift is a very important element in Chinese civil society. In our view, the gift economy is a point of departure, a window into the moral dimension of *renqing* – the central value of affective bonding. But *renqing* itself can be contextualised as part of a broader moral universe defined both through and against history. In other words, while it is important to redirect the discussion of Chinese civil society toward social relations, recognising the ubiquitous importance of affective bonding tells us relatively little about the specific nature and formative processes of civil society in China, and even less about institutions emerging in the *minjian* realm and their critical interactions with the state. In focusing on recreated institutions rather than recycled rituals, we suggest a reading of Chinese civil society that emphasises a sense of community and local identity that cuts across the boundaries of kinship and state, and whose shared meaning is constructed through historical memory. Our case material is drawn from a study of non-governmental organisations (NGOs) in an area southwest of Chengdu in Sichuan province. Specifically, we focus on the relationship between one international NGO and the state in order to demonstrate a particular pattern of cooptation and domination of societal networks. State networks in the area of our fieldwork are still powerful, and cadres still seek to maintain their control over rural society. While predominantly kin-based networks currently function as the principal alternatives to state initiatives, other organisations such as foreign NGOs and temple associations are also increasingly important in the lives of local villagers.

The emergence of non-government organisations in Sichuan has been patterned by their unavoidable need to negotiate with the state for power, but also informed by the expression of local 'interests'. These interests are neither narrowly economic nor simply 'affective', but expressions of a moral discourse created through local identity and historical memory.

PASSING ON THE GIFT IN SICHUAN

From 1991 to 1993, we were attached to an international NGO which has sponsored grass-roots rural livestock development projects around the world for half a century. Headquartered in the United States, it had been involved in China before Liberation, but lost its contacts during the revolutionary period. It returned to China in 1986. Although the NGO continues to have many projects in countries around the world, China is the only country where official government networks manage the NGO's projects. Chinese livestock projects were an exception to its general policy of working with non-government grass-roots networks. This exception was made because such networks were not apparent in the Chinese countryside, and also because the government structure indeed had much to offer. The Chinese government's Bureau of Animal Husbandry (BAH) has offices in every county and contacts in every township across the province. They have trained specialists in animal husbandry who are not only veterinarians and animal technicians, but also have valuable experience in organising and managing livestock development projects of the type the NGO is willing to support. The BAH network therefore provides many benefits, and more than a few of the projects run under their auspices have been excellent, even surpassing expectations.

Nevertheless, at the time of our fieldwork, the NGO began to feel that its contacts within China had expanded enough for its in-country headquarters to operate more efficiently outside of the government network. When it tried to break away from the provincial-level government bureau, however, considerable pressure was brought to bear to keep it within the government fold. A licence from the Bureau of Foreign Economic Relations and Trade was required before an independent office could be set up, but the procedure for procuring it was time-consuming and expensive. The first, and quite significant, hurdle was that there was no category of 'not for profit' corporation under which the NGO could be established. Instead the NGO pursued the approved path of becoming an international joint venture, subject to all the fees exacted by the state. Eventually a corporate licence was issued, but it was revoked within weeks. The main source of resistance stemmed from the bureau's unwillingness to relinquish its control over the benefits it received from 'hosting' the NGO: the prestige from claiming the NGO's successful projects as its own; the opportunity of foreign travel for top bureau leaders under the guise of 'study tours'; and, no doubt most importantly, a share of the funding sent from abroad to cover 'administrative expenses'. Complicating the situation, factional struggles within the bureau were manipulated to increase pressure on the NGO to stay under bureau control.

The US headquarters of the NGO was no doubt disappointed that its efforts to become independent of the government were thwarted. But while government participation in NGO activities may be unavoidable, it does not follow that a 'public sphere' does not exist in China, nor that there is an absence of bottom-up, grass-roots initiatives. The important dynamic is not state participation but the question of control. The state seeks to coopt spontaneous organisations and channel them towards serving its own interests; problems arise when a gap develops between the interests of the state and the interests of the grass-roots organisation. For many international NGOs operating in Sichuan, state participation can be helpful in carrying out their work, but in the case above, the bureau's cooptation served the interests of the state bureaucrats at the expense (literally) of the NGO's interests.

Other trade-offs were involved in working with government networks in the day-to-day administration of the projects. From the perspective of an NGO which emphasises 'grass-roots' development initiatives, government networks are less than ideal because the real locus of power within these projects is not with farmers but with professional bureaucrats. While government networks have deeply 'penetrated' villagers' daily lives, the top-down nature of this interaction means that these networks are often poorly integrated with farmers' perspectives and priorities. Where poor integration occurs, farmers are left without a formal organisation to represent them.

In addition, the NGO's stated goal of encouraging both economic development and a sense of community solidarity was not shared by state administrators of the projects. This goal of holistic community development, central to the NGO's projects around the world, reflects an international development discourse on distribution, individual rights, and 'empowerment', predicated on an opposition between state and society. The project language emphasises regeneration: a vision of a healthy society as one where poor farmers help other poor farmers and thereby create lateral social ties and a stronger social fabric from which to develop other self-organised projects for community betterment. This regenerative ideal of sustainability is contrasted to the 'hand-out'. Indeed, the organisation's commitment to providing aid in the form of livestock underscores the organic dimension of the development scheme.

The goal of community solidarity draws on older ideas of voluntarism and Christian ethics, as well as on contemporary development discourse. The NGO's desire to operate independently of the state and at the grass-roots level is justified in terms of self-help, bottom-up initiative, and a 'spirit of giving'. With on-going ties with American churches, the NGO draws on a (somewhat secularised) abstract universalist ethic of charity. Thus the trademark of the NGO's projects around the world is a practice called 'passing on the gift', whereby individual farmers who receive a gift of livestock from the project are expected to pass on some of the female offspring to another farmer in the area. One of the ideas behind this institution is to make recipients into gift-givers and so build their own self-esteem and sense of empowerment within the community. At the same time, the gift is seen as a tool of horizontal integration, creating community through a circle of exchange. Here the project's conceptual vocabulary combines a social gospel of 'salvation through works', aimed at the individual, with a Utopian, 'barn-raising' ethic of mutual aid and community voluntarism.

If the NGO's concept of the gift exhibits a distinctly western tension between individualism and communalism (hence the concurrent em-phasis on 'self-help', 'self-esteem' and 'community'), the idea of passing on the gift resonates with the non-instrumental *renqing* ethics described by Yang. Chinese project staff working for the NGO have themselves noted the similarity between passing on the gift and native practices of gift-giving. Yet there are differences, too, and the involvement of state agents in the gift relationships has complicated the NGO's original vision. Basically, farmers' perceptions of the NGO's project were coloured by the fact of state (rather than grass-roots) control. In the dairy-goat project to which we were attached, the function of passing on the gift was run by the BAH. Farmers were expected to return offspring to the BAH, which had given them the animals. As it turned out, passing on the gift in this way proved difficult to manage. Farmers saw the gift as just that: a gift from overseas to them, poor farmers. They did not want to shoulder the burden of returning an animal to the government. Significantly, farmers used the term *jiao* ('to hand in, give up, deliver or pay', as in to pay a tax) to describe their obligation to return an animal. Many farmers felt the practice of paying back the government to be unfair and sought to avoid this obligation – they would return only animals in poor health or would pretend their animals only gave birth to male offspring, leaving them without an animal to return. Still other farmers stayed away from the project altogether, saying it was better not to take the 'gift' from their local government because one should try to be independent and avoid complicated obligations with bureaucrats. They saw it as appropriate that the government should seek to help them, but felt that they should not have the obligation to support the government.

The reasons for these attitudes lie in the nature of gift exchange in the countryside, and in the different expectations held by farmers and agents of the state. In the most common village rituals of exchange – weddings, funerals, and the *jiu da wan* (literally, 'nine big bowls') feasts accompanying them – the amount and origin of each cash gift are carefully and elaborately recorded for the recipient family by a scribe writing on ceremonial paper. The donors also keep careful track of how much has been given to whom, and a watchful eye on the amount and quality of the food prepared at the feasts. This apparent parsimony actually serves to preserve a gift equilibrium that underscores the affective, as opposed to instrumental, significance of the gift.

As Yang (1994: 63–4, 317–20) points out, the horizontal ties formed by these ritual gifts can extend to public officials, despite the state's general disapproval of these horizontal loyalties and its insistence on (vertical) loyalty to the nation-state. But farmers also view their vertical ties to the state as governed by a moral equilibrium of mutual obligation, and it is not the sharp distinctions between state and society, or between horizontal and vertical integration, that explain farmers' resistance to incurring an obligation to the state. The reason is, rather, the failure of the state to live up to its end of the bargain. The course of the NGO's livestock project illustrates that the issue of state involvement in village society cannot be reduced to a model of totalitarian state penetration; the problem is not state interference in farmers' civil society, but one of integration and the terms through which it is negotiated.

It was clear that a gift programme highlighted the different perspectives of farmers and bureaucrats. At another livestock project in Sichuan run by the same NGO, project administrators developed a way to avoid these difficulties. Farmers there were provided with a breeding-age cow. In return, after 2 years, they had to repay in cash the value of the cow they received. Many farmers liked this programme and referred to it as the 'loan with no interest'. Administrators liked this method even more. Before, they say, they had to work very hard at educating farmers to the aims of the NGO, its programmes and the idea of 'passing on the gift'. Managing the pass-ons as cash has simplified the obligations and thus made such education less necessary, saving time and trouble. Moreover, from the administrators' point of view there is another benefit. Managing the gift as a loan is a much faster path to development, reaching more families in a shorter period; instead of having to wait until a gift animal matures and gives birth to a female offspring which can be passed on, the money is recycled promptly after two years. Project managers emphasise that this is, therefore, a better, more 'scientific' (*kexue*) method.

The project managers' use of the term 'scientific' to describe the project is indicative of their conceptualisation of project management. As state extension agents (literally, 'technicians', *jishu renyuan*), they view their mission as one of modernisation, popularising advanced technologies to 'backward' (*luohou*) areas, and combating the conservative and 'feudal' (*fengjian*) attitudes of farmers resistant to change. This self-conception reflects the state policy (since 1978) of emphasising the 'four modernisations' (in agriculture, industry, science and technology, national defence) and encouraging the development of science and technology. But, as used in everyday speech, 'science' is more than a discipline or policy objective; it has almost talismanic properties, evoking a whole discourse of progress, modernisation and national wealth and power (Kwok 1965). In its most common sense, scientific means efficient or effective, but it also implies a tendency toward quantification in the design and evaluation of projects, and reinforces a preoccupation with 'fulfilling targets' (*wancheng renwu*). While the latter is most frequently associated with the disastrously inflated reports of crop yields during the Great Leap Forward (GLF, 1958–60) that led to widespread famine, the practice of setting targets continues and feeds into the bureaucrats' love of statistics. The top-down (or what Yang terms 'male') character of the 'scientific' idiom is evident in state management of livestock projects, and may help to explain project managers' preference for the loan rather than the gift.

Yet it would be simplistic to suggest that farmers maintain a 'traditional' gift economy in contrast to the state's goal of modernisation; most farmers in our area of study were neither immune to the allure of the discourse of 'science', nor generally resistant to new technologies. From their perspective the 'loan method' did have disadvantages, which highlighted the poor integration between farmers and the state. For example, one characteristic trajectory of many livestock projects in Sichuan was for a new industry to develop around a given animal (fur rodents, fur rabbits, and specialty breeds of chickens are just a few examples), and for much money to be made by those who got in early –

not just from the regular productive capacity of the animal but also, in pyramid fashion, from selling breeding animals to other farmers who wanted to get in on the business. The cycle of expansion would then outstrip the demand for the animals' product and those who bought animals at inflated prices took a loss. If the farmers had received the animal as a gift and then the price collapsed, they would not be too upset. If they had been encouraged to take a loan they would be more likely to blame the programme that gave them the loan.

In the project where the gift was managed as a loan, the initial capital came in the form of a cow. While this was again 'scientific', because the BAH technicians could knowledgeably select cows of good quality, it also had the drawbacks of limiting the age and the breed available to farmers in need and keeping the burden of project management highly centralised. In some cases, the animals provided by these projects were tailored more to satisfying the BAH's objectives than to the interests of the farmers most in need of assistance. For example, because of a great range in local conditions, there was also a great variation in what was thought to be the ideal family cow. Some farmers identified a cow that could produce 30 *jin* of milk per day and still plough their land as ideal. Nevertheless, the BAH and the milk factory preferred to promote pure-bred Holsteins, which produced far more than 30 *jin* of milk, ate a correspondingly larger quantity of grain, and could not be used to plough fields. The BAH liked the Holstein because the high milk production increased factory profits and because it was a more salient symbol of economic progress (a conclusion borne out by meticulous statistics). Furthermore, while many farmers would have preferred to receive a cheaper immature calf and rear it themselves, the project limited farmers to the purchase of an older, more expensive, breeding-age heifer.[3]

We asked a farmer who had received a full-grown cow with the obligation of repaying cash after two years how he would have felt about a programme that gave him an immature calf that he would raise himself, while in return he would be expected to give a healthy calf to another farmer. He replied, 'Ah, that sounds great. Where do I sign up for this programme? I could have saved a thousand *yuan* this way.' We then asked him to whom he would have donated his calf and he replied, 'To a poor farmer, of course! I attended the classes and I know what this programme is about!' While the BAH had to work hard at educating farmers as to the aim of the programme, it would seem that much of the resistance they were encountering to the original idea of 'passing on the gift' was due to a wariness on the part of the farmers that their gifts were going to the government, or that they were supplying the government with the means to do the work it ought to be doing anyway – the work of helping poor farmers. The farmers who returned live animals in poor health did so because they failed to identify with the programme as it was managed. This scepticism and alienation from the project was not something that 'education' could overcome, since it was not just rooted in a lack of knowledge but in the farmers' observation that the BAH used aspects of these projects for their own benefit. For example, in the case where the breeding-age cows were distributed as a loan with no interest, families of officials were provided with valuable employment in a special farm set up to rear project animals. Thus, educating 'ignorant' farmers was not the problem. The problem was assuring wary farmers that their 'return gifts' were not simply being diverted by bureaucrats.

To us, what was really striking about this and other 'passing on the gift' programmes in China was that, all the while, farmers were informally giving animals to friends and relatives as part of normal social exchanges. This practice could well have 'counted' as passing on the gift from the perspective of the NGO's international staffers, but it was ignored by the BAH. The point here is that what satisfied the criteria of 'scientific' economic planning were those aspects of the project that registered as significant or beneficial to the bureaucracy, while the qualitative object-ives of community-building were in practice ignored by the BAH. Although each had a different understanding of 'passing on the gift', both the international NGO and the farmers at the grass-roots shared a common emphasis on moral values and community objectives – an emphasis that had less resonance with the aims and interests of the bureaucrats.

MORAL ASPECTS OF 'SOCIALIST MARKET ECONOMY'

The wariness of many farmers to become involved with government officials running the livestock gift programme is symptomatic of the changing relationship between farmers and state agencies – a relationship that is crucial for understanding the constraints on NGOs operating in the Chinese countryside. While many of these changes took effect over the entire period of reform (i.e. since 1981), we will focus here on the accelerated pace of change resulting from the 'second wave' of reforms which influenced events during the time of our fieldwork. These reforms, following Deng Xiaoping's 'southern tour' (*nan xun*) in late 1991 and articulated as central government policy in 'document number two' (*erhao wenjian*), intensified the pressure on service bureaucrats to make their services profitable, as regular salaries decreased and 'second jobs' were legalised. Success at the job was no longer measured by gains made on farmers' behalf, but by money earned for the BAH itself. In addition, bureaucrats were no longer constrained from entering into private enterprises while retaining their official positions. Thus employees of the Bureau of Animal Husbandry could use their contacts and their position to push a product that would make money for them, but which was not beneficial – or was even quite risky – for the farmer. As a result of these developments, official corruption worsened and farmers lost confidence in government service bureaus.

The area where the project was located has always been considered a rather poor 'mountain district'. The topography of the region consists of steep mountain slopes, upland valleys and deep rocky gorges. There are terraced rice paddies in the valleys, but the main crop of 'our' village is corn, planted by hand on the steep hillsides. Each villager is allotted a minuscule amount of rice-growing land; rice must be purchased or traded for with corn each year. In the past twenty years, subsistence agriculture has been augmented by wage labour (mostly stone masonry) and sideline occupations such as raising dairy goats. Once prey to famine and chronic shortages of rice, the village has become much more prosperous since the decollectivisation of 1981, but it remains poorer than the rice-growing areas and suburban villages closer to the provincial capital of Chengdu. In recent years, this relative prosperity has begun to erode under the pressure of inflation. The price of milk had not risen appreciably in over a decade. Wages for labour have also remained low, while the price of farming inputs, especially the cost of chemical fertiliser, on which corn production has become heavily dependent, has increased several fold. The overall picture is one of a declining standard of living and little prospect for economic development.

At the same time that villagers began to feel the pressures of inflation, they also saw the tremendous economic boom in urban (especially coastal) areas, and the rise in waste and corruption that accompanied loosening government controls on the economy. Resentment of official corruption and of increased taxation – itself a product of a scramble for local revenues – began to crest after Deng Xiaoping's December 1991 southern tour to investigate the effect of the more liberal opening-up policies being tested in the coastal development zones such as Guang-dong. Deng concluded that these market reforms were beneficial to the Chinese economy and that the benefits of this brand of 'socialist market economy' should be made more widespread. Provisions of 'document number two' also led to a restructuring of government aimed at giving more weight to township or *zhen* administrations. The effect was dramatic. The prefectural government (*diqu*, the level above county) used the restructuring as an opportunity to take over some of the tax base of the county government. The county government, as a result, had to decrease the incomes of its employees by 25 per cent. This was somewhat compensated for, however, by allowing the bureaus and individuals to engage in business to make money. Due to these two changes, the employees of the county government service bureaus (the Forestry Bureau, the Bureau of Animal Husbandry, the Bureau of Agriculture, etc.) ceased almost overnight to dedicate themselves to their former roles. Offices were increasingly empty, and people spent more office time drinking tea, chatting, reading the paper and even playing cards. Work units commonly opened restaurants and convenience stores, or even ran lotteries. Some invested in real estate and built luxury hotels. Worse still, they sought to convert old networks and official powers into leveraged profit-making schemes. For example, the Sanitation Bureau required all restaurants to start using disposable chopsticks which had to be purchased from the Bureau. Open use of substantial cash 'gifts' to win the favour of patrons in the provincial bureaus replaced the more modest offerings of cigarettes, alcohol and local 'specialty products' (*techan*), and became the mode to gain access to programme funds. The money for these investments – in stores, businesses and gift-giving – came from whatever funds the local government had access to and led to a severe credit squeeze by the end of 1993. The cycle of spending also resulted in severe inflationary pressures.

Since 1992, inflation in the area has been severe and basic commodities on which farmers depend, for example fertiliser and grain, are becoming more costly, while the prices they receive for their products and their labour have remained relatively stable. Meanwhile, in the cities and towns, electronic merchandise, foreign cars, and expensive restaurants – much of it the loot of government corruption – are plainly visible. This further fuels farmers' rising expectations and frustration at their loss of social standing. Farmers see the contradictions clearly, and there have been many tax revolts and uprisings in Sichuan in this period of growing discontent.[4]

The political and economic changes that ensued from Deng's southern tour have directly affected agricultural production and marketing. With the change-over in local township personnel, part of the general bureaucratic restructuring initiated by the shifting winds, there was a period of adjustment during which local infrastructure was poorly maintained. For example, the township failed to pay for routine repair of irrigation canals. Leakage from the canal resulted in water shortages when the rice shoots were planted and localised soil erosion on hillsides below the canal. The deregulation of public funds resulted in a severe banking crisis. Farmers' loans were called in, and many villagers found themselves strapped for cash. Reorientation of government-owned factories interrupted the supply and affected the quality of basic inputs such as fertiliser and seed. A retaining wall was built in front of the village where we lived and along the public road following a severe flood in 1992, but due to corruption in the traffic bureau sand was substituted for cement and the first high water in the spring of 1993 obliterated the entire construction. The road was only sporadically passable during the milk season and as a result farmers' milk could not always be transported to the powder factory. Farmers rely on this milk money to purchase their basic rice rations. All of these examples point to what villagers see as an alarming trend toward 'chaos'. Mismanagement and corruption by government officials were commonly compared to the situation under the last years of Nationalist (*Guomindang*) rule. Many villagers complained about inflation and an increase in crime. Higher taxes and pressure to pay back government loans also contributed to growing dissatisfaction. Against the background of an eroding standard of living, villagers saw the changes brought by the 'socialist market economy' as, at best, an economic boom in which they could have no part, and, at worst, a threat to the infrastructure of government services on which they rely and for which they contribute ever higher taxes.

The increased disarticulation between the farmers' situation and the activities of the local government following the second wave of reforms is demonstrated by a severe downturn in the goat economy which took place in the wake of the reforms. In 1992, the corn harvest in the dairy goat project area was the poorest in many years. People estimated their corn yields were down one-third from what they had expected. This meant that the grain available for consumption in 1993 would be less than usual. Exacerbating this problem, the cost of grain began to rise precipitously in 1993 as the price of milk remained flat. Corn went from 0.32 *yuan* per *jin* in 1992 to 0.5 *yuan* per *jin*. If one deducts the market price of the corn the goat eats from the milk earnings, then one sees that the real earnings from raising goats went down 16 per cent. If four goats earned their owner 2 *yuan* a day of gross income in milk sales, the net profit went from 1.2 *yuan* in 1992 a day to just 1 *yuan* per day in 1993.

The milk-powder factories at this time were contending with troubles of their own that made them unresponsive to the needs of the farmers. New policies were being pushed forward requiring that factories be more self-reliant, which had the effect of intensifying competition for very limited funds. In order to reduce their own losses, they delayed both the breeding season for the goats and the milk-collection season. By encouraging the buck farmers to breed later in the year in 1992, they ensured that less milk would be produced in the spring of 1993, milk they feared they could not manage. They followed this up by delaying the date on which they began milk collection in 1993 by twenty days, creating a period during which some farmers had no market for their product. Once the season did begin, they had to contend with very poor transport conditions – conditions made worse by the government's poor road management. When milk is not successfully delivered to the factory, the milk collector deducts the money he loses directly from farmers' incomes. As if this was not enough, the factories were late with their payments to the farmers in June and July, the lean period before the harvest when farmers have to buy corn, fertiliser and rice. In the summer of 1993, the township government made these problems clear in a report prepared for the city government. They stated:

> Prompt payment for milk is extremely important for farm families, for dairy goat husbandry, even for agricultural production. Some farmers say that the price of milk is low; they need money but cannot get any so why bother raising goats at all? At the same time, when milk funds are not disbursed properly this creates problems for the township government in collecting on the animal husbandry project's loans.[5] In July, a township government team of officials visited families to collect loan payments. Some of the farmers said, 'I can't get any milk money; you go ahead and take the goat away and just forget the loan. [We'll just call it even.]'

By the fall of 1993, the goat business had bottomed out, and most families in the village had ceased to keep goats. The number of goats in the village where we lived plummeted from 434 in 1992 to 150 in August 1993. In the face of anticipated corn shortfalls, the rising price of corn, the low price of milk, delayed payments and continued deduction from milk incomes, many farmers simply sold off their animals.

The township-government report cited above drew an explicit connection between the nation-wide problem of the government IOUs paid to farmers and the case of the delayed milk payments locally:

> Through television, radio, newspapers, and other channels, all the dairy farmers fully understand the central government policy forbidding the use of IOUs (*bai tiaozi*) in lieu of payment for farm goods, and they detest the IOUs given them for their milk production.

Although the township government has many times brought this problem to the attention of the relevant government organs, and made it known to the food products factory, this involves problems the township government is unable to resolve itself. Thus we request an appropriate solution from the city Party committee and the city government.

The problem was indeed not just a local problem that the township could resolve for itself, but reflected much broader trends, as the reference to the national policy forbidding the use of IOUs illustrates. This report also demonstrates how the changing political climate resulted in conflicts between different local government bodies as they jockeyed to maintain control of resources. The interests of the township government remained closely aligned to the interests of the farmers, but it too was asserting its right to control more of the milk revenues. In the end, the case study of dairy-goat farming shows that in this climate of competition and conflict among government bodies, it is the farmers who are 'squeezed' as a vital source of revenue.

Many farmers were becoming increasingly disillusioned with the government. Even some aspects of the goat project were coopted to support the bureaucrats and provide them with additional income. For example, there were several initiatives to use project funds to develop feeds and feed additives. These initiatives aimed not only to ensure better nutrition for livestock but also to create an additional source of income for the sponsoring institutions. Extension work thus had a significant top-down component, as officials focused on trying to persuade farmers to adopt practices which were in line with official policies and which were potentially profitable for Bureau enterprises. In fact, the extension provided by the BAH became so removed from farmers' own perceptions of needs and interests that farmers had to be paid to attend 'extension meetings' in which much of the time was given over to exhorting the farmers to pay back the loans they had taken to buy livestock. A popular ditty summed up the farmers' growing disgust with the bureau's extractive practices: 'Before the slogan was "serve the people" (*wei renmin fuwu*); now it's "serve the people's currency" (*wei renminbi fuwu*)'!

As this account suggests, farmers identified corruption as a major problem. Just what they meant by this deserves further attention. One way to conceptualise corruption in the Chinese context is along the lines of Yang's analysis of *guanxi* gift exchanges. Here, the state's objection to the 'feudal' practice of officials accepting gifts and its insistence on the 'universalist ethics' of party discipline are an implicit recognition of the threat that gifts posed to vertical integration through loyalty to the nation-state. In this view, people who seek to establish *guanxi* with officials by giving them gifts are not so much abusing power as subverting the state's normative control by engaging the state's agent in a relation of reciprocal obligation, thereby accruing a kind of 'human capital' greater than any immediate instrumental gain from the transaction (i.e. mere 'bribery'). Yang emphasises that there is a fine line between *guanxi* and corruption (1994: 108), but that the greater the instrumental component, and the less *renqing* ('human feeling') involved, the more likely the transaction will be considered corruption. This kind of analysis aims to qualify and deconstruct our received notions of corruption by emphasising the mutual obligation and reciprocity of *guanxi* relations, and by characterising gifts in this context as 'weapons of the weak' against the totalitarian state.

However, such a corrective should not make us lose sight of the very real and emotionally charged native category of corruption. From another perspective – particularly that of average farmers who have little from which to forge such 'weapons' – corruption is the very negation of the gift precisely because it destroys the affective and fiduciary ties of social relations. The terms used in the farmers' discourse on corruption are instructive. When specifying official corruption, *tanwu*, the emphasis is placed on the misuse of public funds, private gain, greed and covetousness, and the implication is of one who violates the reciprocal bond of obligation, who only takes. The more general *fubai* refers to corruption as decay and rot – the degenerated state of social relations resulting from licentious behaviour and breaking with the moral order of propriety (*li*). The fine line that separates the art of *guanxi* from corruption in urban China is seen more distinctly by farmers, who accept neither the official discourse condemning the personal quality of *guanxi*, nor the behaviour of officials who pursue private gain even as they ignore their obligations to the people.

Significantly, criticisms of corruption were not restricted to the state. Farmers were also concerned about the 'rotting' affective and fiduciary bonds in 'society', often referred to as a breakdown in 'public morality' (*gonggong daode*). Here it is important to note that despite the local perception that the state and its agents are to blame for corrupting the moral order, the realms of state and society were not conceptually separated. Instead, they were joined together in a seamless fabric of moral interaction. In native idiom, this interrelation is expressed in the metaphor of a house: 'if the upper beam is not straight, the lower ones will be crooked' (*shangliang bu zheng, xialiang wai*), meaning that when high officials are 'not upright' (*bu zheng*) the people will be lawless, corrupt, 'crooked' (*wai*). In the village where we lived, *wai* is the word most frequently used to describe this sense of social decay and corruption. It is used in such expressions as 'fake/counterfeit goods' (*wai huo*) or 'his character is crooked to the core' (*ta de xingge wai de hen*). These attitudes are closely linked with the commoditisation of social relations that has accompanied market reforms and given rise to corruption. As much as they resent the official corruption they see all around them, farmers fear a society where money replaces loyalty, filial piety, reciprocity, trust and respect as the glue of social relations. The corruption of these relations is seen as a falling-away from the straight and narrow, a crooked imbalance in the moral order.

It is tempting to explain this imbalance by recourse to a totalitarian model, positing a neat state/society dividing line that ranges the horizontal ties and 'community interests' of the NGO and farmers ('society') against the state's vertical imposition of production targets and rational project management from the top down. However, most of the farmers we spoke with neither conceived of nor wanted a neat separation of state from society. Rather, they incorporated the state into their own moral order. In this moral order, affective bonding and a sense of mutual obligation apply to both horizontal and vertical integration, and are defined in terms of historical memory. Poor integration – breaking the bonds of obligation – is often expressed in terms of 'chaos' (*luan*).

While urban Chinese (especially intellectuals) immediately associate *luan* with the Cultural Revolution (1966–76) – officially sanctioned in the trope 'ten years of chaos' (*shi nian de dongluan*) – farmers in Xiakou have other, more vivid historical associations with the term. For those old enough to remember and pass on the memory, two historical periods stand out as 'chaotic': the civil-war years (1947–9) with their official corruption and rampant banditry, and the totalitarian state terror of the Great Leap Forward (GLF, 1958–60) that collectivised the villagers into huge 'People's Communes', forced them to 'chaotically sow' (*luan sha*) the land and to neglect their crops for work in coal mines to fuel the infamous backyard steel furnaces. The first period represents the absence of social control, the latter epitomises an excess of control. The ideal lies in a balance of local autonomy and state involvement defined against the extremes of *luan*.

The difficulty of negotiating this balance is illustrated in the popular saying 'to release control, but not to the point of chaos; to tighten control, but not to the point of death' (*fang er bu luan; shou er bu si*), and in its wry inversion by local farmers: 'released control is chaos; tightened control is death' (*fang, jiu luan; shou, jiu si*). If *fang* and *shou* describe two abstract extremes – anarchy and totalitarianism – through which government should guide its policy, they also evoke concrete associations, formed through historical experience, against which farmers judge their interaction with the state. For example, *fang* ('to let go, set free, release') is central to the post-Mao policy of *gaige kaifang* ('reform and opening to the outside world'). *Kaifang* ('to open, to come into bloom') is viewed with ambivalence by farmers who at once welcome being 'set free', yet worry they will be 'let go', ignored and passed by. Moreover, the negative historical referent of excessive *fang*, the last years of the *Guomindang* government, serves as the very symbol of official corruption and banditry. Thus when farmers refer to the corruption and crime of today, they almost invariably observe that 'it's even worse now than under the *Guomindang*', and express nostalgic approval for the 'restraining' (*shou*) policies under Chairman Mao that specifically targeted corruption and (allegedly) made crime unheard of.

Shou ('to restrain or control (emotion or action)') is likewise historically and contextually defined, and an excess of *shou* is quite literally associated, in historical memory of the GLF and famine, with death on a massive scale. *Shou* also means 'to receive, harvest, gather, or collect', referring not only to the state's extractive practices in the past (e.g. 'collecting' the great bulk of the village's corn harvest during the GLF), but to the arbitrary imposition of fees, fines and taxes today. This association is reinforced by the widely resented references to 'collecting taxes' (*shou shui*) in ubiquitous wall slogans urging farmers to pay up.

While *fang* is most commonly associated with disorder, an excess of either *fang* or *shou* is linked to *luan*, as in the descriptions of the GLF in terms of the chaotic exploitation of resources (e.g. the chaotic cutting (*luan kan*) of trees, or the chaotic use of human labour in the mines) and in the contemporary problem of officials chaotically imposing levies on the farmers. Indeed, taken together, *fang* and *shou* invoke the capricious oscillation of state power that farmers find so 'chaotic' and destabilising to their own attempts to establish order. *Luan* is thus an essential negative referent for the balance between involvement with and freedom from the state. This conceptual space of moral equilibrium constitutes an important element for the formation of civil society in the Chinese countryside. We describe this equilibrium as 'moral' because, in the view of farmers who seek to balance the autonomy of their community with constructive interaction with the state, affective ties are both 'horizontal' and 'vertical', and are based on feelings of mutual respect and mutual obligation. Many of these farmers feel that 'things today' are *luan* precisely because their interactions with the state lack mutual respect, and because the state has failed to honour its obligations. The farmers voice frequent complaints over what they perceived as excessive *fang* in the licentious behavior of state agents (i.e. corruption), and over excessive *shou* in state control of resources, especially high taxation with no corresponding investment in bettering their community.

CONCLUSION

The problems faced by the NGO livestock project might be attributed to zealous self-serving efforts by agents of the Chinese state to coopt and control 'societal' initiatives, especially when viewed in the light of the farmers' broad critique of official corruption and social chaos. Such a reading also seems to confirm the categories of analysis customary to the 'civil society' model: state versus society, vertical versus horizontal integration, universalist or abstract ethics versus particularist or affective ones. Yet, closer inspection reveals a 'messy' layer of interaction, where cooptation is a mutual process of negotiation, where market reforms and commoditisation are seen as spurring an 'uncivil' unravelling of the social fabric; where gift exchanges and their burden of obligation and expectation extend vertically to involve the 'state' as well as horizontally to embrace 'society'; and where native categories draw state and society together in the pursuit of an encompassing moral equilibrium.

Given these apparent contradictions, what lessons might be drawn from the Chinese experience that speak to the issue of civil society itself? As Chris Hann (1995) points out, the concept is laden with western bias, a major element of which is the tendency to posit a value scheme of individual agents seeking to maximise their interests in the realms of politics and the economy. The villagers we described asserted their local identity and sense of community in an effort to (re)create a moral order against what they perceived as 'chaos' in the world around them. This moral order was derived from historical memory, suggested that the 'interests' around which associations form in Chinese civil society involve not only moral considerations but temporal bonds as well. In the case study of NGO involvement, we saw how managing the passing of the gift as a loan satisfied the criteria of rational economic planning, but fell short of another qualitative goal of the project – that of developing a sense of communal strength and self-reliance. The institution of gift-giving is an important element in the villagers' attempts to redefine a morally balanced relationship with the state. Yet, the western model of civil society fails to capture the flexible interpenetration of state and society in the Chinese context. It also does not account for the moral forces over time underlying the negotiation of interests in the Chinese countryside. Rather than impose a model of civil society as an arbitrary measure of change, we argue that taking the values of villagers seriously and looking at the moral dimension of civil society makes possible a more nuanced, grass-roots view of the relations between state and society in the Chinese countryside.

One implication of this view is that the state–society relation is not a zero sum; an increase in civil society does not necessitate a reduced role for the state. Thus, the notion of a receding state whose functions are taken over by emerging non-government organisations is not wholly persuasive. While much of the safety net provided by the state is being rolled back, farmers will gladly tell you that state presence in the form of fees, taxes and regulation is stronger than ever. Because the civil society model tends to reinforce a western, cold-war, politico-scientistic 'state versus society' viewpoint, we have tried to favour neither the state nor non-governmental organisations, but to focus on the quality of the relation between the two. That said, the details of the account we have provided should make it clear that a severe disarticulation has emerged between the interests of agents of the state and common farmers. The farmers perceive a large gap between themselves and those who wield official power – their opportunities for economic advancement are very limited, and they feel exploited. The balance of power in public organisations urgently needs to move toward the interests of the farmers.

Given all these messy qualifications to the civil society model, we should question whether in China it is a useful concept at all. Perhaps 'civil society' speaks best to the Chinese condition as a metaphor describing a forum or space of interaction. Despite the analytical problem posed by the ubiquitous penetration of the state, the trend toward spontaneous development of social institutions in this metaphorical space suggests that 'Chinese civil society' can also nowadays be given concrete referents in the modern western sense – in NGO projects, township-village enterprises and community temple associations, for example. But it would be more fruitful to ask how the Chinese experience might lead us to rethink the idea of civil society itself. This rethinking would have to involve an approach decentred from the western tradition and open to native categories of conceptualising experience. One implication drawn from China is that there is no necessary link between market relations and the nature of civil society. 'Traditional' affective ties are not only capable of engendering a civil space but, in some cases, these are greatly preferred to commoditisation. Another lesson to be gleaned from China is that the state and its agents are considered members of, rather than mere antagonists to, the civil society. Thus, state-versus-society frameworks need to be broken down to allow room for flexible interactions, and more nuanced analyses of the blurry, multilayered roles of state agents in civil institutions. Most importantly, the limitations of civil society as a spatial metaphor should also be addressed by understanding native categories as historically derived and live in present experience through associations of memory. If we are open to the possibility that the historical development of civil society in the west is at best an imperfect blueprint for understanding its Chinese form – let alone a standard for judging it – then an appreciation of each community's historical experience is essential for understanding its own definition of, and development of, civil society.

NOTES

1 To some extent, these new institutions were a product of western influence. For example, Strand (1989) points out that the YMCA became an important institution for managing the new philanthropic initiatives in Chinese cities during the Nationalist era. Rowe (1989) makes clear, however, that these developments were inspired by new needs arising from the first stages of mass proletarianisation.

2 A common critique of the civil society approach in studies of China is that the concept is historically rooted in the European experience. Thus, any attempt to 'find' civil society in the Chinese historical experience is a distortion. For example, Wakeman's (1993) polemic against Rowe finds inconsistency and exaggeration in the latter's postulation of civil society with true autonomy from the state. By focusing on the interaction of the state and 'public' (in the sense of *gong*, or 'extrabureaucratic', as Rowe understands it), the actual degree of autonomy is less interesting than the process of cooptation and negotiation surrounding it. The corollary to the historical critique, as Rowe himself admits (1993), is that the notion of civil society is inherently western-centric. As we note below, the historically questionable comparative dimension of the concept civil society, like the politically charged nature of the idea of the 'public sphere', should caution against the faddish use of these terms; but they do not negate their abstracted use as analytical tools (Madsen 1993: 186–7).

3 The problem of restricted breed choice was pointed out to project administrators by several analysts, including Pamela Leonard. The BAH responded positively, and promised to work on making hybrids available as well.

4 The most widely reported of these incidents was the violence that erupted in Renshou County over the proliferation of *ad hoc* fees levied by the local authorities to finance a road-construction project connecting the county to Chengdu. Many other 'uprisings' occurred throughout Sichuan during 1993. Although the particular causes varied, the common grievances centred on

local governments' extractive practices, themselves a reflection of the scramble for revenues under restructured government finances, the credit squeeze mentioned above, and the flight of investment capital from Sichuan to Hainan Province. This last implies an echo of the 'peasant emiseration' trend during the first decades of this century described by Fei Xiaotong (1953). Then, as now, local élites (today's party cadres) turned their attention and energies away from the countryside and toward the material lures of the cities, especially the coastal cities. This resulted in 'social erosion' and a moribund rural economy. Eastman's (1988: 94) description of that earlier period of treaty ports, imperialism and rural degentrification could also describe the Sichuan bureaucracy's investment in coastal Hainan Province today, and its consequences: 'This drain of the nation's wealth from the countryside to the treaty ports had incalculable consequences, depressing the rural areas and skewing the nation's financial and industrial development in favour of foreign-dominated cities along the eastern seaboard, rather than investing in home areas, where the sense of insecurity was chronic.'

5 More than one animal-husbandry project was operating at this time, and this reference probably refers to low-interest loans sponsored through an IFAO project, rather than to 'passing on the gift'.

REFERENCES

Eastman, L. (1988) *Family, Fields and Ancestors: Constancy and Change in China's Social and Economic History 1550–1949*, New York: Oxford University Press.

Fei, X. (1953) *China's Gentry: Essays in Rural–Urban Relations*, Chicago: University of Chicago Press.

Habermas, J. (1989) *The Structural Transformation of the Public Sphere*, Cambridge, Mass.: MIT Press.

Hann, C. (1995) 'Philosophers' models on the Carpathian lowlands', in J. Hall (ed.), *Civil Society: Theory, History, Comparison*, London: Polity Press, pp. 158–82.

Kwok, D. W. Y. (1965) *Scientism in Chinese Thought, 1900–1950*, New Haven: Yale University Press.

Leonard, P. (1994) 'The political landscape of a Sichuan village', unpublished Ph.D. thesis, University of Cambridge.

Madsen, R. (1993) 'The public sphere, civil society and moral community: a research agenda for contemporary China studies', *Modern China* 19(2): 139–57.

Rowe, W. T. (1989) *Hankow: Conflict and Community in a Chinese City, 1796–1895*, Stanford, Calif.: Stanford University Press.

—— (1993) 'The problem of civil society in late imperial China', *Modern China* 19(2): 183–98.

Strand, D. (1989) *Rickshaw Beijing: City People and Politics in the 1920s*, Berkeley and Los Angeles: University of California Press.

Wakeman, F. (1993) 'The civil society and the public sphere debate', *Modern China* 19(2): 108–38.

Yang, M. (1994) *Gifts, Favors and Banquets: The Art of Social Relationships in China*, Ithaca, NY: Cornell University Press.

Chapter 11

Making citizens in postwar Japan
National and local perspectives

John Knight

One of the problems of the civil society debate for anthropologists and other social scientists is the persistent dualism of state and society. This dualism lends rhetorical power to an oppositionist discourse, but it should not be accepted uncritically as a basis for analysis. Hence the calls for anthropologists to explore analytically the 'entwining' of state and society (Hann 1993). But even before this area of entwining is examined, it is important to recognise the institutional plurality that exists on both sides. The debate over civil society has tended to be couched in terms of a tension between a totalitarian national state and a national civil society as a site of resistance. Yet national societies do not, as a rule, exist simply as single, undifferentiated national units, but are themselves divided into local and/or regional units of governance with their own greater or lesser powers. This issue of the institutionalised local differentiation of governance may hardly have arisen in the centralised polities of Eastern Europe, but elsewhere, in liberal democratic polities, local government is enshrined as a core feature of the political order.

The existence of local governments and administrations means that localities occupy distinctive institutional niches, and state–society interfaces other than the national one may be important. Thus, while it is important to be wary of the state–society dualism, it is also necessary to be aware of the existence of different sites, levels or scales of state–society tension. This chapter explores the plural character of state–society engagement with reference to postwar Japan, and in particular to upland rural Japan. I begin by giving an overview of the postwar national debate in Japan on the nature of society, pointing out its similarities with, and differences from, the debate on civil society in Eastern Europe. The second part of the chapter looks at upland town-making, a community-building programme aimed at replacing the village as a social entity with a new 'town-wide' citizen society. It focuses on two individuals whose views of rural society and this reform process differ sharply. These two people, of different generations and genders, serve to illustrate the divisions and tensions intrinsic to the rural town-making process. Finally, I consider the relationship between the postwar attempts to create a democratic society at the national level and the corresponding efforts at the local level.

THE POSTWAR NATIONAL DEBATE

Japan has no civil society debate in the manner of Eastern Europe. However, there has been an intense and wide-ranging debate in postwar Japan about the relationship of society to the state, the degree to which 'democracy' has been achieved, the development of a domain of civil associations independent of the state, and the quality of public behaviour. This concern with the nature of postwar Japanese society is also manifested in anthropological, sociological and other writings on Japan by Japanese and foreign scholars. I shall not attempt to reproduce this wide-ranging debate here, but instead highlight what I see as the two major themes to emerge from it.

The first concerns the postwar Japanese state. A recurring representation of Eastern European socialist societies has been that of the civil 'vacuum' caused by strong, totalitarian states 'squashing' society (see Hann 1993: 18–19). A somewhat similar representation is evident in the Japanese context. A key explanation of postwar economic success in Japan has centred on what McKean (1993) has called 'the strong state thesis', according to which the state is strong enough to override sectional interests in society, in order to apply itself single-mindedly to national development. Postwar Japan has thus been depicted variously as an instance of 'state-led capitalism', as a society run by a 'capitalist development state' characterised by 'soft authoritarianism' rather than real democracy (Johnson 1982), as marked by a 'passive' political culture (Pharr 1990: 29), and even as a crypto-communist society (Kenrick 1988). A recurring theme is that, while the institutions of democracy were adopted during the Occupation period, the basic political values of the Japanese have not really changed.

For Matsumoto, a key feature of these recalcitrant political values is 'the assumption that the state is a prior and self-justifying entity, sufficient in itself' (1978: 38). He argues that the Japanese idea of the public realm is defined in stark opposition to the private realm. '[T]he public, rather than conceptualized as an amalgam of private interests, is thought to take shape only at the expense of the private as a higher, self-contained realm' (1978: 48). In similar vein, Smith argues that '[t]he distinction between public and private, which in the West is ultimately connected with that between church and state, cannot exist where [as in Japan] the state itself is conceived to be a moral entity' (1983: 129–30). The formal conversion to democracy notwithstanding, there are clear signs that the state continues to assume moral leadership in postwar Japan. Smith remarks on the irony that, despite their deep ideological differences, both the political Left and the Right in postwar Japan are agreed on the need for a component of ethical instruction in public education (*ibid.*).

The point is that there exists a chronic inability even in postwar Japan to imagine a public realm separate from, or independent of, the state.

> The state today is deprived of its erstwhile monopoly on morality and the household lacks its former authority over the individual, yet there is no church or any other analogous institution invested with the moral character that once inhered in the state.
>
> (Smith 1983: 130)

As a result of this absence of countervailing institutions, the state continues to dominate the public realm.

One major difference between this debate on the state in postwar Japan and the debate on civil society and the state in Eastern Europe concerns the place of business. McKean points out that scholarly discussion of the Japanese state has failed to achieve any agreement on its boundaries, with some writers using the term 'state' as a synonym for the bureaucracy, others including in the term the elected party regime, and others still including private interests, such as business, deemed to have inordinate state influence (1993: 77).

This power of business over the state, and therefore over Japanese society as a whole, has been a major issue. The recognition that state power tends to be allied with certain private or corporate economic interests means that civil society in the Japanese context cannot be defined as something other than the state, or in terms of imperatives of whittling down the state through privatisation, as is found in parts of Eastern Europe (see Ray 1991). Rather than being viewed as a civil counterweight to the state, business tends to be placed on the side of the state. Thus, in contrast to the 'individual capitalism' of the United States or Britain, postwar Japan is characterised as an example of 'corporate capitalism' (*hojin shihonshugi*) (Okumura 1992). With the focus on this state–business nexus, some Japanese intellectuals in the 1960s declared postwar Japan to be a 'managed society' (*kanri shakai*) (Koschmann 1993: 415–16).

The second area in which what might be called a civil deficit has been noted is in relation to particular or sectional interests. 'Groupism' or *dantaishugi* has been a prominent theme in the writings of Japanese intellectuals in the postwar period, particularly from the 1970s on (see Dale 1988: *passim*; Yoshino 1992: 17–22). That Japan is a group-centred society is now part of the conventional understanding in western anthropology and sociology. Robert Smith draws attention to 'the intense identification of the individual with small groups of affiliation', which therefore claim primary allegiance (Smith 1983: 127; see also Coulmas 1993).

On the positive side, this group-centredness is seen to contribute to public order. Smith argues that the intensity of group commitment among Japanese has been 'of critical importance in the decline of crime rates in the postwar period' (Smith 1983: 127). This is because, for the Japanese individual, 'one's actions will reflect on one's group' (*ibid.*). For Smith, citing a famous passage from the Analects, a Confucian principle is at work here: 'Their persons being cultivated, their families were regulated. Their families being regulated, their states were rightly governed' (1983: 129). Social control comes not from society as a whole but from the particular groups within it. In a 'group-oriented society' like Japan, therefore, order in public space is not a function of public norms strictly speaking, but of the power of particular group norms to regulate public space (see also Pharr 1990: 31). The image conveyed is of a sort of honeycomb society which, although it might appear unitary from the outside, is actually constituted by so many separate cells or holes. The civic whole is not greater than the sum of the group parts.

On the negative side, this intensity of partial attachments (particularly those of company affiliations) in Japan is seen to preclude any significant commitment to the public domain beyond. Japanese society, as a consequence, is marked by a dearth of voluntary activity, low standards of public behaviour, and contracts which lack a binding quality (Coulmas 1993: 130–1).

One common characterisation of group-centredness in postwar Japan is that it represents an enduring village mentality in an urbanised society (Irokawa 1978; Kamishima 1961; Kanzaki 1983; Tamamoto 1995). The groups making up modern Japanese society represent the 'village' of the person concerned (Nakane 1973: 62). The village represents the core model of Japanese organisation, such that companies, clubs and neighbourhoods are structured by its principles. It is as though, in the course of urbanisation, a 'transfer of community' has taken place (see Ben-Ari 1991 for discussion).[1] This persistence of a village mentality has tended to be seen negatively, as a problem. Even for the founder of modern Japanese folklore Yanagita Kunio, otherwise a champion of village tradition, the divisive legacy of village exclusivism – of sharply distinguishing in-group from out-group – in urban Japan was a cause for concern, as it posed a serious danger to urban social harmony and national unity (see Kawada 1993: 53–60). It has been commonly viewed as an obstacle to the achievement of a mature civil society in Japan. On the other hand, the tradition of village communality and its wider social legacy in modern Japan has been defended as consistent with, even a precondition of, democracy – or rather *Japanese* democracy (Irokawa 1978; Kawamura 1994). The argument is that village communality ensures a social solidarity and interdependence among Japanese in everyday life which can serve as a bulwark against a potentially oppressive state (serving the interests of monopoly capital, from Kawamura's perspective).

These two points, about state power and group-centredness, are mutually consistent. The honeycomb society is firmly encased by state power. There is public order in Japan, but this is *derivative* in character, an effect of the power of lower-level group affiliation, and it does not contradict the claim that in Japan there is an absence of 'civic consciousness' (Smith 1983: 129; see also Robins-Mowry 1983: 145). The state is able to assume moral leadership in the public sphere because of the vacuum that exists there. This is the social context that breeds state tutelage of public conduct, in the form of recurring campaigns to improve behaviour, whether this be driving, the saying of greetings in public, the removal of discriminatory attitudes, or the undertaking of voluntary activities. Public social interaction becomes a key domain of state activity.

DEMOCRACY AND UPLAND JAPAN

Postwar Japan has emphasised the key role of local government in a democratic polity. The occupation authorities explicitly stressed the importance of local government to the overall goal of democratising Japan, and sought to establish a political system sufficiently decentralised to preclude any re-emergence of the state authoritarianism of the prewar years (MacDougall 1989: 139–43). 'The message of the American reformers was clear: a democratic society requires an independent grassroots administrative network; local self-government is the school of democracy' (Samuels 1983: xx). New local government units, with their elected mayors and assemblies, would mirror the new national democratic polity.

Debates have ensued as to just how decentralised the postwar Japanese polity really is, or the extent to which Japanese local government is actually popular self-government (Fukutake 1967: ch.10). Furthermore, there has existed a strong counter-argument to the view which equated decentralisation with democratisation. This held that the main bastions of traditionalism within Japan were in the regions, and that therefore any decentralisation or empowerment of localities would only allow these provincial forces of reaction the chance to thwart progressive national reforms (MacDougall 1989: 143).

Upland regions (consisting of around 4 per cent – 5 million people – of the national population) are of particular concern in this connection. While an agrarian land reform was carried out as part of the modernising democratisation measures aimed at removing the old landlord class and attacking rural social hierarchy, forest land was not included. In upland regions, therefore, where forest land often makes up 80 per cent or more of the land area, considerable concentration in land ownership has remained. In the postwar period these remoter areas have been perceived to be still dominated by a landlord class, and therefore as the most socially backward part of the nation.

The attempt to create a new public sphere in such places must be seen in the context of the government's commitment to maintain the rural periphery. In the postwar period upland Japan has undergone large-scale depopulation (through outmigration) in response to urban industrial growth and the decline of the rural economy. But while upland areas may appear socially backward and economically marginal, they are also of some political importance. In 1970 the Japanese government passed the 'Depopulation Act' (*kasoho*), providing assistance to such areas in an effort to stem the loss of population. Fujita (1993: 50) argues that this piece of legislation was motivated by the governing party's fears that, were this scale of population redistribution to continue, it would eventually lead to a reduction in the number of Diet seats in upland areas, to its serious electoral disadvantage. The Right's control of national electoral politics was at stake in the preservation of the upland periphery. It was their very conservatism, in other words, which made the central government so concerned to save upland areas. Upland communities therefore occupy a distinctive niche within national political and economic space. They are included in national debates over the nature of Japanese society, the promotion of democracy and civic participation, and the need to improve standards of public behaviour, and so on, but they are also subject to state policies specifically targeted at more remote rural localities.

Like other upland areas, Motomiya has been seriously affected by depopulation. Between 1955 and 1995 it lost 60 per cent of its population. What remains is highly skewed, made up disproportionately of older people. Outmigration has separated younger family members, including the family heir, from parents left in the village. It has caused the number of school-aged children to fall sharply, leading to the closure of village schools. Moreover, many of those younger men who have stayed behind in Motomiya find it increasingly difficult to attract a bride, resulting in a serious problem of rural celibacy. In short, Motomiya is faced with a major crisis of social reproduction.

The postwar Japanese state has been committed to elevating the rural standard of living to that of urban dwellers through farm subsidies, other forms of revenue transfer, the relocation of industry, and so on. The state has enhanced local infrastructure as a means of promoting economic revival and improved living conditions and welfare provisions. The most prominent manifestation of this national commitment to the well-being of more remote areas is the expansion of municipal administrations.

The Motomiya town-office plays the role of a *sakigake gyōsei*, a 'pioneer administration'. It is charged with the responsibility of leading the local population out of its present state of decline and towards social progress and development. The municipal state intervenes in the economy, for example, advising on rationalisation measures for existing industries and obtaining subsidies for new enterprises. It also intervenes in health and welfare, and community-building. Community-building in Motomiya takes the form of *machizukuri* or 'town-making', the process of making a new 'bright town' (*akarui machi*) for the twenty-first century to which local people will be happy to belong.

Town-building consists of two main strands. The first is the physical integration of the Motomiya area through the resettlement of the more remote parts of population into more central, lowland areas, the extension and improvement of the road infrastructure, and the integration and centralisation of public amenities such as schools. The second involves the social reform of existing village populations into *chōmin* or 'town citizens'. A new sense of *chōmin* identity is to be achieved through the establishment of a set of town symbols (the town flag, song, bird, tree, flower, etc.), a town citizen's charter of civic aims (to value nature and history, to labour and study, to train mind and body, etc.), new civic spaces (community centre, sports hall, etc.), new patterns of town-wide civic association in the form of citizen leisure pastimes (sports activities, self-improvement classes, board-game groups), annual and periodic town-wide events (festivals, sports' days, artistic performances), and a wide-ranging programme of public education including the publication of local history texts (see Knight 1994 for details). The larger purpose of this state-promoted community-building plan is that, by modernising and rationalising upland rural areas in this way and instituting a new single *chōmin* community in place of the fractious, parochial village society that has existed hitherto, these areas will be better able to overcome their present-day economic marginality and demographic decline. The construction of the new *chōmin* community ultimately has the *remedial* purpose of elevating the most backward rural hinterlands to a national standard of living and thereby integrating them into national society.

This is a highly condensed account of the *machizukuri* initiative from an official point of view. How do local people respond to this official campaign to replace the village as a social entity with a new *chomin* community? There is no simple answer to this because local people differ sharply in their evaluation of the village, and therefore of the merits of the plan to erase it socially. In order to convey a sense of the range of local opinion, I shall present two contrasting views. The first is that of a young single woman highly critical of what she sees as a claustrophobic rural society in which young people like herself do not belong. Hers is a viewpoint that is quite common among young people, that sector of the population that has abandoned Motomiya *en masse*, and helps to account for the need for the *machizukuri* social reforms in the first place.

MICHIKO

Michiko is a young woman in her early twenties who returned to Motomiya the previous year from the city where she had worked in a bread factory since graduating from high school. She is now contemplating her future, whether to leave for the city again or whether to stay in Motomiya. On the whole, she has not enjoyed the past year back in Motomiya and is highly critical of life in the *inaka* ('countryside').

In conversation, Michiko repeatedly characterises the *inaka* as an 'uncomfortable' (*kyūkutsu*), 'narrow' (*semai*) and 'closed' (*heisateki*) place. Although she does not clearly distinguish between them herself, it is clear that there are two social sources of this discomfort. The first is her own family. Since her return from the city, she has been regularly admonished by her parents for going out with friends, for staying out late, and for spending money too freely. 'Don't do things that cover your parents' faces in mud' (*oya no kao ni doro o nuru yō na koto o suru na*) and 'Don't shame your parents' (*oya ni haji o kakasanai yō ni*) have been her father's favourite expressions. Her parents' attitude towards her friends particularly annoys her. They always want to find out who she associates with. 'For them, people are always the child of so-and-so' (*naninani san no ko*), and are judged accordingly. She points out that if she mentions somebody whose family they do not know, her parents, especially her father, immediately become suspicious (literally 'make a strange face', *hen na kao o suru*).

The wider source of constraint is what Michiko calls the *inaka*, which might be translated as 'village society'. 'In the country, there is peace as long as you don't stick out' (*inaka de wa hamidasanakattara heiwa*). In explaining to me the meaning of this expression, she draws a circle on a piece of paper, makes a cross inside it, and then draws an arrow as far as the circle perimeter. In the *inaka* if you stay within the *en* or circle – that is, if you conform to village ways – there is peace. She then reminds me of the similar, but more common, Japanese expression, 'the nail that sticks out is hammered down'. She elaborates on the narrowness of the *inaka*: 'Because the number of people is small, relations with others, and within the locality, become extremely thick (*sugoku koyukunaru*), and so locally a single person becomes something extremely large.' As a result, there is a feeling that one is always 'being watched' (*shisen o kanjiru*) or being gossiped about.

This is not just something that she feels, but is something that preoccupies 'country people' like her parents, who constantly worry that she will shame them in front of other villagers. The constraints imposed by the village make family life that much harder to bear:

> Country life means living in a narrow society, living in the same house with parents or parents-in-law, living in a boring place where there are few chances to meet the opposite sex, where there are no places to have fun, and where there are stiff, narrow human relationships, a narrow world where everybody knows about you and where, just on hearing the names of others, you know all about them. This is what I really hate. . . . Unity [*danketsu*] might not be the right word, compared with the scattered nature [*barabarasa*] of the city it is a word you can use for the country. Looked at as an ally, unity is something beneficial and comforting, but when it turns around and becomes an enemy it is something very frightening.

There is a strong allusion here to the authoritarian character of the village. It is 'narrow', 'constraining', and it potentially infringes people's *rights*. It can demand 'unity' of those within it and make life very uncomfortable for those who try to resist. This sort of critique of local society is widespread among young single people like Michiko, but I have also heard it from young wives, especially those who originate from outside. This is no abstract criticism, but one that refers to the quality of everyday local life.

Recently, Michiko joined a youth group. The *seinendan* is an association encouraged and supported by the town-office, and its activities include assisting in the preparation of public events, holding discussion evenings and debates, as well as various sports activities, group outings and other informal get-togethers. Michiko has become happier with life since she joined the group. She has made friends and developed an enthusiasm for townmaking activities. In 1994 she was selected by the town-office to participate in a publicly financed 'international exchange' (*kokusai koryu*) trip to Britain where she stayed with a rural English family and learnt English for two months. This was part of the Motomiya's 'pioneer development' (*kaijin ikusei*) programme. Through this local youth are encouraged to acquire experience of the wider world in order to develop a different, more constructive perspective on their hometown and on the process of town-making. Although she continues to be dissatisfied with daily life in the *inaka*, Michiko has none the less become one of the town's 'pioneers' (*kaijin*) or young leaders in whom it has invested municipal funds and on whom it depends for the future.

One of the things Michiko was encouraged to investigate in Britain was 'volunteer activities' (*borantia katsudo*) among British youth. There is a long-standing Japanese interest in western volunteerism, particularly voluntary activities among housewives. In 1970 the Ministry of Education endorsed a nation-wide programme to mobilise 'women volunteers who will work to build up a sense of solidarity within their respective communities' and thereby combat the rise of 'human alienation' in an increasingly urbanised postwar Japan (in Robins-Mowry 1983: 150). The official promotion of volunteerism in rural Motomiya – among housewives, the elderly, as well as youth – is similarly aimed at securing a *wider* sense of social solidarity, one quite different from the old, exclusive solidarity of the village.

An example of the youth volunteerism sponsored and coordinated by the town-office is litter collection. On the main roads between village settlements, the town youth group collects litter and rubbish in order to make a 'beautiful environment' (*utsukushii kankyō*). This is an example of civic mobilisation for a specific purpose: to deal with the build-up of litter caused by the rise in tourism, thereby ensuring that Motomiya remains an attractive place that tourists will continue to visit. Until this volunteer clean-up began, the landscape beyond village settlements was totally ignored by villagers. This is not the only form of road-clearing Michiko is called on to do. She is sometimes asked by her mother to represent the household in 'village path-clearing' or *michibushin*, a long-established customary duty for each village household which arises two or three times each year. Michiko therefore performs path or road-clearing twice over. But within the village this activity is obligatory, beyond the village it is 'voluntary'.

KURIMOTO

If the 'bright town' can be seen as a response to the dissatisfaction with village life on the part of young people like Michiko, and therefore a means to overcome present-day decline, older people may experience the whole town-making initiative rather differently. Kurimoto is the heir of a landowning family. Now in his fifties, his is a three-generational household consisting of himself and his wife, their children and his mother. With the decline in domestic forestry due to wood imports, this 'mountain-owner' (*yamanushi*) family no longer has quite the wealth and power it once did. Kurimoto has responded to this situation by building a tourist guest-house which he runs with his wife, while managing his extensive family forests part time. His family line boasts influential regional politicians, but, even though it is widely believed he would easily be elected to the town council if he ever stood, he has stayed out of politics. He remains none the less one of the most outspoken critics of the town-office.

For Kurimoto a key aspect of rural decline is the weakness of the Japanese family, which he claims has been under attack from the state both nationally and locally. The background here is the American-inspired postwar civil code which, as part of the wider strategy of promoting individual autonomy, disestablished the patriarchal *ie* or stem family – the continuity of which was made into a legal duty in the late-nineteenth-century civil code – as a legal entity (Edwards 1989: 10–11). Kurimoto points to what he sees as the overtaxing of the family as proof that Japanese governments do not really support the family. He cites inheritance tax as further evidence of this antipathy to family continuity. Given the scale of the family forest landholdings, his son will have to pay a large tax when Kurimoto dies. A common response to this situation is to split up the estate between the children in order to minimise this payment. Many landowning families find that they have to sell off part of their land just to pay the tax. Hence the cry of forest landowners in

Japan that 'after three successions, the mountains are no more' (*sankai sozoku suru to yama ga naku naru*) (Tadaki 1988: 189). In the wider area of which Motomiya is part, movements have been formed to call for a change in these laws (Ue 1987: 326–7).

Rural areas such as Motomiya have been inordinately affected by this national state disposition towards the family. But Kurimoto also sees an antipathy to the family on the part of local government. For example, he sees the modernising town-making initiative of the Motomiya town-office, with its stress on local people coming together as *chomin*, as fundamentally misconceived.

> I think that for town-making (*machizukuri*) what is important is family-making (*iezukuri*). If the three generations of parents and children lived together, there would never be depopulation. Where a family is independent, with children succeeding as heirs and everybody living together as three generations, they will be able to care for themselves instead of the town-office caring for them. It is in this sense that I think that town-making is not something that the town-office should do, but something that each independent family and all local people must do themselves.

For Kurimoto the postwar decline of Japanese mountain villages is directly related to the decline of the rural family. If the family had stayed strong, if first sons had stayed behind in the village to succeed as heirs instead of migrating to the cities, and if younger couples were willing to reside in three-generation households to live with and take care of older parents and grandparents, there would be no such thing as the 'de-population problem' (*kaso mondai*), as it is officially termed. His point is not just that the town-office efforts are misplaced, but that they are actually counter-productive because the family is further weakened through the dependency on the town-office that develops.

The same point applies to the village. For Kurimoto the problems of rural society are firmly related to the decline of the village as a *kyodotai* ('collectivity'). He points out that some villages are marked by strong solidarity or unity (*danketsu ga tsuyoi*), citing a half-dozen local villages, including his own. Even today in these villages everyone (i.e. someone from each household) turns out for communal occasions such as *michibushin*; they help each other at the times of rice transplanting and harvesting, or, if somebody is lost in the mountains, form a village search party to find them; when somebody dies, other villagers take time off work to help prepare the funeral. However, Kurimoto stresses that in most villages this unity is weakening, with diminishing participation in village festivals and other customary communal occasions. In his view, a contributory factor in rural decline, is that rural people now increasingly expect the town-office to undertake everyday tasks that before they would have performed themselves. For example, when an animal – a feral dog or a raccoon dog – is killed on a village road, it will just stay there until somebody calls the town-office to come and dispose of it, whereas before a few villagers would have soon got together and disposed of it themselves (in the mountains). Kurimoto sees this as an example of a deeper malaise afflicting places like Motomiya in recent years. Motomiya is faced not with a 'depopulation problem' but with a 'problem of the heart' (*kokoro no mondai*). In his view, depopulation will be overcome not by mountain villagers depending on others (i.e. those beyond the village) to do things for them – the effect of town-office functioning – but only by undertaking to do things themselves as they did in the past. This sentiment is expressed in what has become a rallying cry in Motomiya: 'if we don't *dare mo yatte kurenai* do things ourselves nobody will do them for us' (*jibun de yaranakereba*).

Kurimoto criticises the town-office not just for inducing passivity among local people, but for wilfully undermining local traditions and customs. A prime example of this is the 'empty custom abolition' (*kyorei haishi*) campaign. This is presented as a 'movement' or *undo* in which groups of local residents spontaneously decide to discontinue certain traditional gift-giving practices at times of births, weddings, sickness and funerals, on the grounds that they impose onerous financial and psychological burdens on local people (see Bestor 1989: 204–5; Knight 1994). The 'movement' is widely seen as promoted by the town-office as part of its town-making plan. For Kurimoto, however, village ways 'have nothing to do with the town-office' (*yakuba to kankei nai*) and such interference is completely wrong. The strength of rural society, he stresses, lies in the way people care for each other, and gifting at times of joy such as weddings or at times of bereavement is an expression of this.

We might see all this as nothing more than the predictable anguished outcry of rural conservatives in the face of modernisation initiatives targeted at those key bases of traditionalism, the stem family and the village. Kurimoto is after all the heir of a powerful *yamanushi* family of the sort that has long dominated Japanese mountain village life (Ushiomi 1968: ch.2), a hierarchical situation that has persisted into the postwar era because of the exclusion of forest land from the postwar land reform. As such, he has an obvious stake both in family continuity and in preserving the village collectivity within which his family wields great influence. Yet, on closer inspection, this sort of neat categorisation comes to seem less clear-cut. For the conservative Kurimoto also attacks what he sees as the overbearing, even authoritarian manner of the town-office. He argues that, behind the language of popular participation, it relies on a pervasive civil deference, that it has itself been instrumental in creating, in enacting its agenda of reforms.

In Japan, working for the state carries a certain prestige, and this extends to employees of the town-office. There is no little envy in Motomiya towards those who work for the town-office, for they have a security of livelihood denied to many other local people (such as forest labourers). I heard it said of one town-office man that 'his father is the rising sun' (*chichioya wa hinomaru*). The town-office man is secure in life because of his association with the state (symbolised by the rising-sun flag). If one is to stay and live one's life in Motomiya, the ideal is to become attached to – to be adopted by – the town-office. Kurimoto deplores this and argues that the authority of the state in a place like Motomiya is such that a wider dependency orientation arises towards it, even on the part of those who do not work for it. In the intrusiveness of the town-office into local life, it is as though the state is seeking to become the father of all the people in the town!

One of the most striking areas of civil intervention by the town-office is marriage. In Motomiya, as in much of rural Japan, there is a growing problem of male bachelorhood, with women reluctant to marry local men. Thus in Motomiya one-third of men in their thirties remain unmarried, compared to a figure of 20 per cent nationally. The reasons for this situation are regularly discussed and debated locally, and a recurring theme is that the 'go-betweens' (*nakodo*) no longer exist. The *nakodo* was a prominent local man who would lend his authority to a match – either in suggesting it in the first place, arranging it, or presiding over it formally at the wedding. Few people are now prepared to undertake the task on account of the responsibility it carries with it, particularly if the marriage develops problems. Kurimoto is an exception, a man who has acted as *nakodo* on many occasions. The town-office has responded to this growing problem of rural male celibacy by itself taking on responsibility for marriage brokerage. At both prefectural and local level, events are arranged for local men to meet potential spouses (see Knight 1995). From the point of view of the town-office, it is a vacuum in local society that necessitates state intervention. The institution of marriage has broken down locally, in part due to the decline of traditional leaders, and it therefore attempts to take on this role itself. Yet for local leaders like Kurimoto, this development appears as part of a larger process of increasing dependency.

VILLAGE INTO TOWN?

Michiko and Kurimoto illustrate the complicated character of the local debate on civil society. One tends to see the old ways of the village as, unfortunately, very much alive, and as deterring young people like herself from leading a rural life, the other tends to stress, with no less regret, the decline of village ways. Both refer to the notion of *danketsu* ('unity, solidarity'), Michiko to point to the 'frightening' side of rural life, Kurimoto to highlight his perception that some villages have managed to retain their integrity in this age of decline. Moreover, both use or allude to a language of rights. Michiko complains about the village society which restricts the freedom of young people like herself. Kurimoto inveighs against an interfering local state and challenges its right to carry out its reforms.

Town-office staff quote voices like that of Michiko to justify the town-making reforms. By 'widening the circle' (*wa o hirogeru*), making a large town community out of so many small villages, they seek to bring into being a civic space in which Michiko and others can feel comfortable. As the example of the youth group's road-clearing shows, the town community, no less than that of the village is based on collective action. The village is an obstacle to town-making not because it is collective but because it is exclusive and therefore, from the town perspective, divisive. Of course, the difference between the two forms of road-clearing, apart from one of scale, is that one was 'voluntary', the other compulsory (failure to participate in village *michibushin* typically leads to censure, even sanctions). Formally, Michiko and other members of the youth group undertake the road-clearing because they are committed to building a new, bright town, not because they are obliged to do so. In practice, however, once instituted, such activities may become obligatory – the duty of *chomin* to the town. Although the town uses the idiom of volunteer, it sees local people as having responsibilities to each other and the town community as a whole by virtue of their status as *chōmin*. The civic volunteers cannot but be obligated in so far as they live in the town.

The difference therefore between town and village, or between the two forms of road-clearing, may be less one of motivation than of scale. Municipally promoted volunteerism can be understood as a means of translating the collectivist tradition of the village into an idiom suitable for the new town community. Town-making involves not so much the erasure of the village as its social upscaling. From this perspective, the views of Michiko and Kurimoto may not be so irreconcilable after all. For if the town is village-like, Kurimoto can be reassured that local communal traditions will not be discarded, but reapplied in an enlarged context. At the same time, Michiko and her peers need to be convinced that the town community is fundamentally different from the village. This is achieved in large part through the emphasis on youth. Town-making, especially in depopulated rural areas, requires young leaders – hence the investment in foreign study trips. The 'pioneer-raising' programme seeks to foster social innovation and *sōzōryoku* ('creativity'). But this is not incompatible with cooperation among citizens. Indeed, in her foreign trip, Michiko was assigned the task of exploring a new form of ('voluntary') collective activity. The point is to ensure that young leaders should ultimately contribute to the mobilisation of the community.

For all his concern about the loss of village unity and his objections to town-office rhetoric and campaigns, Kurimoto himself knows only too well that the new town community is a long way from being realised. At town assembly election time, for example, the single formal constituency of the town in practice becomes so many village elections, in which candidates seek support only from their own natal and surrounding villages. Accordingly, these small units become the informal con- stituencies of the 'town' assemblymen afterwards. In such village-based politics, moreover, wealthy *yamanushi* families like Kurimoto's continue to exert considerable influence, even if, as with Kurimoto, their own family head does not stand.

Rural municipalities like Motomiya cannot, however, be reduced analytically to an agglomeration of villages. Villages will remain important social units in these larger localities, but their significance will not be the same as before. If the village forms a support base in municipal elections, this certainly does not exhaust the vote-getting process; other associations, such as the workplace and kinship ties, which cross-cut village ties, also have a bearing. The village does not dominate local politics as it did in the past. Similarly, new town-wide associations such as the youth group, while they do not erase village collective activity, do none the less reconfigure them in so far as they place them in a new larger (municipal) social context in which they become one axis of association among others. The new situation of associational pluralism means that the village is not the 'social cage' it was before: it may still be an ascribed, as opposed to a voluntary, form of activity, but it has become an overlapping one (Hall 1995: 15).

Against the sort of charges that Kurimoto makes, the town-office would defend itself by citing an ubiquitous, if diffuse, desire in Motomiya for something to be done to alleviate the seemingly relentless trend of depopulation. That the sort of sentiments Kurimoto voices can be readily heard among older people in Motomiya suggests that there is still some way to go before the town-office convinces most local people that the creation of the 'bright town' will achieve this demographic goal. In the meantime, as it attempts to create a new public sphere or civic community marked by town-wide social interaction in place of the parochialisms of traditional rural society, the local administration is itself criticised for high-handedly undermining actual local communities and fostering state dependency.[2]

CONCLUSION

Finally I turn to the relationship between these national and local debates. That the nation serves as a model for the municipal locality is indicated by the prominence given to the forms and trappings of nation. This is apparent in flags, songs, history textbooks, the office of mayor, the assembly, the bureaucracy, mayoral 'summits', olympic-like sports' gatherings, explicit self-characterisations as mini-nations with the issuing of 'passports', and so on. This municipal adoption of national forms does not, however, amount to municipal nationalism. In Japan these formal local identities typically accord with the formal national identity: every Japanese citizen should have a local allegiance, for the two are not in conflict. The locality of Motomiya is a constituent unit of national governance. On the wall of the Motomiya town assembly hang two flags side by side: the Motomiya municipal flag and the Japanese rising sun. There is no evidence of what might be called centrifugal state localism or regionalism – that is, one antipathetic to the national state – in Motomiya.

Yet there is a tension in the relationship between Motomiya and the wider nation. Although part of a national domain, Motomiya also represents an *institutionally distinctive* local state domain by virtue of its status as a depopulated, economically marginalised locality, one that is at odds with larger trends in the national society. It is this discrepancy between advanced national development and local backwardness which structures the relationship between local state and local populace.

It has been pointed out that civil society emerged in eighteenth-century Europe against the background of 'an enormous jump in fiscal extraction' on the part of the state (Hall 1995: 7). 'Struggles for citizenship' on the part of the national bourgeoisie are a response to the state-tax demands made on it. Here, by contrast, I have been concerned with the local state in a rural periphery where the relationship is one of fiscal subsidy. The starting point of state activity in this local theatre is a depopulated, economically backward rural society, and a nationally assigned administrative responsibility to remedy or at least mitigate these conditions. The solution is seen in terms of a new town community which both transcends village divisions and provides a social and demographic basis for a renascent civic and economic vitality.

It is against this background that we can understand how the two (local and national) civic orders above relate to each other. Despite the different social scales involved, there are clearly major parallels between the terms of local and national citizenship. Just as at a national-level critics have diagnosed a civic vacuum between powerful primary groups and the state, so in Motomiya the diagnosis is of a social vacuum at the level of the town, in between village parochialism and state dependency. Just as the middle way nationally is for Japanese to develop a civic consciousness, so the middle way locally is for these mountain villagers to become full social members of the 'bright town' community.

Some of the terms of the local debate are clearly extendable to the national context. In particular, the failure to achieve a civil society nationally has been attributed to the power of primary social groups, a 'groupist' disposition believed to be genealogically related to the particularism of an earlier village society. The village therefore has a double presence, local and national. Village parochialism appears as the obstacle to rural town-making, while in the wider debates among academics and intellectuals a sort of extended or applied village sociality emerges as an obstacle to creating a national citizenry.

I began this chapter by stressing the plural character of civil society, and arguing that one corollary of this was the need, analytically, to recognise state–social interfaces other than the national. Once this plurality is recognised, however, the task then becomes one of *relating* the different interfaces. The tracing of an idiomatic affinity between nation and region – showing how in Japan making citizens is doubly associated with breaking villages – is one way of doing so.

NOTES

1   See Lebra 1992: 15–17 for a similar 'transfer' approach according to which the traditional stem family associated with rural Japan is viewed as a model for urban group formation.
2   This criticism of the local state has also been made by Japanese academics. See Irokawa 1978, and Bestor's discussion of Japanese sociologists (1989: 120–1).

REFERENCES

Ben-Ari, E. (1991) *Changing Japanese Suburbia: A Study of Two Present-Day Localities*, London: KPI.

Bestor, T. C. (1989) *Neighbourhood Tokyo*, Stanford, Calif.: Stanford University Press.

Coulmas, F. (1993) 'Responsibility allocation and networks in Japanese society', *Japan Quarterly* 40(2): 126–35.

Dale, P. N. (1988) *The Myth of Japanese Uniqueness*, London: Routledge.

Edwards, W. (1989) *Modern Japan Through its Weddings*, Stanford, Calif.: Stanford University Press.

Fujita, Y. (1993) 'Changes in mountain villages and policies for the development of mountain areas in Japan', in J. Sargent and R. Wiltshire (eds), *Geographical Studies and Japan*, Folkestone: Japan Library, pp. 47–52.

Fukutake, T. (1967) *Japanese Rural Society*, Ithaca: Cornell University Press.

Hall, J. A. (1995) 'In search of civil society', in J. A. Hall (ed.), *Civil Society: Theory, History, Comparison*, Cambridge: Polity Press, pp. 1–31.

Hann, C. (1993) 'Introduction: social anthropology and socialism', in C. M. Hann (ed.), *Socialism: Ideals, Ideologies, and Local Practice*, London: Routledge, pp. 1–26.

Irokawa, D. (1978) 'The survival struggle of the Japanese community', in J. V. Koschmann (ed.), *Authority and the Individual in Japan*, Tokyo: University Press, pp. 250–96.

Johnson, C. (1982) *MITI and the Japanese Miracle*, Tokyo: Charles E. Tuttle.

Kamishima, J. (1961) *Kindai nihon no seishin kozo* ('The Mental Structure of the Japanese'), Tokyo: Iwanami Shoten.

Kanzaki, N. (1983) 'Waga kuni ni okeru tabi no rekishi to shuzoku', in *Nihonjin no tabi to rizoto* ('The Holidays of Japanese and Resorts'), Ise: Chiku Rizoto Kaihatsu Projekuto.

Kawada, M. (1993) *The Origin of Ethnography in Japan: Yanagita Kunio and his Times*, London: Kegan Paul International.

Kawamura, N. (1994) *Sociology and Society of Japan*, London: Kegan Paul International.

Kenrick, D. M. (1988) *Where Communism Works: The Success of Competitive Communism in Japan*, Basingstoke: Macmillan.

Knight, J. (1994) 'Town-making in rural Japan: an example from Wakayama', *Journal of Rural Studies* 10(3): 249–61.

—— (1995) 'Municipal matchmaking in rural Japan', *Anthropology Today* 11(2): 9–17.

Koschmann, J. V. (1993) 'Intellectuals and politics', in Andrew Gordon (ed.), *Postwar Japan as History*, Berkeley and Los Angeles: University of California Press, pp. 395–423.

Lebra, T. S. (1992) 'Introduction', in T. S. Lebra (ed.), *Japanese Social Organisation*, Honolulu: University of Hawaii Press, pp. 1–21.

MacDougall, T. (1989) 'Democracy and local government in postwar Japan', in T. Ishida and E.S. Krauss (eds), *Democracy in Japan*, Pittsburgh: University Press, pp. 139–69.

McKean, M. A. (1993) 'State strength and the public interest', in G. D. Allinson and Y. Sone (eds), *Political Dynamics in Contemporary Japan*, Ithaca, NY: Cornell University Press, pp. 72–104.

Matsumoto, S. (1978) 'The roots of political disillusionment: "public" and "private" in Japan', in J. V. Koschmann (ed.), *Authority and the Individual in Japan*, Tokyo: University Press, pp. 31–51.

Nakane, C. (1973) *Japanese Society*, Harmondsworth: Penguin.

Okumura, H. (1992) 'Corporate capitalism: cracks in the system', *Japan Quarterly* 39(1): 54–61.

Pharr, S. J. (1990) *Losing Face: Status Politics in Japan*, Berkeley and Los Angeles: University of California Press.

Ray, L. (1991) 'A Thatcher export phenomenon? The enterprise culture in Eastern Europe', in R. Keat and N. Abercrombie (eds), *Enterprise Culture*, London: Routledge, pp. 114–35.

Robins-Mowry, D. (1983) *The Hidden Sun: Women of Modern Japan*, Boulder, Colo.: Westview.

Samuels, R. J. (1983) *The Politics of Regional Policy in Japan*, Princeton: Princeton University Press.

Smith, R. (1983) *Japanese Society: Tradition, Self and the Social Order*, Cambridge: Cambridge University Press.

Tadaki, Y. (1988) *Mori to ningen no bunkashi* ('A Cultural History of Forests and Man'), Tokyo: NHK Books.

Tamamoto, M. (1995) 'Reflections on Japan's postwar state', *Daedalus* 124(2): 1–22.

Ue, T. (1987) *Seishun o kawa ni ukabete: ki to ningen no uchu II* ('Youth Afloat in the River: The Universe of Trees and Men, vol. II'), Tokyo: Fukuinkan Shoten.

Ushiomi, T. (1968) *Forestry and Mountain Village Communities in Japan*, Tokyo: Kokusai Bunka Shinkokai.

Yoshino, K. (1992) *Cultural Nationalism in Contemporary Japan: A Sociological Enquiry*, London: Routledge.

Index

Rowe, W. 200–1
Russia 13, 72–3, 98–119

Sadowski, Y. 156
Said, E. 157
Sampson, S. 2, 9–10, 13–15
Samuels, R. 227
Sarageldin, A. 180, 190
Schmit, L. 15–16, 18, 186, 188, 190
schools, folk 148–51
Scruton, R. 81
secularism 144, 147, 151, 158
security 182–5
self-sufficiency 38–9, 233–4
Seligman, A. 2–6, 10, 18, 146
Shepherd, J. 58
Shils, E. 146–7
Siberia 13, 98–119
Simmel, G. 39–40, 64, 72
Simpson, R. 62
Sino-Indonesians 189, 190–1, 195
Siriprachai, S. 195
Smith, A. 4, 146
Smith, R. 224, 225, 226
Smolar, A. 89–90
social reproduction 28, 33–8, 44, 46,
    109–11, 204–5
society: American 38; does not exist
    (Thatcher) 11, 59; linkage between
    individual and society via state 165;
    linkage between individual and
    society via family 165; see also
    state, as distinct from society
Soeharto, President of Indonesia 178,
    182, 183, 185, 191
Soekarno, former President of
    Indonesia 182
Solidarity (trade union) 87–90, 93–4
Spülbeck, S. 12
Staniszkis, J. 79, 89
Stasi 12, 66–71, 73–4
state 21, 150–2, 202; dependency on
    21, 40–6, 232–5, 238; development
    of modern state in Middle East
    159–60; as distinct from civil
    society 4–10, 46, 80; as distinct
    from society 7–10, 21, 23, 200, 218,
    219–20, 222; and economic
    development 178–97; as employer

54, 235; as encompassing private
business 224; and gender roles 155,
161, 173, see also gender; as
included in civil society 22, 157,
220, 224; naturalness of 156; as
ostensibly gender neutral 155–6;
receding involvement of 199, see
also decollectivisation; reducing
size of 54, 199, 219; state capitalism
223; strong state thesis 223; ties to
state via gifts 47, 206, 214–15, 218,
see also gifts
state socialism 104, 106, 107–10,
112–13, 134, 161, 190, 200–1; and
collective 'we' 13, 106–7; and
everyday activity 12–13; and moral
aspects of socialist market economy
209–18; see also communism; post-
communism
strangers 64, 72, 76–7, 135
Strathern, M. 27, 37, 42, 45
surveillance 66–71
sustainability 190, 195, 204–5
sympathies, natural 4, 146
Syria 15, 155–6, 159–73
system export 125–6

Tadaki, Y. 233
Tamamoto, M. 225
Tarkowska, E. and Tarkowski, J. 84,
85, 91
Taylor, C. 27
technocracy 16, 181, 185–9, 196; see
also politics of expertise
Tester, K. 2–3, 27
Thatcher, M. 11, 54–9, 62
time: as indivisible 31–3; as not
equivalent to money 32
Tjiptoherijanto, P. 187
Tocqueville, A de 5, 13, 21, 23, 51, 52
Toprak, B. 149
totalitarianism 74–6, 79, 84, 206, 215,
216, 217, 222
town citizens (*chomin*) 228, 236
town-making 221–39
transition 121–42
trust 6, 13, 22, 23, 67
Turkey 14, 143–52
Turner, B. 159